Rio2016
XXX Olympiad London 2012
Rio2016
London 2012
Rio2016
XXXI Olimpíada Rio 2016
XXXI Olimpíada Rio 2016
XXX Olympiad London 2012
XXXI Olimpíada Rio 2016

# Laura Jason
# TROTT & KENNY
## THE INSIDE TRACK

# Laura Jason
# TROTT & KENNY
## THE INSIDE TRACK

written with Tom Fordyce

Michael O'Mara Books Limited

First published in Great Britain in 2016 by
Michael O'Mara Books Limited
9 Lion Yard
Tremadoc Road
London SW4 7NQ

A CIP catalogue record for this book is available from the British Library.

Papers used by Michael O'Mara Books Limited are natural,
recyclable products made from wood grown in sustainable forests.
The manufacturing processes conform to the environmental
regulations of the country of origin.

ISBN: 978-1-78243-796-3 in hardback print format
ISBN: 978-1-78243-797-0 in trade paperback format
ISBN: 978-1-78243-799-4 in ebook format

1 3 5 7 9 10 8 6 4 2

Front cover image: Dan Rouse Photography
Back cover top: Bryn Lennon / Getty Images
Bottom left: Eric Feferberg / AFP / Getty Images
Bottom right: Xinhua News Agency / REX / Shutterstock

Cover design by Ana Bjezancevic

Designed and typeset by Mark Bracey

Printed and bound by CPI Group (UK) Ltd, Croydon, CR0 4YY

www.mombooks.com

For our parents, Glenda and Adrian, Lorraine and
Michael, for putting up with us for all these years and
supporting us throughout, for turning childhood fun
into something so much bigger than we could ever have
dreamed of. And to our siblings, Emma Trott and Craig
Kenny, from pain-in-the-backside childhood companions
to the best friends we could ever hope to have.

# Contents

# Prologue

Tuesday 16 August, 2016.
The Olympic velodrome,
Rio de Janeiro, Brazil.

**JASON:** It is just after 6 p.m. I am sitting on a remarkably uncomfortable plastic chair next to one man with huge legs and another whose legs are even bigger. My feet are in tight cycling shoes. My torso, legs and arms are encased in a skinsuit that feels tighter than my actual skin. I am wearing white gloves and a helmet that squeezes the side of my head, and under all this it is hot and sweaty.

I am a sprinter. I am waiting for the final of the Olympic keirin, and I am waiting for history. In the five days before this I have won my fourth and fifth Olympic gold medals – one in the team sprint, one in the individual sprint. In these same five days the woman who will shortly become my wife has won her third and fourth golds. She now not only has my engagement ring on her finger but more gold round her neck than any other female athlete in British history. She is sitting no more than ten paces away from me, but there can be no communication, no hugs or kisses. Not now.

**LAURA:** I'm happy, but I can't relax. These Olympics are over for me, but they're not over for us. I won a gold medal in the team pursuit three days ago and a gold in the omnium less than an hour ago. I have just been standing on the top step of the podium while they played the national anthem, watching the Union flag go up. I need a rest, I need a shower and want to celebrate, but I can't. Not yet.

Four finals down, four gold medals. One final left. Jason against five other riders. Jason, my partner for more than four years now, due to walk down the aisle with me in a few weeks' time, my housemate, my best friend.

One more race. One more win for a perfect Olympics. One more race and we can at last sleep in the same bed again. Olympics can do strange things to you. Your relationship takes second place to other demands, even if the two of you will be sharing the same surname by the end of the next month.

Always together. In this nervous moment, alone.

**JASON:** Laura gets more anxious watching my races than I do. My mum Lorraine, up there in the packed stands, has to bury her head in her hands until it's over. I'm the calmest man in the race. I might be the calmest man in Rio. I have planned how to race this final, and I know I have the speed to make my tactics work.

There are some things I don't know. I don't know that there are nearly 12 million people watching all this live on television back in the UK, or that BBC One has delayed the ten o'clock news to let them see these last few minutes of flat-out action. I don't know either that the *News at Ten* is going to be waiting much longer than its presenters ever thought.

In an Olympic final you fret about nothing except the Olympic final. There is no room for doubts, for emotion, for looking across at your fiancée and trying to tell her to stop worrying. It is just me, strapped into the pedals of my bike, my coach pushing me on to the track, two rivals lined up to my left, three to my right.

I know my rivals and I know my tactics. The German, the reigning world champion, has a fierce kick. I have to be ready to follow him when he accelerates. The Malaysian and the Colombian will finish strongly. I sit behind them as we all follow the derny, the electric motorbike that controls the pace for the first six and a half laps before leaving us to fight it out.

Round we go. Everything as I expected – two in front, three behind. Round goes the derny, picking up speed. Fifty kilometres an hour now, and as it dives off the track the German is hammering past. I get out of the saddle and give it absolutely everything I have, because I need to get on his wheel, otherwise ...

BANG.

The restart gun has fired. Gasps all around. Riders slowing, looking at each other, looking up at the big screens at either end of the arena.

This doesn't happen often. This doesn't happen unless there is something wrong, unless a rider has gone past the rear wheel of the derny before we are meant to, getting a jump on his rivals, almost false-starting the final two-and-a-half-lap showdown.

Someone must have done it, because they don't fire the restart gun in the Olympic final on a whim. But who?

**LAURA:** Hands to my face. They had looked to be going too fast too early. Riders right up on the derny and Jason shouldering his way to the front.

Heart pounding. Staring at the big screen. Not now, please. Not when everything has been so flawless; when he's got the form and the legs; when we are so close.

**JASON:** Riding round, trying to keep my face and body language from betraying any emotion. I don't think it's me. I wouldn't make such a mistake, certainly not in an Olympic final, would I? The bigger the battle, the more intense the pressure, the calmer I feel. And then, as I watch the replay on the big screen, it hits me: this is far too close for comfort.

**LAURA:** I stare at that big screen with a sick feeling in my guts. Jason looks out. I watch again. It's so hard to tell – it could be Jason, it could be the Malaysian, but it could be both, and it has to be someone, or why else would they fire the gun?

Our British Cycling coaches are rushing over to the officials. Arguments and gesticulations. Jason's mum not looking in the first place and now pushing her head even lower in her lap. Millions back home, hands on mouths, waiting, and wondering, and still waiting.

And me in the middle of the track, watching Jason pedalling slowly round the pale brown polished boards, powerless to do anything about it, waiting and wondering and thinking: Is that it? Is it over?

# One: **Reality Bites**

**JASON:** We spend our lives turning left.

Left on to the first bend, left into the back straight, left into the final banking, left into the home straight. Round and round, day after day, lap after 250-metre lap. Glamour? There's no glamour, not in the long hours and fallow years between Olympics. Not in training sessions designed to push your body further than it wants to be pushed, in gym sessions when you squat and try to stand with two and a half times your own body weight on your shoulders, in laps ridden so hard that you fall off your bike and throw up everything that's inside your stomach and a fair amount of stuff you didn't even know was in there.

This has been my life since my early teens, and Laura's life from younger still. If you're not an Olympic athlete, the point when you start puking during your working hours is the point where you go home and have a few days in bed. For us it comes as a strange kind of relief. You come off the track and think your head is going to explode. Your helmet feels like it's stopping you breathing. Your skinsuit feels as if it is crushing you from the outside in. You rip off that armour and suddenly, left vulnerable, human once again, your body responds. Except it's not like throwing up after drinking, or with a stomach virus. When you throw up from physical exhaustion it's like someone's flicked a switch: it's an emotional release, as if all your demons have come out in your vomit. It almost feels good.

So broken can you be sometimes that you lie on the ground with your feet up in the air, trying to get some blood to flow to your brain, except there's no position you can find that can make you feel better. You try sitting in one of the plastic chairs on the infield inside the track, and you think, 'This chair is the most uncomfortable chair in the world.' So you lie on the floor, and sometimes that's the best thing to do: to curl up into a ball and hope it all goes away. To wait for the pounding in your head to slowly die away and the air to come into your lungs, and your limbs to gradually feel like your own again, the feeling to come back into fingers that have been useless and numb.

**LAURA:** I get this weird thing sometimes when I go flat out. If someone pointed at a patch of unoccupied floor as I came off the track and told me I could fall asleep without any recriminations or danger, I would sleep as quickly as clicking fingers. Gone. Trotty down. It's almost like your body wants to shut everything down. No thoughts, no strength, nothing left. It's, 'Please don't hurt me any more.' It's gravity taking over; it's nothing in your head at all except to find a safe place to wait for the bile to come.

The best thing you can do is to ride it off, jump back on the bike, pedal on. It's the best thing and it's the worst thing, because it doesn't feel possible, and even when it does, it also feels horrendous. There are rollers set up for you to put the bike on – allowing you to pedal it as if on a treadmill – and you've ridden rollers every week of your cycling life, and still you sit there and think, 'Why isn't this bike freewheeling? Why aren't those rollers moving?' And then you look down and your legs look the same as they did ten minutes ago except now they belong to someone else, and that someone else is moving them, and – hold on, I think I'm going to be sick again ...

Sometimes the big rush comes along to save you. Endorphins, hormones, all that good stuff, racing through you, coming to save the day. But you can't call it like the emergency services. You might have gone hard and hit your numbers. You might have produced the power the coaches want and kept clipping the lap times the analysts had asked for. Then it's a good feeling, and suddenly everything is all right in the world, and you love your job, and although there's nothing left, you want to go back out and do it all over again. Or you might have thrown in the same efforts, gone just as hard as you can, left it all out there ... and come up short. Then there's no rush, no elation, no love of the game and a 'Let's do it again.' None of that. Either way, you've got no choice. The next session's on the horizon. Whether it's gone well or badly, you bank it. Fuel up for the next one, recover from the pain as best you can. Because there's more pain coming. It's always coming, the pain.

**JASON:** You do it because it matters, because it makes the good stuff happen. Without the prosaic days in the velodrome, without emptying out everything you have, there could be no golden crescendo on those three days every four years when the whole world is watching.

It matters, and then it doesn't matter at all. Months and months of chasing form, and as soon as you stop racing there is absolutely nothing you can do with it. You can't go for long relaxing rides in the Peak District, because your body is trained to go flat out for forty-two seconds. You can't race again, because the Olympics are over. It is not like road racing after the Tour de France, when there are city-centre criteriums in which champions can be paraded and seen to do their choreographed thing once again. All the effort we throw in to build ourselves up, and it's all for one final. The final went well, the final went badly. It doesn't matter: it's done. You're sat there at home, with this really specific, incredible form in your legs, and it comes in handy for absolutely nothing else at all.

It's not just that – as a speed merchant who trains only on the track – I can't ride a road bike for more than an hour during the last couple of months before an Olympics without hurting all over. I also can't walk. I can't walk to the shops because they're more than ten minutes away, and ten minutes of walking is enough to make my back hurt. Twenty minutes is enough to leave me wrecked. In that period, you stop everything that isn't exclusively designed to make you go faster in your most particular of chosen disciplines – not just specific in the general sporting sense, or specific to cycling as a sport, or even specific to the one tight aspect of cycling that is track racing, but specific to a single aspect of track. And so out in the wider world, where it is all about adaptability and being able to do a little bit of everything – walking, lifting, jogging, carrying – we are like improbably cut jigsaw pieces that fit into no other puzzle. You become really sensitive to everything around you. Living becomes almost like a challenge.

**LAURA:** After the World Championships one year we went to stay in a little Derbyshire village called Flash, which is less than an hour's drive from our home. The idea was to enjoy the Peaks' countryside. To unwind. First day there we went for a short walk. That was me done. Never again. I went back to our room and slept as if I'd just walked to the North Pole.

Take me to an ordinary gym and I'm useless. I can't manage five minutes on the running machine. Burpees? No chance. Don't ask me to do anything with my arms, like press-ups or tricep dips. All my muscle and power is below the waist. Jason purposely doesn't build up his arms, because he sees them as extra weight. They're just anchors, extra drag. Keep them skinny. Keep them light.

I go to a steep hill near our house in Cheshire after the Olympics. I'm a double gold medallist: I'm going to fly up it, right? Nope. One of my events lasts for four minutes. None of them involve hills. I'm a racer, spotting gaps and accelerating into them, jumping on to wheels, holding a line a couple of centimetres from the rear tyre of the woman in front. I'm not a climber, grinding away up the Wizard in Alderley Edge or Blaze Hill further out east past Bollington. We lose the resilience to do normal things. Even standing hurts. Show me a chair and I'm in it.

We don't go food shopping, because we can't walk for that long. Twenty minutes pushing a trolley is horrendous.

Vacuuming? Before Rio, that got reined right back in. You should have seen our house. No way would I clean it: too much time on my feet, too much pushing and shoving the vacuum. Jason would mow the lawn, but only because it's tiny and he's got himself a mower that pulls itself.

It sounds like a joke, I know. We are weird creatures that have evolved to do only one thing. Take us out of that habitat and we're goners. I can't take a bus or a train because there's a chance there might be no seats. No standing, remember? The bus might be late, or the train cancelled. More standing. Public transport, germs everywhere. Illnesses galore. Can't do it. Can't risk it.

**JASON:** Driving you on through it all are your coaches. Some might be coercive, all stick and no carrot. Mine have to be collaborative, because I am an awkward sod.

If there are a lot of riders on the track, you have to stick to a strict schedule, so that endurance riders aren't getting in the way of the speed merchants and the speed merchants aren't dive-bombing four sitting ducks of team pursuiters. And so the coaches will shout, 'Sprinters on the track!' Me being me, I then pretend to go to the toilet or something, all because I don't like being told what to do. I may have my shoes on and be good to go well before we are due to start, but it's my grumpy way of telling them to ask rather than order, to treat me as an adult who knows what he needs rather than a naughty kid who's trying to get away with it.

**LAURA:** I love being first on the track. Track is where the racing happens. Let me at it.

Now, I'm late all the time, but never for training, and never for the start of sessions. Arrange to meet me for coffee and I'll be leaving the house when I'm meant to be kissing your cheek.

If the programme says we're doing an effort at 9.10, we girls are on the track by eight minutes past, rolling round getting ready for it. When we share the track with the lads in the morning, lunch is at 11 a.m. If we're not done by then we won't eat lunch on time, and if we don't eat lunch on time we won't be ready for our next session at 1 p.m. And if I'm eating at 11.30 and racing an hour and a half later, I'm going to be throwing up that lunch long before the exhaustion turns my guts inside out. Schedules matter. When they go wrong, so does everything else.

**JASON:** You can spot the riders who have been in the national squads from an early age. On the Olympic Development Programme – the first step on the pathway from promising junior to senior success – there was a ten-minute rule: be ready to start your session ten minutes before it is actually scheduled to begin. Then, if you have a puncture, you have time to fix it. If there's a mechanical issue with your bike, you can sort it out. That was the ODP culture, and those who have grown up with it still arrive with that window of leeway in place. Those who have come on the squad quite late think 9 a.m. means 9 a.m. The old ODP gang will be there at 8.50.

As a sprint squad now, we will just begin without riders. We will start doing team warm-ups, and we will almost take pleasure in watching the clock count down. Who's going to be late? Will anyone be caught out? A minute to go; anyone pushing it? It's an attitude I love; in some ways a small detail but really an indicator of wider attitudes. Being on time shows respect to the team. Being the last one there is as good as being late for me; I hate being the last one so much that if I'm ever that rider then I'll be the first the next day. When the hour starts, you have to be ready to start too. Not walking out, or fiddling with your gear ratio, or chatting to the mechanics. Because typically, when you're kept waiting, it's always by the same people. You're stood outside on a wet Manchester morning getting cold, or you're in the gym itching to go but unable to push on. We have days when we train both morning and afternoon. When you start late, you finish late. Your eating is cocked up, your day is cocked up, your ability to perform when it really matters, on those few days every four years, is incrementally weakened.

**LAURA:** When you're an Olympic athlete, everything else fits in around your training. Nothing else comes before bike riding, whether it's traffic on the way in or a haircut on the way out or taking the dogs for a walk. If you get the priorities wrong you're messing up yourself and you're messing up everyone else.

Those sacrifices don't come easily. All those laps of the track. Forty of them in the warm-up alone, before every session, and then the training itself, round and round in circles, like clockwork toys, to get to an end point that could be three years away. You remember to be thankful for little things. When you're staring at the black line that runs round the bottom of the track you're glad you're not a swimmer, watching another black line on the tiles under your nose, head in the water for four hours, no one to talk to. When we're putting in a shift on the track there's no breath for chat. But when we're warming up or cooling down we can share a moment, and that helps you get through it, reminds you you're not on your own. Jason can talk when he's on the rollers before a flat-out effort, although because it's Jason he won't talk like I would talk. There's sociable and then there's Laura sociable.

You can't vary it. The path to an Olympics only goes one way. Runners can mix it up – they can do their 400-metre laps the other way round, saving legs, saving injury from overusing the same muscles in the same way. Our tracks don't work that way. You try turning right, even on an empty track, and the boards will fight it. Those bends aren't symmetrical, and the transitions off them into the straights only work properly in one direction. If you're going the right way it all feels completely natural. You don't even need to steer, not by using the handlebars like you would on the road. The first time people get on the track, that's the common mistake: the track wants to move them round, and they try to resist it. When you get good on the track and you relax into its curves you realize you can use it. If you're pedalling at a certain speed, you roll naturally around the track, whereas going the other way doesn't seem to work. Ride the wrong way and it will tip you outwards, and you don't want to be falling outwards, because that's the way the big crashes come. Fall to your right, if you're going the proper way round, and you'll generally be okay. Fall left and it's a long way down.

They'll try to mix it up for us, with different training camps at different tracks. Hot ones, cold ones, bumpy ones, old ones, so that we've got a mental resilience when the big days come and it doesn't all feel as familiar and easy as our home track in Manchester. As an endurance rider I can go out on the road or on the turbo-trainer, putting a roller under the rear wheel and a block under the front to turn my bike into a stationary trainer, and I can train with the girls and make it social as well as effective. The repetitive nature of cycling doesn't hurt us physically, not until the lactic acid comes and the legs go and the vomit arrives. Because it's both the track and your body that steer the bike, you're using both legs to the same extent. Run on an athletics track and one leg is always dominant, because there's no banking to get you round. Go fast round the boards and it all balances out. It feels natural, and it feels good. And that's why the track never feels like a prison; it never feels as though those big banked turns are walls closing in on you. When you know the track and trust it and learn about it, letting it do what it wants, it gives you loads of free speed. If you want to go fast on your bike, then that's the place to do it. Of the various forms of training we do – velodrome, roads, turbo, gym – the track itself is what I love the most, because it's the closest element to the race. And racing is fun, and racing is why I do it.

**JASON:** That's the track. In the gym, the weights can hurt you just as much. When you start again after even a little while off, your body rebels against the forces you are putting through it. It's not just that you get out of bed like an old man; you don't even get out of bed. You lie under the duvet thinking, I do not want to stand up; I'm not sure I can stand up. Could I live today entirely upstairs? But when you are deep in training, squatting under a bar holding weights that are more than twice as heavy as you are naturally, it's less the muscles that ache than your actual body structure. You build up resistance to the muscular aches, and you can adapt and cope with greater training loads. But your body will always remind you that what you are doing is not natural, not within the limits of what most human bodies can handle. You can at least walk down the stairs at this point, but you do so with heavy tiredness. The strain is so great that you can feel the ache in the bones themselves, as if your skeleton is being compressed, as if no massage or hot or cold bath could ever shift it. You're not stiff; you're simply desperate for immobility. You try to sit down and you collapse into the chair. At night the pain keeps you awake – not the sharp jab of a torn muscle, but a relentless dull throbbing, an unnatural instinctive physical alarm clock that refuses to let you rest.

You take your relief where you can. On warm summer days I can find myself wishing I were an endurance track rider like Laura, able to go floating round the countryside, stimulated by the world around me, relaxed by the rhythm of the road and the sights that speed by. Walking into a windowless building can feel depressing, like shutting the door on a vast cave when instinctively you want to play outside. I am not a natural gym person – I would not be lifting weights if it wasn't so essential to my chances of success. Later in the year, though, comes the rain, and the sleet, and the dark mornings and damp afternoons. Then the gym becomes a refuge, and the cave of the velodrome becomes a place to hide.

You search for the fun, and you learn to tap into pleasure wherever it shows its face. I love the speed, and I love the stimulation of training with others, because that is when you are faster than ever before. On your own you can travel. Together you race, and the brain gives you extra free kilometres an hour. Interaction and stimulation, turning bad sessions into good, horrible efforts into eyeballs-out excitement.

You can find comedy in the pain. You laugh at the efforts and errors of others, not in a vindictive way but because you are all trying, and with trying comes failure. My team sprint lead-out man Philip Hindes was asked before Rio to take the first of a series of flying 200-metre efforts, the rest of us following him high up the track and then sweeping down on to his back wheel before our own turns, and because Phil usually comes in a little too slow and then kicks a little too hard, we asked him to come in fast. Except he then arrives as if he's been shot out of a cannon, much to our amusement, and in our competitive desire to chase we destroyed our legs before the session had really begun. But it works, because you are getting your training done without realizing. Fun disguises the hard work, but the hard work is still there, and the hard work is still banked.

All of it is specific. Lads who use gyms to stay fit or build beach muscles will also do squats and power cleans. But while they might do sets of ten, we are doing two or three, for the weights are so big and the explosiveness we need on the track is so critical that doing more would not only build the wrong sort of muscles but also frankly be impossible. Three lifts, maybe ten times, and you have blown your doors off. We are sprinters: everything is about the power. Everything is about the speed.

**LAURA:** Specificity again. Jason goes big and brief. We endurance girls go the opposite way: light weights, lots of times. Leg presses, leg extensions. Big belts around our waists to support our backs. And when we're on the leg-press machine, we're pushing 230 kilograms away – light weights compared to those used by the male sprinters; huge weights for girls our size.

I get through it all by thinking about racing. My next race, my next opponents. It can be weeks or months away. It doesn't matter. I will convince myself that if I slack off here, if I fail to finish or cut the weights or come off the track an effort or two early, I will be crap come the next domestic meet, the next World Cup, the next Olympics. I will make every session count, and I will obsess over it, and when I obsess over something I can't shake it out of my head. I see a car I don't recognize near our house, I convince myself we're going to get burgled. Jason can't talk me out of it: it's in there, it's happening. I tell myself that if I'm not doing this training session then one of my rivals is, and then I go into a weird mood. I've got to do this session now. I can't not do it.

It never gets easier. Food is your big comfort, and then you have a new physiologist, and his new idea is to take you off carbs for three days. Usually I eat porridge for breakfast, avocado on toast, an omelette, a yoghurt. Suddenly that's gone. Just a three-egg omelette, no orange juice, no milk in your coffee. A two-hour road ride, feeling like there's nothing in the tank, only a protein gel to eat, and then home to a lunch of twelve marshmallows. Instant sugar; instant sick feeling in your nose and guts. A flat-out track session in the afternoon, emptying your stores. Dinner? One slab of meat. No pasta, no potatoes, no bread. So hungry you feel sick all over again. Then there are the ice-baths, 12 degrees, like standing in the North Sea off the Essex coast at Christmas.

You do it for the races. As a kid it was the only time you would ever have a crowd, and crowd means atmosphere means excitement. The Revolution series, the elite domestic track meets, the supporters coming for the big names but sticking around to watch us young ones too. You know the coaches are going to be there. You know you have to perform to be selected. As you progress through the ranks your sights shift upwards, to World Cups and beyond, and you have to train through those events you used to target, but you still care about every one of them, and you still want to win every time you ride out on to the track.

Every race matters, and every race changes the rider I am. There are some girls who are always fantastic in training. Of the gold medal-winning team pursuit squad, Jo Rowsell and Ciara Horne are total machines in training. Their sessions are unbelievable. Not mine. I can be riding like a dog, then all of a sudden I get a sniff of a finish line and I'm a rider transformed. Before London 2012 I was finding the training in itself so tough that I forever felt I was teetering on the edge of illness. How could I succeed at an Olympics if I could barely make it through training? It was the same in 2016. Before the World Cup in Hong Kong I was horrendous. I couldn't finish a team pursuit with the girls. But when I get there, I blow it apart. I won the omnium like I wasn't even trying.

It works because I love it. I've done two Olympics now, I've been racing since before my age hit double figures, and that love has never died. I get asked about being an inspiration to young girls. Well, I still feel exactly like the eight-year-old kid who raced because she loved it. I didn't want fame for this. I didn't want money from it and I didn't want admiration. I just did it because bike riding is my life.

My dad Adrian says he can see it when I race. In Rio he said that when I was riding round I looked like I was just having fun. Everyone else was tense – it's an Olympics, you're supposed to be nervous. But I knew how to deal with it, and I knew that the scale of the occasion didn't mean it shouldn't be fun too.

**JASON:** You have to hold a balance between obsession and everyday life. British Cycling have a well-known fixation with hand-wash gels. You are supposed to use it before every meal, after every handshake. It cuts down on germs, and if it cuts down on germs, it reduces the chances of you missing training with illness or – far worse – having four years of preparation destroyed by a runny nose on the morning of your Olympic final. We have had medical experts come to our training camps, hold a special light over our fingers and show us all the areas we missed when we thought we were washing our hands correctly. We have had talks at Celtic Manor about being careful pressing buttons in hotel lifts and then letting the same fingertip scratch your nose or rub your eye.

You try to be sensible. You don't bite your nails. You wash your hands with soap before meals, and if you've been glad-handing at an event you might think about washing them again before you leave. Some riders are almost addicted to the sight of that foam on their fingers and the smell of the alcohol rub, or they start polishing their phones with hand-gel each morning. We still let our two dogs lick our faces, even if the chances are they've been licking each other's backsides just before. When we were warned about touching lift buttons with our fingers we asked whether we should use our tongues instead. But if our parents were coming to stay and one had a chest infection, we would delay their visit. If we bought a bacon butty in the local shop and the guy behind the counter sneezed all over it, we would drop it in the bin on the way out. We try, though, to hang on to any normality we can, because so much of what we do is not normal. So much of it separates us from the real world.

But that separation can pay off in the most beautiful way. When your training times are improving with each week that ticks by, your mood changes. When you go into qualification unsure and come out as the fastest rider on the track, you feel a wonderful sense of confidence and certainty. When you clock a personal best – and so finely tuned are you that often you know you've done so, just from the sensation, without needing to wait for the numbers – all the privations and the eccentricity seem worthwhile. Strength feels good. Form feels like authority.

And then there is the thrill of going fast, of going faster than your body could go any other way, far quicker than you could ever run, yet all of it still under your own power. You feel superhuman. Your brain almost overloads with the sensory rush.

No matter how many times you hammer down from a steeply banked turn, it still gives you that same thrill. A thrill that so few others ever experience; a thrill that you chase in all the dark hours that allow it to happen.

# Two: **The Sprinter**

**JASON:** I am a sprinter. I am speed.

I never feel more fully alive than when I am racing. The sensation of swooping down the banking, the adrenaline rush of flying past your opponent knowing with complete certainty that you have them beaten and there's nothing they can do. The challenge of trying to find perfection under extreme stress. And going fast, so fast, faster than anyone else could in that moment.

I need stimulus. I need someone to race against, even if it's the illusion of racing. At the velodrome in Manchester they call it the Lynx Effect, because often it will be one of the girls on the track at the same time, following our efforts, but it doesn't have to be a female. When I'm doing efforts with someone I just go faster. Put me on the track with no one else and I am quick. Put me on the track with someone to beat and I find a little extra. I have no idea why, and it doesn't make sense to my logical mind, but it is a fact I have come to accept.

Sprint races at major championships begin with a flying 200 metres against the clock. One rider at a time, and the fastest man becomes top seed for the man-against-man first round that follows. I used to struggle with flying laps as a young rider and I struggle with them today. In the competition proper I race beautifully. Even if I have someone behind me, no threat at all, just knowing that they are there will make me ride that bit quicker. I can empty the tanks.

Physically I am all fast-twitch fibres. Mentally I am patient and calm. You might think sprinters are all naked aggression and muscle-bursting machismo, but the best are all about cool judgement under immense duress. Knowing when to go and when to wait. Knowing you have that supercharged speed to unleash, but understanding that you can only switch it on when it really matters. Perversely it is the endurance track riders who are the ones always raring to go before training, twitchy before races. Laura will do her flying lap as one of the six disciplines in her omnium, and it's all, 'let's go', and 'bang bang bang'. My Olympic sprint final starts off instead almost in slow motion: 'Dum de dum, de dum de dum …'

We can ride slower than anyone else in that first lap, so slowly that Laura would be worried about crashing. And then, when we ignite, it is like opening a tank of nitrous oxide. We can burn incredibly brightly for a remarkably short period of time. Our warm-ups last forever; the key moment in our race is over in a flash of carbon and straining muscle.

**LAURA:** Sprinting suits Jason because he's so chilled in everyday life. He has to be, because he has to be able to read people. It's like a game of poker in which you play your winning hand at over 70 kilometres per hour. If you are fired up and feisty from the word go then you're never going to win. Calm beats chaos every time.

**JASON:** Sprinting is speed, but it is speed in the right second. You are a tactician and you are a problem solver. You will analyse each rival in the months before and you will work out what they are most likely to do in any given situation. They will want the race to unfold one way. There is one move that will suit their physical ability and competitive character more than any other. You must be capable of both spotting that move coming and knowing exactly what you can do to counter it.

Thinking is good. Thinking is good unless you overthink it. In those flying 200 metres, that's sometimes what I have done. But when another rider is on your wheel you just act without thought. Instinct – which is really experience and race understanding built up over thousands of skirmishes over a lifetime of sprinting – can be your best friend and only answer.

The thrill of riding a bike fast never fails. Going fast, going well. The last few weeks before an Olympic Games are the most fun of all. Everyone is riding express because all the training has been about peaking for now; the engineers and mechanics have given us the new technology and new bikes that will take us round even quicker. No compromise in your preparation, everything else stripped away and burnished in the search for more speed.

We tend to go fastest in the keirin – six big guys going fast on big gears. But it doesn't feel as fast as the sprint, because you are all together going the same pace. In a big sprint final, nothing feels faster than when you are in second place and you have that carrot of victory dangling in front of you. That's when you feel it. That's when you get the rush.

Fast can feel slow. When you are in form, everything happens more easily. You see the race and all its problems unfolding leisurely in front of you. When you are riding well your ability to read the moves is an entirely natural thing. Particularly in the keirin, you just know what is going to happen and how you should react. You just do it. When it's going badly, it's all doubt and worry. You're thinking, I hope he doesn't go there, I hope that rider doesn't do that …

When form is there, you feel like you're two moves ahead of everyone else. It is an amazing sensation. The panic can come if you think you're in form and someone is in better. I have had big semi-finals when I have beaten great riders in super shape to get there and felt really good about how I was going. Then suddenly one man has more power than you. They can simply drive it round the outside, and there is nothing you can do. From flying you come crashing back to earth.

You can plan as much as you want, and these days we tend to plan it right nine times out of ten. When I first started with GB we would only get it right half the time. But you must be able to think on your feet, too. If somebody goes, you have to go with them without thinking about it. Hesitate to assess what has happened and you are already a goner. British Cycling head coach Iain Dyer used to say, if you're thinking about it, it's already too late. When you are going well you call everything right; it's the magic of form and experience reacting to things that happen. You know the individuals and you know you can beat them. When everything's going badly you get it wrong every time. The frustration is intense.

My mum Lorraine says that I was born strong. Or at least that's what she thought. My brother Craig, four years older, struggled early on with asthma, but in my first eight months I had no asthma, no colds, no snotty noses. When Mum took me for my first full check-up with the nurse, I failed the hearing test, my head was apparently too big and I had a heart murmur.

As Mum was leaving, the health visitor waved at her and walked over. 'How are you doing? I haven't seen you for ages!' Mum looked back at her. 'When I brought Jason in he was perfect. And now ...'

Craig was the talkative one. Like my mum, he would chat all day. I would hide behind him, saying nothing, watching it all. But while I was quiet from the start I was competitive. I wanted to be like my big brother, and I wanted everything he had. Just before my first birthday I was drinking my milk from a bottle as usual when I noticed Craig was drinking his from a cup. I had to have a cup too, even if I couldn't use it properly, even if, when I was put back on the bottle, I had forgotten how to suck and couldn't use that either. Aged three I was in the back garden on my bike with stabilizers when I realized Craig wasn't using any. Right. Neither would I. We had a long lawn down the side of the house. Dad took the stabilizers off, Mum did the running up and down, pushing me and holding on to the saddle. When her back failed her, she went back inside to do the washing-up, only to look through the kitchen window and see me go sailing past. 'Mum! I've done it, I can do it!'

My forenames were both chosen for a logical reason. Mum was a teacher. As a teacher you know not only which names are common at a given time but also which you will forever associate with the naughty kid in your class. There were only a few Jasons, and all were well behaved. Francis was chosen as my middle name because that was my grandfather's name, and my parents wanted it to stay within the family. Francis lived long enough to see me win my first Olympic gold in Beijing on television. I would have loved him to see me do it again at London 2012, but he passed away a few months before, while I was away racing in Melbourne at the World Championships. He lives on in me though, just as Mum had hoped. One of his quotes is always in my head and Laura's before a big race: Don't bring home any scrap metal. Silver counted as scrap. So did bronze. Job done, Granddad.

So I was JFK. It didn't raise too many eyebrows in Bolton. My riding would. At three I would pedal off with Mum when she went to pick Craig up from primary school. She would be running alongside me, trying desperately to keep up, and all I cared about was making sure my teddy Sweep was still attached to the handlebars and facing forwards so he could enjoy the speed too. Sweep had been given to me by my Aunty Maria at birth, and after repeated washes had not only faded from his original bright blue but had also lost the loud squeak he used to make when you squeezed his middle. Mum heard me explaining to a friend of hers at the school gate: 'Sweep used to squeak, but now he just whispers.'

As an adult I am sometimes quite shy. That came on in my teenage years. At nursery I was one of the most confident children there, rough and tumble on my bike, ruling the playground on my feet. One morning, the mother of one of my friends took my mum aside. 'Thomas was being told off by his dad last night. He wasn't happy about it. "If you don't stop, Dad," he said, "I'm going to tell Jason Kenny about you."'

Mum glanced over at where we were lining up to go into the classroom. I was first in line when a friend tried to push in front. I held him off and told him to get behind me. Thomas arrived and ran to the front. I stood back and let him in. All about teamwork, even at that point. Find yourself a good man to lead out the sprint; don't let anyone past you on the back straight.

Not all of my early habits were so indicative of a successful cycling career. I used to have a tendency to run into trees. Off ahead of my parents, chasing Craig, I'd fail to notice the large trunk right in front of me. That was the point when Mum and Dad may have first suspected that I was a little shortsighted.

School started off badly: I began on a Wednesday and cried until the Friday. But I settled in, and enjoyed the playground games and the maths lessons – since in the future I'd be working in hundredths of seconds, a first year trying to count to a hundred was a decent start.

It was never just about cycling. We were allowed to try everything: a term of tennis, a year of karate, football all the way through. We were lively boys, and our parents wanted us to burn that energy off without us hanging around the streets of Farnworth in Bolton and putting it to the wrong sort of use. Nothing was ever forced, and nothing was ever taken too seriously. If it looked as if we were getting bored with something, if it was becoming routine rather than fun, we would leave it behind and look for something else. Swimming was a big thing, because we boys always want to be around water. At one point the club we swam with wanted us to start early morning training. Neither of us fancied it, and Mum and Dad were absolutely fine with that. Another parent with two sons came up to Mum. 'This could be their last chance. Why don't you push them more?' Mum, aware from her teaching experiences of how competitive some parents could be, was thinking, 'They're nine and thirteen – how could this be their last chance?'

I hadn't always been so grateful for parental intervention. Aged eight, I was becoming aware of my appearance. One evening, Mum caught me doing my hair in the mirror.

'Mum, how old do you have to be before you can use hair gel?'

'Oh, at least eighteen.'

'Okay. What about mousse?'

Cycling round a track rather than the streets and parks of Bolton came about, when I was eleven, through good fortune rather than deliberate design. Mum's brother booked a taster session at the Manchester Velodrome, which had only been opened for a few years. You could borrow a fixed-wheel track bike, have a little bit of instruction and be let loose to ride around for the rest of your hour. He had ridden with some friends from work and thought it was something Craig and I would enjoy. He was right. I loved it.

We were already on the lookout for the next sporting fix. I was too old for my former football team, and Britain's Jason Queally had just won gold in the kilo at the Sydney Olympics. Something was in the air. We found a cycling club for kids my age called Eastlands Velo, which was based at the Manchester

Velodrome. Mum wanted to keep me occupied, and professed herself happy to drive me the half-hour around the M60, so I was in – Monday evenings at first – learning how to keep pedalling on a bike that gave you no choice, learning how to steer and react in a world without brakes. Soon I'd be going on Saturday mornings as well, 8 until 11.

Mum's ability to talk to any available bystander kicked in again. Another mother told her that one of the other boys went after school on Wednesday nights too. Eastlands Velo had that sort of programme, which may be why, as well as me, they also produced Steven Burke, who won Olympic gold in 2012 and 2016 as part of the team pursuit, and road riders Simon and Adam Yates. I wasn't sure if I could cut it. Was I actually good enough? More Mum chat: The coaches say it's fine.

And so the routine developed. Mum would get home from her school to find me waiting at the door with my kitbag and bike. Into the car and straight off. If she was late I would give her an adolescent earful.

She didn't always enjoy watching me, but she preferred what I was doing to motorbiking. She was afraid that I would end up riding one, so when Craig and I each reached seventeen, she paid for our driving lessons in the hope we would skip that teenage obsession and go straight to cars instead. It didn't work – both of us now ride motorbikes. In the velodrome she used to hate the group races, where there were riders diving around all over the place and often sliding down the track. Rather than watching the mayhem unfold, she would stare fixedly at the lap counter and will it to turn over more quickly. But she liked the atmosphere, the fact that it was run by volunteers, and she was thrilled that it was indoors. Having had two sons and having pined for a daughter, she had reached her limit for standing in the pouring rain watching us play average football.

A year on from moving up to training three times a week, aged thirteen, I borrowed a bike and rode the National Track Championships. I finished tenth. Later, Laura and I would work out that she had been there that same day, me racing the under-14s, Laura yet to turn ten but racing with the under-12s.

The fixation was taking hold. I had always been a doer rather than a watcher – playing football rather than watching Bolton Wanderers, riding my own bike rather than sitting in the stands watching the legends. I wasn't necessarily good at everything, and I certainly wasn't the best. I was fast but never the fastest. On school sports days I was a perpetual runner-up – I once won the 400 metres at the Bolton Schools championships, but that was because it was chucking it down. I was pretty much the only one who turned up and tried. Other than that, I was always the nearly man – second, third, fourth. Decent at everything, excelling at very little. My coordination kicked in late: I can now catch and kick a ball much better than I could in my teens. But I have always tried really hard and got stuck in to whatever I do. I would invariably be the one pouring sweat, breathing loudly.

Craig could always beat me easily at pretty much every-thing. He was stronger and faster, and was charged with looking after me when we were out and about. That was good for me, because it meant I was exposed to a lot more than I otherwise would have been. I was forever chasing him, just as

Laura, another second sibling of two, was constantly chasing her big sister Emma.

It dragged me along, and it made me relaxed in the company of lads older than me. When I was still thirteen I got thrown into training with a load of sixteen-year-olds, and I got on with them really well, better than I did with kids my own age.

Craig and I would argue, as brothers do. If you left us in the same room there would be trouble. We would grow up just fine, though: him still protective of me, very proud of what's come since, and me in awe of his ability to make friends and talk almost as much as our mother. And even back then there was no jealousy that Mum was ferrying me to the velodrome three times a week. She saw it as the perfect chance to have a chat with her otherwise recalcitrant younger teenage son – or at least chat at him – and Craig was just as happy: he was supposed to be doing his homework but was thinking instead, 'Great, I can go on the computer while Mum takes him ...'

There was luck involved. The country had just one Olympic-standard velodrome at that point, and it just happened to be fifteen miles from our house. Had I been brought up in Newcastle, Leeds, Birmingham or Bristol, there would have been no indoor cycling and no Olympic gold medals. I wonder sometimes how much talent slipped through the net. My father Michael might have been a top track sprinter, for example. We'll never know. Kids from the same street as me in Bolton born ten years before me would never know what they could have achieved on the track. For all the precision of the training I have had and the technology I have used since, I was gifted the chance to experience all that by geography and inadvertent timing.

But I was competitive, and I could handle the pressures that those competitions would bring. Mum used to enjoy sport at school but hated the start line. Before she even set off she would have worked herself up into such a state that she believed all hope of success had gone. Even now she can wind herself up in an instant. I was just able to hold it in. Just like my dad Michael, just like my granddad Francis. What I did get from Mum was a lack of fear, a lack of expectation. When I was beaten – and I was beaten more than I wasn't – they used to say to me, 'Oh, never mind – you'll beat him next time', or, 'He's a good rider, he's the one to watch.' Always chasing the next rider, never worrying how many more were ahead after that.

I loved competing and I loved trying hard, and you can try really hard on a bike. You can really push yourself. With a burgeoning love of speed came a quiet satisfaction that I could somehow stay totally relaxed in a situation where others were panicking and falling apart. Even then, had you seen me riding, you would have noticed my poker face, in contrast to the grimaces and gurns of my rivals. I was thinking about what was happening, analysing the situation. Pausing on the throttle, using it as and when I needed to rather than letting emotion take over in a sudden uncontrolled explosion. With hindsight, I was showing all the signs of becoming a classic man two in a three-man team sprint: holding that fine balance between going 100 per cent and 99.9 per cent, juggling not only my needs and sensations but those of others around me.

If you were to meet me down the pub now, you would find me relatively quiet. I'm a slow starter with new people. Your first impression might not be the best. I'm bad at small talk;

if I don't want to talk to someone, it leaks out of my face, whereas Laura can and will chat to anyone, even if she doesn't like them. I will warm up, though. There is chat within me, and once I'm relaxed in your company it can flow.

As a teenager I couldn't manage any of that. I wasn't confident in who I was, or in the fact that anyone would want to talk to me. I hadn't opened up as I have now; I couldn't express myself as I can today. Now I have just accepted who I am: if people don't like me, who cares. It doesn't matter.

Back then it was more difficult, on and off the track. One year, as the British Cycling system began to work through its long revolution, all the kids who owned a racing licence were tested. If you turned out to be good enough, you would get on the talent team. Big stakes, a high bar. On a turbo – a stationary trainer – they put a mountain bike. The endurance part of the test was to do a flat-out three-minute effort and see how far you would have gone. The speed test involved turning the pedals under no resistance to see what the maximum cadence was that you could hit, and then a five-second sprint.

We were the first wave of youngsters to go through it, and it was clear they were stabbing in the dark. The standard you were expected to hit was ridiculous. I failed the sprint element, but I had done well enough in the three minutes to make the grade, even though I was the youngest rider they would take on, aged thirteen. The man who came up with the test? Iain Dyer, who years later would coach me at Great Britain level to Olympic gold. Other good riders made it through – Matt Crampton, another future GB sprinter; Adam Blythe, who went on to beat Mark Cavendish for the British road race title and to ride the Tour de France; Lizzie Armitstead, World road race champion. For me it was the point of no return. I loved cycling so much that I stopped trying to make the school team in other sports, save for one glorious late run in the football team that saw us make the final of the Bolton Schools trophy, only for me to be subbed off as we lost, my calves – which by then had become all about track rather than turf – having cramped up to nightmarish effect.

I got my own proper track bike, a Fort bike, bright yellow and imported from the Czech Republic. I loved it so much that it slept in my bedroom with me, got transported to the car for training sessions and then carried into the velodrome at the other end. I had a tank of a road bike, and from my talent programme I could borrow a BMX and a cyclo-cross bike too. This was the visionary thinking coming through: let these gifted kids try everything, develop their skills all round, and stay interested and fresh rather than one-dimensional and bored. Instead of pushing us reluctantly down one path they were allowing us to naturally find our own. It both fed my developing fascination with the sport and allowed my understanding of it to grow.

At those first Nationals, where we had competed in an omnium, I had been knocked out early in the sprint. I had assumed that was me done, and headed out to the canteen to eat my sandwiches with Mum and Dad before we drove back to Bolton. It took a steward to intervene, to run to find me and point out that no, I wasn't out, and yes, I'd better get my kit back on and dig the bike back out of the boot of the car. Getting on that talent team and being taken to events across the country was a cycling scholarship in more ways than one.

I sometimes wonder where I would be had cycling not arrived in that auspicious way. At school I stayed on to do my A-Levels but drifted through, starting with maths, physics and PE, dropping physics after a year and finishing with two Ds. Pretty average. I knew I couldn't stand being in an office, so, if it hadn't been for cycling, I would have done something physical, chosen a skill that would come in handy to other people as well as me. My brother became a car mechanic, which has turned out to be rather useful for the family, so maybe I would have become a builder. I wouldn't be unhappy doing it either. You fix the van, Craig, I'll sort your extension.

I am a contented man, and not only because of those six Olympic gold medals. I will laugh at most things. All the times we were getting beaten at big races with the British sprint squad developed a dark sense of humour that was already there. Laughing at how bad we were sometimes was the only thing to get us through. It doesn't matter how humiliating or depressing something is; eventually you can laugh at it, even if a little wince or lingering disappointment goes with it too.

Not much makes me angry, not even drivers who try to run us off the road. When I lived in Manchester, I was so used to hopping on to the kerb to avoid stroppy taxi drivers that I could remain quite placid about it. In the Cheshire countryside, having your life put at risk because someone is unwilling to add ten seconds to their journey seems rather unnecessary. People will pass you with a gap that starts at an inch and narrows as they accelerate away. There are riders who have just taken up cycling who might not have the handling skills to stay upright, and there are professional track riders who might be about to win gold medals for your nation. A week before the World Championships in 2016 I was nearly sent into a hedge. That would have been it: broken arm, world title gone because some numpty in a van didn't want to deviate a foot from his chosen path. There wasn't even anyone on the road at the time – it was as if he was trying to prove or score a point by overtaking me as close as he could.

I'm a contented man, but I can get sad when others don't expect it. I hate thinking I've upset anyone, or let someone down. I try my best not to, and I will rationalize it by telling myself that we make the decisions we do with the information we have at the time. And I try not to worry, because worrying has always seemed pointless to me. Can you change something? Then change it. If you can't, let it go.

One of the characteristics that defines me is that I make lots of mistakes but don't tend to make a mistake twice. I am the same with my emotions. I worried once, found it did nothing to help and decided not to do it again. I got nervous once before a race and decided not to get nervous again. At some point in my life I would no doubt have panicked; having experienced that, I don't panic.

It helps me. After the Olympics in 2016 I went racing at Brands Hatch in a borrowed car. It had been a few years since my last track day and I was rusty, not yet aware that my skills had taken a massive step back. I tried to take a corner fast, way too fast. Massive spin, heading in rapid circles for the fence. I don't want to hit the fence. Broken car, broken leg. I'm trying to sort it out, slow it down, and at no point during that frantic few seconds do I panic. Panic and you tense up and end in a far worse mess. So I didn't. I stayed relaxed and kept it out of the fence. Back to the pits, fresh underpants, tried again.

A few years ago I had a sleepless night worrying about something stupid that I had no control over. The next morning I drew a mental line under it. No more will I let this affect me. When issues crop up now – and they always will – I do the same. I've trained myself to let them go.

I can't take all the credit. My granddad was always like that, no nonsense, sort it out, crack on. My nan was the same. When my brother was born they gave up smoking overnight. No gradually cutting down, no nicotine patches. They just stopped. One night later in his life Granddad just stopped eating crap. He decided one day, I'm going to eat well, walk the dog, and stay fit. He walked the dog every day until he died. I think I have inherited that attitude. Maybe it's a northern thing: just do it.

I am a private man. There are things about me that even some of those close to me don't know. Every Sunday of my life I've gone to church. I still go now, to the local Catholic one. I kept that to myself for a long time. There will be people I'm with every week at the velodrome who don't know. I wouldn't describe myself as religious. It's just a little release at the end of the week, a little moment to yourself. I support it because it supports others: the old dears who go for tea and biscuits, the lonely people with no one else in their lives.

I arrive at the last minute and leave as soon as it finishes. Laura doesn't come. I sit in the same spot every time, quite near the back. I don't talk to a soul. I don't sing the hymns. I'll shake the hands of people close by when the time comes for the sign of peace. You'd look a bit weird if you didn't shake people's hands. The priest says hello, and then I go.

**LAURA:** Jason is a caring man. He looks after both of us; he does pretty much everything. No matter how upset I am, he will put up with it.

If I come second, I'll be devastated. He understands. He'll take the mick afterwards too – 'You came second? Second?' – and sometimes he'll do it too soon. If he gets knocked out in the first round he will laugh about it straight away. With me he has to leave it about a week or so. It's got to be history.

He is much more sociable than he lets on, certainly more sociable than he comes across in television interviews. Yet he can be awkward when we're with strangers. When someone is chewing his ear off and he's not giving much back, I'll be stood there thinking, 'Come on, just speak to me instead, save both of you the trouble.' When he doesn't want to speak to someone he has a tell that only I can spot: a long, slow blink. It's a subconscious thing, but when I see it I think, 'Uh oh, trouble,' because it's either going to be silence or it's going to be something blunt, but either way it isn't going to be good.

Jason is good at lots of things. He taught himself to play guitar. He cooks. He does a pie that could win prizes. He washes up. He's good with DIY around the house, if you ignore the fact that he isn't the best at hammering nails into awkward spots. He would argue that his dad makes him look bad because he is the greatest hammerer in the north-west of England. Michael has an initial whack so accurate and firm that the job is almost done in one blow. Jason has to build into his. Classic sprinter. Slow slow slow, fast fast fast. Classic man two in a sprint: his dad does the hard shift up front, Jason just keeps the momentum going.

He says he is just as he was as a kid: enjoys everything, excels only at cycling. To me, he gets most things right. The oven in our cottage is an Aga, and it has hot spots and cold spots. Jason not only works out that the heat comes in top left but then figures out where each different item should go to be finished at the same time. He knows when the spuds need turning – I don't – and remembers to turn them. I never would. I'm the woman who tried to grill a baked potato, and set fire to my flat.

He is terrible at being tidy. One corner of our bedroom is taken over by his floordrobe, a big pile of clothes that all smell. He claims it is a system: clean clothes in the traditional wardrobe; dirty ones in the clothes-basket; ones with another wear in them in the floordrobe. He'll wear a t-shirt for one day round the house. Into the floordrobe. The next he'll wear it to the gym. Back into the floordrobe. On the third day he will retire it for dog walking.

I don't agree with it. It just stinks, so it should be put into the washing machine. Occasionally I'll take things into my own hands and just put the entire floordrobe into the wash. He goes ballistic. I come back in and he's rooting through the machine after its cycle like he's left his wallet and phone in there.

That's not the only thing. When I come home from being away on camps or racing, it's very rare to find he has vacuumed in my absence. I have to make a point of phoning him: 'Is the house going to be tidy when I get back?' Except then he's cleaning up ten minutes before I arrive. And he will only have vacuumed the bits of the floor he can see. Never under the chairs or under the mats. The throws will have migrated from the sofa to become mats on the mats.

He will never throw old food out. It can be rotting. It doesn't bother him. Admittedly, I stockpile. I automatically buy potatoes and onions every time I go to the shops. We've got months of them piled up in one of the corner cupboards. We would have to have days of potato soup followed by mashed potato and potato pie for pudding to get through them. He will never just bin them. I've seen him eat four out-of-date yoghurts in a row rather than throw them out. He won't have been hungry, and he doesn't like yoghurt. Same with eggs. He'd rather have a twelve-egg omelette and then lie motionless on the sofa for the next two hours with the egg-sweats rather than see them go to waste.

I admire him. I admire the fact that he can have really bad days on the track and still get up for the next one. If I had gone through three years as bad as he did between the 2012 and 2016 Olympics I would have cracked. And I worry about him when he's out on his motorbike, not because I doubt his skills but because of everybody else around him. Apart from that, I wouldn't say that I do worry. I want him to be happy. If there's something that's wrong with him, then he tells me anyway. What is there left to worry about if he shares it all with me.

He likes the easy life. He likes being at home with the dogs, he likes messing around in the garden. To me it's another household chore. We're not meant to be on our feet. An hour out and about in the sun is not good for us. Get a gardener. Let the grass grow.

He finds it therapeutic. He loves messing about in his garage with his bikes, and he loves racing them at track days. When we went to Silverstone to watch the British MotoGP, we spent some of the race in hospitality. People were there who had very little interest in the racing. Jason not only avoided them, but had no interest in small talk when he was cornered. Tyre pressures, Cal Crutchlow, Valentino Rossi, fine. Anything else and the long, slow blink came out to play. Uh oh.

**JASON:** My motivation to train and ride can climb and dip at random times. It's not that I ever fall out of love with cycling, it's more that I'm a creature of habit, and if I fall out of my rhythm, that's the worst thing for me. When I've got a good routine going then riding is never a chore. When I'm on top of everything, all is fine. It's when I go away to train or race or something breaks that rhythm that I can struggle. The Olympics are a natural stimulus. When they appear on the planning horizon it focuses the mind and gives you a clear target. I slip into the Olympic-year routine. I get up, I have breakfast, I get to the track.

Training on the track hurts, but the routine is established. There will be inescapable pain, but you welcome its onset. It is the easier rides in the less intense periods after big competitions that perversely can be harder: getting out on the road when you're on your own at home, getting out when it's wet and cold and the sofa is warm and you're only supposed to do a couple of flat hours anyway, and it would be so easy to forget about it until the next hard session on the track comes round to kick you up the backside.

You try to think your way through it. I now have a proper

winter road bike – bigger tyres, solid wheels, mudguards. As a man schooled in the temperature-controlled indoors, I used to loathe the horrible cold spray that comes up off the road in the dark wet months, the sludge on the small country roads, the frozen feet. Stick mudguards on, wear decent thermals and it completely changes the experience. Obvious stuff to road riders around the country; essential to us accustomed to the smooth boards of the velodrome.

Laura helps, because Laura will never slack. If it's on the training schedule then she will do it. She takes considerable pride in ticking the sessions off. If it's a road ride then it happens early: done so that she can have the afternoon to do what she wants. A lot of her sessions are double days – mornings in the velodrome, lunch, more schooling on the boards in the afternoon. It makes her appreciate her time off, so on the single days, even when she secretly wants to lie in bed, she will get up and do it, get out and get it done. I fight the inertia. Leave it until later. Watch the weather. Find an excuse. When the sessions matter I am always there. When they feel less important, it can be easy to treat them as such.

I stay in love with it because I love the brainpower as well as the leg speed. Everyone talks about tactics in sprinting. We all have a mental video library of rivals' best rides and worst nightmares. What people don't realize is that if you break it down, you find that almost everyone has one or two rides that they favour. Particularly if they're under pressure, they revert to the rides they prefer. After Rio 2016, Laura and I appeared on *The Jonathan Ross Show* with three of the Great Britain hockey team that had recently won gold. Goalkeeper Maddie Hinch had saved all four Dutch penalties as the favourites were beaten in the final. She put that success down to exactly the same thing: when the pressure came on, each Dutch player in turn did exactly what Maddie had expected them to do, from having watched replays again and again beforehand.

Sprinters revert to their safe ride. If you know what they're doing, that will give you the upper hand. Whether you can do anything about it is another question, because they tend to be successful in that ride, which is why they have stuck to it.

You look for the little physical twitches and tells. It's more subtle than it used to be. When I first started racing, riders would pull a lot more shapes than they do now. Support teams grow. Video evidence proliferates. Word gets around, and riders rein it back in. You have to watch for a hint of what was once a clear sign.

A strong rider will want a gap over the man behind him. That's fine. You can work that out. What you have to watch for is when they are going to try to create that gap, because it can open out so quickly, and if you're not quite on it then the race is gone.

There are bigger tells. In the man-on-man showdown of an individual sprint final, three laps, best of three races, we alternate which rider leads it out. A typical ride from the back is to push on the person at the front and then pick up the tow from their slipstream and pass them at the finish. To ride like that, you don't actually want to take the front. So the plan for the rider in front is to offer the other man a big opening to take the lead. If he doesn't take it, then you know he wants to be at the back, and you don't need to push on. You don't have to feel that pressure to defend the front.

I watch for every tiny clue. That first slow-motion lap can be like circling a crime scene. Count your opponent's pedal revolutions. Go slow around the bottom of the track and you can roughly figure out what gear they're on. Once you work out whether it's a big gear or small one compared to yours and their usual one you can transpose that into what they'll want to do in the race.

Some riders claim they can spot a gear ratio by glancing over at the start. In the past, maybe you could. We all rode with similar set-ups. Now the spread is so large that you can never be sure. Someone could be coming up on a random gear, and a random gear means previous tactical scenarios go out of the window.

You find a way. If you are at the back, you count their pedal revolutions against yours as you cruise slowly round on that first 250 metres. You know what gear you have on and you know you are going the same speed. So you watch their foot as it goes over the top of the pedalling arc and do the mental maths.

It's harder if it's your turn on the front. You're looking back under your armpit or craning your neck past your shoulder while also trying to hold the optimum position on the track. You watch for their positioning and you calculate where you are in the competition. If they're keen to get moving, if they want a smooth, gradual acceleration from standing start to flat out rather than a slow dance and then a sudden shoot-out, the chances are they're on a bigger gear. If they go high up the track they're also likely to be on a higher gear, because they're looking for the descent from that height to give them the momentum they need to launch in that gear. If they're not really interested in pumping up the track then you flip it round: chances are they're on a smaller gear, so I'll tweak my tactics and make this as difficult for them as I can. People tend to go big when they feel the pressure to progress. The closer you are to the medal races the more likely a rider is to stick a meaty gear on. It all comes with experience.

I stay in love with cycling because of the Olympics. It's the only time we do a full taper, cutting the length and intensity of our training so that it is all about perfection in one race rather than day after day of hard work; cutting it all back so, for those few special moments, we feel physically fresher than we have in three years. It changes the sensations in your body as you spin laps around the track, and it changes your mental outlook. We will do mini tapers for a World Championship, but it doesn't have the same effect. Taper too early and your legs lose some of their strength. Taper too late and all those thousands of training laps are still holding your legs back.

It can freak you out. You're so used to working so hard for so long that when you wake up one morning and your legs are no longer hurting it actually feels wrong. Sometimes you want them to hurt, because that's the feeling you've been aiming for every evening over the past forty months. There can be panic for some. This isn't normal, this isn't right. What we do well to forget is that life will carry on after an Olympics. It's as if the world ends when the flame is extinguished. Our focus is totally on those few moments of racing, and that is one of the reasons why we perform at an Olympics like seldom before or after. We don't worry about holding anything back for the next World Championships.

We give more, both physically and mentally, than we do at any other point.

I stay in love with cycling because my relationship allows me to. Laura and I are not identical characters. I always get up first, as soon as the dogs wake me; Laura will stay in bed. She might tell you that I'm messier than her, but we just approach tidiness in our own ways. I will keep it at a general level; Laura will let it slide for days and then have a hissy fit and subsequent blitz-clean.

The floordrobe will wind her up. In the kitchen the same rules don't appear to apply. I can be cleaning the kitchen and Laura will just happily sit on the sofa. If I'm sitting on the sofa and Laura is starting housework, she won't actually say anything, but she'll put the vacuum on its noisiest setting and start jabbing me in the ankles with it until I get up and say, 'I'll get involved, shall I?'

We'll argue about that. We argue about what we argue about. Laura will send me detailed essays on WhatsApp, specifying the sub-clauses in her position and the contradictions in mine. I'd like to say we have found a good way of resolving our disputes, but they usually escalate until someone says something they regret and then we end up apologizing. Apologizing is good; being able to do so without escalating first to a point of destruction might be even better. They always say never go to sleep on an argument, and that seems fine, but if you've got a very logical position you think makes complete sense then it's much harder. Or if you're just really tired, and the pillow has a greater attraction than another hour of detailed negotiation. When you're going to be pushing yourself beyond normal physical limits early the next morning, sometimes you just have to go to bed.

We'll argue on bike rides. If Laura feels bad on the bike and I am there, that's usually my fault for some reason. If Laura feels bad in general, that's probably my fault as well. If she's not slept well that will be my fault, too. We'll be on the bikes and she'll be hungry, because she has failed to eat enough before we left the house. She'll want to stop for food, except she hasn't brought any money, so when she insists on a flapjack it's me going into the shop to get it and my money that's paying for it. When I emerge without a flapjack because the shop didn't have any, but with a carefully chosen selection of confectionery that I think she might like, I get the blame for the absence of flapjacks and the stinging criticism that she doesn't like those sweets and shouldn't I know that. And then she eats all the sweets anyway, because I suppose those will just have to do, Jason.

And it's all fine. These are normal arguments between a couple who, outside of those ten Olympic golds, are a normal boy and a normal girl. It doesn't mean our relationship doesn't work or that we shouldn't be together. We have stood strong through far worse, and we will stand strong into the future. They are the usual little tiffs that every couple has, and at their core is the deep affection that binds us together. We know we each have flaws and we accept them in the other person. We don't pretend to be perfect. We don't pretend to be extraordinary.

We do almost everything together. Getting through the box set of *Nashville* on the nervous nights before the Rio Olympics. Watching *EastEnders* even when it's not my first choice. We split for the morning commute in to the velodrome on the east side of Manchester, but that is because each has such a definitive training timetable that you cannot compromise. Laura takes her bike in the car; I hop on my motorbike and pick my way through the traffic as I would against my rivals in an Olympic keirin final. It's not good for the carbon footprint, but we cannot afford slack in the schedule. You cannot mess up your meal times, not if you want to squeeze every little benefit out of those training sessions. You cannot sit around the velodrome for too long, or muscles will tighten and moods shift.

When our two programmes briefly synchronize, or when we are allowed to merely tick over in the giddy few months after an Olympic triumph, we can ride out on the roads together. Sometimes your head is full of white noise, and you just want to be out on your own and let the miles and pedal strokes clear it all away. Other times we can ride together towards the climbs and fast descents of the Peak District, Laura having the route knowledge for the longer pulls because of her endurance background, me wary of going too far because I am all about speed, and speed over distance is not me and not my engine.

We started off our relationship doing everything together, and that's how it continues to flourish. When I need a little time on my own, I take my motorbike to a track day just across Cheshire at Oulton Park – just about the most fun I can have. I commute on a Kawasaki Z1000SX, a different beast entirely to the Royal Enfield that I'll potter about on, itself a rational swap for the KTM Duke I had before that – a hooligan of a bike, a bike that wanted to wheelie and do all the sort of stupid fun stuff that a man who rides a pedal bike for his living and country can't really afford to be doing. Laura doesn't like the bikes. They're nothing like her Vespa, and she extrapolates the danger in her own mind. The happiest she's been around my bikes is when a chap we met at the British MotoGP promised to sort me out with an airbag suit.

Motorbikes apart, I might appear not to get ecstatic about anything. I do cry a lot; I'm far more emotional than people might imagine. But I don't cry through happiness, so it can be harder to spot. I keep it in, at least to those who don't know me. But the happiness is there. Going fast makes me happy. Laura makes me happy.

I am controlled. I am speed, too. And when I sprint, I come alive.

# Three: **Man Two**

**JASON:** At the start of 2008 I was certainly in the mix for the Beijing Olympics, but I felt that my age and lack of experience might go against me. I was nineteen years old, and my twentieth birthday was not until a few days before the World Championships in Manchester that March. And while I'd been working through the fresh-faced ranks with some success, winning the junior world sprint title, and coming up against some of the big boys in the Revolution events in the UK, my future was supposed to lie along the development pathway to London 2012. I was living in Fallowfield, a modest student area a couple of miles south of the velodrome, sharing a small flat with fellow young sprinter Matt Crampton. Chris Hoy was already an Olympic champion, the big name and biggest legs on the scene, while Jamie Staff was the experienced old hand and Ross Edgar the greased lightning that kept those two pistons pumping. The three of them finished second behind a mean French trio in the team sprint at the Worlds, and Chris and Ross seemed nailed on for the two spots in the individual sprint come August in the Laoshan velodrome. All three were pre-selected as the Worlds came to an end.

But there was a fourth spot on the team – a slot for a reserve, really, but a shot at an early Olympics all the same. I thought I had a pretty good chance at being that reserve. Hidden among all those World medals in Manchester I'd come home fifth in the sprint. I could ride a good team sprint, and I could also ride the keirin. Three events covered by one man. A word with my coach, and the plan started to come together. Get in shape for the trial that the selection panel would set up, make myself the ideal back-up man.

It worked. Always better with a battle to fight, always able to handle the nerves that wrecked others on big occasions, I hit the numbers and made the squad. Maybe I should have been intimidated. I barely knew Chris, who would become the defining teammate, role model and rival throughout those first two Olympic campaigns. The first time we spent any proper time together was at the pre-Beijing holding camp in Celtic Manor in Newport, South Wales, where the team would fine-tune our training and test-run all the new kit that the so-called Secret Squirrels Club, our blue-sky designers and crack engineers, had been developing over the past two years. We had shared a track during those Worlds yet never ridden together; while I'd finished unnoticed in my lonely fifth place in the sprint, Chris had won gold with a devastating display of raw power and flawless execution.

Born on the same day in March as me but twelve years before, he was the Man. I was the Kid, except I was too unknown to warrant a nickname. Then there was Jamie, three years older still than Chris, the dad of the team, and my roommate in the hotel at Celtic Manor for maybe exactly that reason. I would share with him again in China, and I would listen and learn from everything he said. Jamie had begun in BMX cycling and still had that explosive jump out of the gate, which made him the natural man one in that team – the rider who blasts away at the start, dragging his teammates with him, fighting the big gear, chewing up the track and all the muscle fibres in his legs on that first of the three laps. Chris was the finisher, man three, the one to launch the final assault on the line with the last blistering lap. Which left Ross as man two, strong enough to get on Jamie's wheel so that all that initial speed was not lost to the warm air, clever enough not to leave Chris flapping around in his slipstream so that he too could get the tow he needed before igniting his own fuel tanks.

Ross was quick. He had set one of the fastest laps ever recorded a few years before, and was tight with Chris from their successes with Scotland at the Commonwealth Games. Breaking up that trio was going to be a huge task, not only because they had just run second in the Worlds but because they all trusted and liked each other. Instead, I tried to look at it another way: because this was a team capable of winning, certainly capable of medalling, I knew that if I could get in the team, I was potentially standing on an Olympic podium. It stripped away all the pressure, and it cleared my mind. Forget about the racing. Forget about the Olympics. There was only one goal for me: get in the team. The rest could take care of itself.

The sheer scale of an Olympics is supposed to be over-whelming. The Games are bigger than any sporting event, more important by far than a track World Championships, on a scale that can leave a first-timer out of his depth and unable to cope. The athletes' village is more like a town. The food hall is a cycle ride from your apartment. There are superstars in the queue for pasta, athletes of every shape ambling down the corridors. You watch the opening ceremony on television (no British cyclist attended, for who would want to be on their feet for four hours just before the most important race of their life?) and you are suddenly aware that the whole world is watching this few square miles of the planet's surface. What would it be like to lose now, here, when there is no hiding place and only the best to beat?

And this was my great advantage. Worry about losing? I had nothing to lose. While others were standing around in shock – 'Oh my God, it's the Olympics!' – I was in the unique position of having absolutely no pressure or expectation on me at all. If I didn't make the team, my development path was still geared towards London. My ability was still there; my peak years were still coming on tap. Nothing to chase, nothing to fear. A great team of riders around me, an atmosphere where success was not a wild hope or gamble but a proven fact. The other three were relaxed: they had seen these things before, and they had proven themselves equal to it. Not all of the wider squad were so content – as July slipped away and others hunted for form or selection there were arguments and tears and recriminations around us – but I was genuinely happy to be there. I obsessed about getting in the team, but without fear anywhere near me. The greatest show on earth can trigger the greatest stage fright. Not for me. I actually enjoyed it.

**LAURA:** Sweet sixteen, that's me when Beijing comes around. Who's staying up late to watch it in Cheshunt? My dad and my big sister, but not me. Done with my GCSEs, I'm not really a watcher of pro cycling yet; I'm certainly not a cycling geek. The team sprint would happen when I was asleep. So would the individual sprint, and Brad Wiggins in the pursuit, and Brad and Geraint and Ed and Paul Manning, my future coach, in the team pursuit, and Rebecca Romero, and all those other golds that kept on piling up, all those other medals that Britain won.

It was the female role models I was interested in and thought about. Nicole Cooke in the road race up by the Great Wall, as it chucked down with rain, that white kit all turned to grey and mud, coming out of the final corner and the mist and climbing that last hill and her all over the bike and then the big celebration, the big roar, clenching her fist and then slamming it down, and my sister jumping around all over the sofa. Nights later, watching Vicky Pendleton winning sprint gold on the track, a personal connection to it all because I'd seen her riding the same grass track as Emma and me at Mildenhall, said hello to her, and borrowed equipment and kit from her dad.

I took in Chris Hoy, because who didn't, but I could hardly think of me and the Olympics in any way that made sense. Even 2012 seemed so far, though also so close. There was a little scheme in Hertfordshire in which they chose twenty kids from twelve sports to celebrate the fact that London was coming round, but it didn't really mean anything apart from hearing Heather Small singing 'Proud' every time they got us together.

I was training hard and I was taking what I did seriously, but I was taking it seriously because I hated to lose, and so training all made sense – two hours a night, going up to the velodrome in Manchester for regular camps, hating the trips because it was so far from home and because they were squeezing me into the role of a sprinter, something I could never be. It wasn't me then and it's not me now. But it was the only way you could get on to the Olympic Development Programme a year early, and it was the only way I was getting noticed. We would sometimes be coached by a legendary figure in British cycling named Geoff Cooke, national champion more than sixty times as a rider, now in his seventies, and the most enthusiastic man you could ever have training you. He was so encouraging, wonderfully so, but it made him a little trigger-happy on the stopwatch. You're riding, you're riding, you're head down, you're coming down the home straight. He presses the stopwatch … and then you cross the line.

I clocked a crazy time for a quarter-lap. I only weighed 48 kg at the time, so naturally I'm going to go fast, but suddenly the talk is all about Laura Trott and her times, and word apparently even reaches the podium boys heading for Beijing, and I'm the talk of heroes I have never met and one boy I've never heard of but will one day fall in love with. All because of Geoff Cooke and his twitchy stopwatch finger.

And even with me on the ODP, and on training camps riding those same boards as Hoy and Vicky and the boy I don't know, riding for Great Britain seems like such a jump I don't even dream about it. It's just me, racing and hating to lose, racing and getting faster, racing and clocking those dodgy quarters.

**JASON:** Some people chase form. Other riders wish for it. Others lie there each night and pray to the great god of form:

please let my legs feel good, please let me feel like I'm floating round those polished boards tomorrow morning.

I didn't have to do anything. Young legs, nothing to lose; everything to fight for. A few days out from hostilities in Laoshan, I was told I'd got the nod over Ross as man two in that sprint team. There were no guarantees – if I went badly in qualification, he could come back in for the first round. He would also keep his place alongside Chris in the keirin. But I would be racing again too, in the individual sprint, and by making the sprint team I had already hit the only goal I had. You might expect I was already satisfied. That's supposed to be the worst possible feeling for an elite sportsman. Satisfied means you're no longer hungry; when the hunger goes the motivation slips away too.

Except it was still all so simple for me. As we warmed up on the rollers on that Friday morning, the very first day of competition in the velodrome, I had two thoughts in my head: Get on the back of Jamie. Deliver Chris nice and smooth.

There was noise in my ears, but not deafening. Laoshan was not how London would be. The great revolution that would shake British cycling and turn it into the hottest Olympic ticket in town was about to begin, but only the insiders had guessed: there were empty seats and a sense of calm. Our skinsuits looked space age but felt more prosaic, more like the simple stretchy rubber they were.

Simple it stayed, if by simple you mean untroubled. That qualification race was the first time I've ever glanced up at the scoreboard at the end of a three laps and been surprised, because, while I'm occasionally a miserable sod, I'm always an optimist. I always think we're going to smash the world record, even in training. I always think the best is going to happen. This was the first time I'd looked at the board and immediately thought, 'Oh my God, that can't be right. That doesn't look right. That can't be true, because we've just taken a massive chunk off the fastest time ever ...'

We had clocked 42.95 seconds. If those numbers mean nothing to you, if you have no idea how long it should take three men on fixed-gear bikes to complete three laps of a 250-metre oval of pale wood, take it from me: it was ridiculous. And I'm an optimist, a man who doesn't get excited easily. No one had ever come close to that time. And now no one thought there could be any changes to our line-up, or that the US trio would get close to us in the first round a few hours later. They didn't.

Which left the big boys. France, reigning world champions, the power and the glory, for the gold medal.

Grégory Baugé, a massive man, looking even bigger in his skinsuit and with his visor pulled down. Kévin Sireau, leaner and meaner. Arnaud Tournant, their finisher, more medals in his house than I had shoes. We don't have to look at them, because they start across the track, and this is probably no bad thing. Jamie on my left in the starting gate, me in the middle with my head bowed, saddle held by a blazer-wearing official, Chris on my right, our own man with more medals than he knows what to do with.

I have my own problems. There's the fear that I won't be able to get hold of Jamie's wheel. It strikes me that I really don't have that much experience at man two, and that the man in the blue blazer holding my wheel is holding me in a way that is making my inexperience very apparent: slightly awkwardly. Jamie is fine. In a mechanical gate you are always rock solid, and you are always released at exactly the right time. Humans, by contrast, come with habits and flaws. One official might not be quite so used to holding still a hulking sprinter as another. He might not have the strength to hold you absolutely straight. He might have a belly that nudges you in the small of the back and keeps your backside from going as far back in the saddle as you need it to go to get your starting power. He might even hold you a little too long, not out of malice or favouritism to the French, but because he isn't quite concentrating, or he doesn't react to the gun quite as quickly as the finely tuned athlete he is hanging on to.

Jamie is held steady. For me and Chris, this is our first challenge, before a single pedal crank has been turned. We have trained with our coaches holding us. With coaches who know what you are like and who hold you every day, you can shuffle and they will just absorb it all. If you're being held by someone who is not really used to it or not that strong or just doesn't care, they'll not bother to adjust. If you shuffle, they will just let you lean to one side.

There are tricks of the trade for a young man to learn. The official rule is that when man one throws his leg over the bike, the entire trio has fifty seconds to get settled. So we try to get man two and three on the track as quickly as possible, to get in as good a position as we can in the time we have left. You can communicate to Mr Blue Blazer, but not by words muffled through your helmet. Put your arm out straight to the right and they will tip you slightly right. Do it again and they'll tip you a little further still. Fail to have them sort you out in the allotted time and that's it. You just have to suck it up.

It's something that I've got used to over the years. At the time, I knew I didn't have any margin for error on the start line. My only strategy was to just go flat out, but to get out fast you need to get out of the saddle. If you can't get back, you can't push, and if you can't push you feel stuck.

The technique I was taught was to go up on the count of two, back on one and then go go go. That way it should be a fluid movement, and all your power and strength is thrown forwards into the bike. But after a bad experience in my first senior championship, I worked with Iain my coach to change it. Go back early. Really early, so that Mr Blazer knows exactly where you're going to be. The only problem with going back really early is that it can hurt your neck trying to hold your head up. That is why, to this day, I'm always looking down at the start of a team sprint.

Away we go, and suddenly the sensations are fractured. We are flat out and frantic, and all that sticks in the mind are little pieces of reality, small fragments that the brain can cling on to as you throw the conscious and subconscious into doing something which is simultaneously straightforward and enormously complicated, entirely familiar and yet matters more to more people than anything you have ever done before.

Either the colour and clamour is only in one pocket at the end of the back straight, or it's only there that I recognize it because that's also where all the British supporters are gathered. Round we go, round in what seems like the eye of a rotating storm, and then we get to that point, and suddenly it's impossible to ignore. I feel like I'm riding right into the British fans, right into the waving Union flags and screams and shaking fists.

Jamie has detonated from the gate, blown it to pieces, but I'm with him just where I want to be, and I've got enough comfort to find time for the thought: I hope Jamie gets out of the way. In fact, I'm not just comfortable, I'm easy. I actually feel like I'm floating. There is no sense of stamping on the pedals or fighting the resistance of air or ground. It's not hurting, and it doesn't even feel like I'm going flat out.

My first Olympic final, and I've hit a wonderful little window where all the training and preparation and hours turning left around the cold boards in Manchester have come together. I haven't prayed to the great god of form, but he's blessed me anyway. I don't see myself as the engine of this team; I don't suddenly see myself as a hero. I'm just a link, keeping up the revs that Jamie has established, keeping my lap super-smooth so that I don't go too hard in the first half to leave Chris adrift and then die in the second to force him to spread his final effort across 400 metres rather than 250. The last lap is the one that wins the race. All I have to do is deliver Chris fast and easy, but it has never felt like this before, floating around, holding my speed at 99 per cent so the link in the chain does not break, no lactic in the legs, no burning in the lungs. There isn't even any stress about where we will swing up and let the next man through, because they are still relatively relaxed about the rules at this point and will allow you a little leeway around the official line and regulations.

I can't know that Chris is fighting to stay on my wheel. You can't see, not with your head low in its tuck and every wiggle of the helmet or waggle of the shoulders throwing you from aerodynamic perfection. But I do know as soon as I flick up the track after my lap that we have won, because as I start to cruise high up the boards I can see France's man three Tournant coming through, and he's pulling the sort of shapes on his bike that speak of a man beyond his limits and a man who is fighting speed rather than ruling it. Chris is up, ahead and away, and when Chris is up you know he is not going to lose that lead. He's Chris Hoy. You'd back him every day.

There was no immediate elation. Man two is the lonely one, left decelerating on the opposite side of the track as man one and three come together to grab gloved hands and wave them at the sky. So it was that Jamie and Chris came together, the 'b' of the bang and the exclamation mark at the end, leaving me to drift slowly to a halt and climb off my bike an Olympic champion at the age of twenty.

I unzipped my top as they made their way over. In the days to come I would get stick for revealing a hairy chest to the world. I would also find myself with too many things to hold on the podium and not enough space to put my hands, draping one awkward arm across the shoulders of the bronze medal winners to my left and then accidentally waving the bunch of the flowers I'd been given in Chris's face, blocking the iconic gold medal photos of the man who would shortly be made a knight of the realm. The hairy chest I could do nothing about, in itself not necessarily manlier than those of the smooth-chested champions around me but certainly more manly than shaving it off in an effort to look just like the others.

There's an expectation around winning Olympic gold. As a child you see it as an absolute: you're an Olympic champion, everything has changed for evermore. As an adult, particularly if you've been chasing it for a long time, you expect an explosion of joy, the sensation of all your dreams coming true at once, a plateau of happiness to stroll along into the future.

It was all different for me: it was my first attempt, so I was never left with any of the yearning and wondering. My individual event was still to come two days later, so there would be no wild partying or dancing in the cleats. Call me a Bolton boy, but I knew instinctively that nothing had changed at all apart from the fact I had a medal hanging around my neck.

It can feel lonely. Those in the team who are finished can let go of all that emotion and pent-up desire to drink and dance and do everything else we can't do for the long months before. Chris had the keirin and sprint to come, and anyway, he was Chris. But if you're in the team pursuit, and the only one racing again, you can see three of your teammates head off together into the boozy sunset while you pedal back to the athletes' village by yourself. By the time they are on their second drink, you're tucked up in bed hoping they'll remember to keep the noise down when they come back that night. If they do come back that night.

In future years I would celebrate gold medals with a press conference, or a pizza, or a half-hour lie-in. In some ways that rather suited me, because I find pleasure in being by myself sometimes. I like to keep it low level. And on this night Jamie behaved himself, no matter that his gold had been a long time coming; that it should have come in Athens four years previously, only for illness to mess up the team's qualification and cost them a podium place; that at his age he had no more chances left. I remember him coming in, but if there was dancing and shouting it had already taken place earlier in the evening. And while our gold on the first day of competition had put a rocket under the entire track team, confirming in every riders' mind that what we were doing in training was bang on, that our secret squirrels had cracked it, that we were peaking collectively in a way no nation ever had before, I let all that excitement and adrenaline wash past me. On my day off I could hear all the cheering coming from adjoining apartments as teammates watched Brad Wiggins tear it up in the individual pursuit, but I was happy to watch it on my own, feet up, only moving to get to the coffee machine that Chris and Jamie had brought over in their luggage to ensure that none of us went short of a cyclist's favourite beverage. At one point Vicky Pendleton stuck her head in to see if I was okay. I couldn't have been happier. Save the legs, protect the head. No fuss. Drama on hold for the velodrome and the cameras and the crowds.

Because, really, I was still floating. Going into the individual sprint, I had no expectations whatsoever. I'd hit my goal of making the team: I'd made it into the trio. I had a gold medal that a few months before had not even seemed a possibility. Not only did I still have nothing to lose, but I had over-achieved. So much credit built up, so many years left in which to cash it in.

That sense of ease and calm showed up in spectacular fashion in the qualifying round. Only Chris rode a faster flying 200 metres than me, and even then only by four hundredths of a second. No one else broke ten seconds: not Germany's Stefan Nimke, not our old team sprint rival Kévin Sireau, not his compatriot Mickaël Bourgain. And on it went, Chris chewing up his opponents, me smooth against mine. In the quarter-finals I saw off Sireau again, winning the best-of-three 2–0, and then doing the same to Germany's Maximilian Levy in the semis. It was as if Chris and I were drawn together, racing inexorably towards an all-British showdown, depressing even more the hopes of those other nations lined up in the track centre, underlining, as all our teammates had, that this British squad had something special about them that no one had ever seen before.

There was no discussion between the two of us before that final. There didn't need to be. No one is going to cede anything, no matter that two days before you were cogs in the same machine. We looked slightly different, me in the white helmet with red and blue stripes, Chris in a black and white one because he wasn't happy with the helmet we were given late in the day. Inside we were feeling very different too, although I could never have guessed it at the time. Because while I felt no pressure, that meant Chris was under it all. He was the experienced one, the proven champion, racing at his third Olympics, knowing this was in theory the one that should never get away. It would be eight years until I truly understood what was going through his mind, when I would come up against a similarly unproven teammate in Callum Skinner in the corresponding final in Rio. On the start line in Beijing, I knew that the worst I could do was second. And silver to go with a gold when you are that young and that callow is a haul that no one could be disappointed with.

Floating floating, and this time stung by the big old bee. Chris dominated those two races, letting me lead it out both times, coming over the top of me late in the first and then eating me up on the final bend in the second. You could see what it meant to him in the way he ripped off his helmet and squeezed shut his eyes in relief and exhaustion, in the way he was teary as the anthem was played on the podium while I just smiled and tried to remember to keep my jersey zipped up this time. Even in the aftermath I was content, watching him soaking up the plaudits, becoming the epitome of that British team as it returned home first-class with British Airways, his entire life changing in the space of three finals and three gold medals, never to be the same again.

As for me, I was out of the village before the sun had risen the next day, at the airport at 7 a.m., ready for a flight I'd requested before the whole giddy madness had even begun. I just wanted to get home, back to my family, back to the life I had put on hold to make this whole adventure happen. A life that mainly involved sitting in a flat in a dull part of south Manchester, waiting to go cycling again with everyone I was leaving behind in China.

**LAURA:** All that, and I didn't even notice he was there. It wasn't until that Christmas that I read in my dad's copy of *Cycling Weekly* about this young track sprinter they had stuck in at fifth in their annual ranking of British riders. Wow, I thought – twenty years old and two Olympic medals. Fair play, whoever you are. Fair play.

# Four: **The Devil**

**LAURA:** All the races I do, all the medals I've won, and I'm defined by the devil.

The elimination race. Every two laps, the rider at the very back of the field is removed. The devil takes the hindmost. I won it in London and I won it in Rio. I've won it in Australia and Belarus, from Paris, France to Cali, Colombia.

I've not always been good at beating the devil. The first few I did, I was terrible. Then it just clicked. Everyone had been telling me that the safest place to ride was second wheel – tucked in behind the leader, no danger, no worries. They forgot that there were eighteen other riders all trying to do the same thing all the time. You sit in second wheel, everyone comes over you. You're stuck. You're in the worst possible position. No getting out of there. And then it hit me one day: my strength is my speed. If I stay at the back, all the way round, I can line up the last woman, get out and get round her. When the numbers are big, ride the bunch a little, make it easy for myself. Hide in the middle and don't get caught out. Tick them off, girl after girl. When it gets down to seven of us left – well, seven's my favourite number, I'm not being beaten from here.

Six riders left, it becomes less cat and mouse and more like a sprint. Watch everyone else a little bit more. I know my rivals. I know what they fancy. I know that none of them has ever tried to take a long one on me, blasted off the front and tried to hang on for the entire 500 metres. Even if they did I'd try to catch them anyway.

My eyes are constantly tracking. Who's doing what? Where are they? Who's travelling, and who's boxed in? Some riders will try to pretend they're not bothered about me. If I swing up the track and drop in at the back, the woman whose back wheel I'm on won't even look at me. That makes sense if that rider knows they can outsprint the woman in her slipstream. Just leave them there. With me, that's suicide. I'm coming round you.

If they take me to the top of the track, that's fine. I just don't let them trap me up there. If I drop down, I make sure they can't drop down on my outside. Then I'm boxed in. And remember: it doesn't matter if you're at the back for 499 of those 500 metres that make up each two-lap showdown. As long as you go round one rider in the metre that matters, on you go.

You have to get up to speed fast. Some people are terrified by the calculations. The constant pressure. At my first senior World Championships, Apeldoorn in the Netherlands in 2011, I ended up as nineteen, same as my age, the fifth rider to be hooked of the twenty-three girls who started. It was so fast compared to anything I had ever raced before. I didn't want to go over the top of everyone by smashing it really hard, because that seemed a lot of hard work, and at nineteen you don't have that much hard work in you. I hadn't worked out that you make that one big effort and you're on the front and you're safe for at least two lots of two laps. Then you're going your speed, rather than someone else's. The bunch tends to follow you and let you dictate.

The other girls might want to watch me. To use me as a pilot, to steer them through the traffic and the chaos. I'll mess with their minds by mixing it up. One race I might do most of it from the front. If I've got good enough form I can race it like an individual pursuit – three kilometres hard hard hard. I know that I can ride at what we call zone 3, somewhere between 84 and 94 per cent of my maximum heart rate, for an hour. I can do threshold – harder still, not quite flat out – for twenty minutes. Work any harder than that and I'm going into the red, and in a multi-event race like the omnium, that will mess you up for the tests to come. That gives me a fall-back: ride at threshold pace at the front for the whole race, which is generally under eleven minutes. In my head I'm safe there. But do that all the time and my rivals will read me like a comic. So sometimes I'll go to the back and do it solely from there.

None of it is preordained. All the time you're resetting. If you don't make the decision in the first half-lap you're screwed: a lap and a half isn't long enough to sort yourself out. I let my instinct make those constant calculations for me. No two of my races are ever the same. You can't read me, not with the weapons I've got, not when I hate to be overtaken like nothing else.

The devil follows me away from the track. When I'm in the car I don't like letting other cars out. I hate it if another driver comes up the inside of me; I refuse to let them pull out. On the road I can see it all unfolding ahead of me long seconds before anyone else because of my experience. I can pre-empt it all. Reflexes, mental maps, confidence in the tightest of squeezes.

The bike and I are part of the same machine. Yet there are times when the strains of constant competition can show. I remember after the Olympics in 2012 being really upset over nothing, not quite feeling like I didn't want to do it any more, but not really knowing why I was doing it. It wasn't that I'd fallen out of love with it, but I was going out to ride my bike because I felt like I had to. There was no racing coming up. I was going out to ride because I didn't know any different.

That lasted a week. That was it. Never a doubt since, never a fling anywhere else.

But I get nervous. I always have and probably always will. Legs going up and down. The sound of my cleats tapping: an attempt to ease my nerves, if an annoyance for my teammates. I've got butterflies in my stomach doing a scratch race. I get on my bike and it's gone. It's gone, like a switch being hit. I can feel it running out of my legs.

When I get taken to photo-shoots, standing there in the big white studios, all tripods and make-up and mirrors and glamour, I say give me my helmet. I only feel natural when my helmet is on – it's me, it's part of me. It would be like somebody else bleaching their hair or getting their nose redone. They would look in the mirror and see a stranger staring back.

My sister Emma always loved riding the roads. I'm a track girl, through and through. All the things that terrify road riders about the track scare me in reverse on the roads. When I'm riding the boards, there are no brakes, no gears. Some idiot cannot just slam on in front of me.

It's 2012, I'm out on the roads in a weaving bunch. I look up and I can see a massive crash happen ahead of me. I stop. I'm at the back of the main group, because that's safest in my head, riding round and not wanting to be there. Someone who is chasing to get back on to the peloton smashes into me and sends me over the handlebars. Into the tarmac, chin all mashed up. I feel like my earrings have been ripped out. I think my ear has fallen off. Blood everywhere, no idea what my team manager's name is, running up to her all cut up and messed, and saying, 'Do I still have my ear?' 'Okay, get in the car, you need to go to hospital.' Getting into the hottest ambulance in the world, passing out, waking up in a ward with bright lights and dried blood with both my ears still on.

Maybe it's because I've always seen road racing as second to the track. I'm only doing it to benefit my track work, so if I crash out on the road, I've crashed out in something I don't enjoy, which isn't even the event that I'm practising for. Despite winning the National Road Race Championships in 2014, when I outsprinted Lizzie Armitstead to claim the title, you couldn't have convinced me to do road World Championships. It was bad enough that I had to do the Commonwealth Games road race. Right girl in the wrong event.

On the track I love that close proximity. I barge people out of the way. In the elimination race I like going through small gaps. Mark Cavendish always says to me, 'I don't know how you do it.' But that's my fun. There's no way you'd get me going as fast as he does around a corner. I wouldn't do it.

It's not the injuries I fear. Had I fallen off in the points race at the Rio Olympics, the last of the six events in my omnium, I would have got back on. I would have finished that thing, even with a broken arm, even with a broken pelvis. Some competitions, I've been in points races and looked up to see I've got sixty laps to go, thinking, I've got a stitch, I'm not going to finish this race. Then at the Olympics it all just felt like fun, and I simply rode round.

You react and you hold on to control when your form is there. When you're going well, a rival will throw something in and you'll think, 'All right then, bring it on, let's have it.' You know how you have to respond and you do it. When you're going badly and someone does something sudden, it's, 'Oh my God, no …' When you're struggling, you think you know what you have to do but you're not sure if you can do it. By the time you've thought about it, the moment has passed and you've lost the race.

Sportspeople talk about being in the zone. Being in the zone for me is being on my bike, on the track, and it all feeling effortless. The riding, the tactics, the timing, the big moves. All of it without thinking, all of it without consciously trying.

I started small and I started in trouble. Born six weeks early, with a collapsed lung, I spent the first weeks of my life in intensive care at Princess Alexandra Hospital in Harlow, Essex. I had asthma from that point on, and never wanted to sleep again after all the time wired up in the confines of an incubator. I didn't sleep through the night at six months, and I didn't at a year. Always on the go, never wanting to settle. I would be nursery age before my parents Adrian and Glenda had an unbroken night's sleep. They could always calm my elder sister Emma by sticking her in front of the TV or a video. That would bore me rigid. It would keep me quiet for about ten minutes, and then I would be off, looking for the next distraction, hunting the next excitement. My grandparents called me the little two-minute wonder: yes, okay, I've done that. Right, what's next? I'm bored.

I now like my sleep. In regards to the other character traits, I'm still the person at twenty-four that I was when I was the little girl on Mum's nerves and Dad's knee. Noisy. Curious. Always on the go. Dad remembers me having a perpetual cold or a cough, and that was the legacy of the asthma. Mum says I was the more outgoing of her two daughters, maybe because I got a slightly easier ride – they were frightened of breaking the first one. They didn't know how far they could push us, or how robust little girls could really be.

Because television didn't work for me, it had to be physical activity. I had to be stimulated and amused. The first thing I tried was something called Tumble Tots – like gymnastics for pre-schoolers, balancing along wooden planks an inch off the ground, climbing through hoops, clambering up foam slopes, sliding down the other side. Some singing at the start and finish. I loved it, and Emma joined in too. That led into trampolining – first at the Grundy Leisure Centre, on the road between the railway station in Cheshunt and the big roundabout on the A10, now rebranded the Laura Trott Centre, and then up the road in Harlow at the old sports centre there.

It was basic stuff at the start, a bit of a bounce-around session for those of us who hadn't started school, the sort of thing you might put on for a kids' birthday party. The cycling came a year later: me aged five, Emma already on her bike and flying around, Dad deciding to take the two of us across the level crossing and towards the safe, car-free paths around the Lee Valley Park.

It was the day the stabilizers came off. Dad was pushing me along, grabbing my shoulders as I veered towards the bushes, picking me up as I crashed. Which I was doing a lot. Emma went on ahead, confident on her own, heading down the biggest hill she could find. A few seconds after we lost sight of her we heard her scream. I told Dad to ignore it. We had to get me riding.

A stranger came round the corner, carrying Emma. She was really screaming now, crying the place down. Dad was similarly lacking in sympathy. 'What's the matter with you? Stop making such a silly fuss.' Emma sobbing, just managing to get the words out. 'I can't walk, Dad. It really hurts ...'

Dad had no choice. He sat Emma on his handlebars, carried her bike in his other hand and told me to get on with it. And that's how I learned to ride – on my own, through necessity. I either rode or I got left in Lee Valley Park.

The no-nonsense parenting continued at home. Mum looked at her sobbing elder daughter. 'Oh, just walk it off. You'll be fine in a minute.' Emma tried to walk down the hallway. Louder screams. We called on our neighbour, who happened to be a nurse. A quick examination, and a brisk verdict: take her to hospital. Emma had broken the ball and socket joint in her ankle. Badly. Plaster for two months, and when she finally found herself free, she still couldn't control her foot properly. It turned out they had trapped a nerve while setting it. All because of my stabilizers, all because I had to get riding.

It took a while for cycling to grab hold. In those early days I hated riding out in public, because I didn't want to pedal down the high street with my helmet on. Ironic, given how I would turn out, but at that time there was a little courtyard of shops off the street where all the so-called cool kids would hang out, and they would shout at you as you went past. Mum didn't like us playing out, but she didn't like our friends coming round to ours, either. She wanted to keep the place spotless. So out we would go, Emma and I, and we would have to run the gauntlet of the cool kids with the big mouths and nothing else to do but hang around a little parade of shops.

It wasn't the only thing that put me off. We struggled to find bikes that fitted me. Not many girls my size were after road bikes. We used to borrow one, give it back, borrow another. One morning, when I was eight, my dad saw a little Peugeot up for sale. It's still there in their house, along with everything else we ever rode or wore or won. On my first go on it we were cruising round Broxbourne as a family, easing down a little hill that got steeper further down, when I realized my hands wouldn't reach the brakes on the dropped handlebars. I tried to pull them with my hands on the brake hoods, but it did almost nothing. Roundabout coming up, hill getting steeper, me letting go of the brakes entirely, past Mum, her shouting and screaming, straight over the roundabout and on to a one-way road. In the opposite direction. Into some railings, no broken ball and socket joint but the question in my mind: Why are we Trott girls doing this cycling lark?

It wasn't until Mum's weight-loss regime played its fateful

role that the bug bit. She decided the pounds were piling on quicker than she would have liked, and while at the swimming pool she soon got talking to another mother, who had two daughters roughly the same age. The woman recommended cycling with a club. Mum went over to Welwyn Wheelers and, because we girls couldn't sit about the house on our own, we went with her and signed up. Gosling Sports Park had a velodrome, an old-school one, a big outdoor concrete oval around the outside of an athletics track, which itself encircled a football pitch. It wasn't glamorous – grey and lumpy, one small stand along the home straight with changing-rooms underneath it – but it was fun. Proper fun. Racing now, aged eight, not just pedalling, and chasing others, kids much bigger than me, not just Emma but boys, and boys who didn't like getting beaten. Some would start having to get used to it.

I was still doing as many sports as I could. Never settling, always trying more, always seeing how fast or high or deep I could go. The trampolining at Harlow was my true first love. I would keep at it until my mid-teens. Only two things held me back. The first was my own ability: I was racing through the grades at a much younger age than was usual, throwing in somersaults, relishing the sensation of being up in the air and weightless and free. The coaches became very nervous about the degree of difficulty that would have to be in my routines. Maybe they lacked the confidence that a girl my age could do those things. Either way, they started to hold me back, tried to consolidate what I could already do rather than let me see how far I could go.

The other was the blackouts. In a training session, rolling out the somersaults, one of the coaches spotted that I was badly out of position mid-air. He tried to catch me, and I nearly broke his arms, because I was a dead weight. Out like a light, as if the batteries had suddenly failed. By the time I had hit the trampoline bed and bounced back up I had come out of it, but the alarms were going off for those who had seen it and those who heard about it.

A few months later, after arriving home from a swimming lesson. Dad was standing up by the TV. I ran to grab a cuddle off him, as daughters do. Next minute I was sliding down Dad's legs and narrowly missed cracking my head on our fireplace. I came back round, Dad still totally unaware anything has happened.

I looked up at him. 'What happened, Dad? Did I just die?'

Appointments and investigations. Referred up the A10 to Addenbrooke's Hospital in Cambridge. Wearing a crown of wires for forty-eight hours, going through scanners, working out what was going on between those two Trott ears. Nothing, or rather nothing they could find that explained the loss of consciousness.

While I was being studied and sent for other tests, the trampolining was off. No jumping around for six months, no flying free. We never would find out conclusively what had happened. I was a bad eater and I wouldn't remember to drink during the school day, so it might have been sugar-outs – me out of fuel, my brain with no option left to it but to reboot. I had always been a fussy eater. Baby food and nothing else until eighteen months old, no toast fingers or carrot sticks or liquidized whatever that Mum and Dad were having for tea. That first thing I ate that was technically solid was on a family holiday to Portugal, and even then it was only crisps. Crisps, beautiful crisps. I can still polish off a family pack almost without noticing.

The blackouts understandably terrified my parents. They had endured those setbacks with my struggles at birth, thought they were through them, had to cope with the asthma and constant illnesses, and now this – no proper explanation, all that uncertainty, all that paranoia parents have anyway, multiplied by the country's top specialists holding their hands up and saying, 'We're really sorry, but we don't know what's caused it, and we don't know if it will happen again.'

At the time I didn't pick up on it all that much. You're a kid, you're in your own happy world. When your parents are caring, loving ones like mine, they protect you from your own fears, let alone theirs. But I knew I couldn't trampoline again for a long time, and in that gap cycling took a tighter hold.

I swam, too. Both Emma and I would compete. But when the chance came to train more often and more intensively, neither of us wanted to take it. I think it helped us in our distant futures. Both of us preferred freestyle, and that was more conducive to building a cyclist's physique than breaststroke or butterfly, which would have given us bigger upper bodies. There was also athletics. I ran cross-country in winter and middle distance on the track in summer. One year I went a whole season unbeaten – in the cross-country, and in the 800 metres and 1500 metres on the track. Mum had been to the same school, and the 800-metre record dated back to her era, twenty-six years before. In Year 10 I was finally old enough to have a crack at it. Ran it, broke it. Someone told me the next race up was the 1500 metres. Cool, I'll do it. Ran straight into it and broke the school record in that one too.

There are still photos of that afternoon knocking around on Facebook somewhere. The records still stand, too. I won a prize for outstanding sporting achievement from Year 7 onwards, and it was athletics that started it all off, not cycling. I was even offered a scholarship at Herts Phoenix, the same athletics club that produced GB 200-metre runner Jodie Williams. No one had ever turned them down before. They were shocked when I did. I just knew I preferred cycling.

Running must have helped build my engine. It was certainly an outlet for my fierce competitive spirit. You might wonder if it also helped my tactical awareness for the velodrome scraps that were to come – working within a pack, deciding whether to hug the kerb for the shortest racing line, not letting yourself get trapped by those coming round on your outside, mixing the endurance base with the speed to respond to sudden moves or to kick away at the end. Trouble was, it was all much simpler for me: I would just run away from all the other girls. If there were boys in the session or ahead in the race, I'd go out and tag on to them instead.

The cool kids were still hanging around the same small parade of shops. I would be out mountain biking around Lee Valley with Mum on our regular ten-mile loop, or doing the Welwyn Club 10 with my dad behind me. From that point on, even subconsciously, I thought, I don't mind this now; I don't care what the kids think.

I preferred the friends I was making through cycling to those I could make in school. My cycling success gave me confidence. When I went back to school after wins, I used to think, I don't care what you lot think any more. And of course once you start winning, they shut up. They want to be associated with you. I was in every school team except basketball and football. Everything else I loved. My best mate Kristi understood. We had done trampolining and swimming together. The others I would hang around with were Emma and her friends. I went through a shy phase in my teens, just as Emma was going through a talkative one. I didn't like the other girls that Kristi would hang out with, so I would stay with Emma instead. As long as I had my big sister there, it was fine. She could deal with the problems.

I was winning on the track, but I had so much to learn, too. When I made my first forays into racing in Europe, I struggled in the big bunch races. On the UK scene the groups would never be that big. What gave me an edge there was that I was now racing constantly in the Friday-night track leagues. When I had been eleven and twelve I would often find myself racing fourteen- and fifteen-year-old boys. They didn't enjoy being pushed around by a girl who barely came up to their chests, and they gave it back. As a response I developed an aggressive, bullish attitude myself: I'm coming through that gap, you're not stopping me. I'm coming past you, and I don't care what you think.

I couldn't catch. I couldn't hit a tennis ball and I never got the hang of golf. Emma could do all that, and more. She would have made an incredible triathlete. I wondered a short while ago whether I could still succeed in athletics. My dad told me to try some cross-country again, go and knock out a five-kilometre parkrun one Saturday morning and see if I could manage a reasonable time. But he did also say that he wouldn't want to be around me on the Sunday morning when I woke up and realized I couldn't walk, and that the only way

I was going to be able to get down the stairs was by bouncing down on my backside. It may be true, I don't know. I was lucky. I found the right sport. I found the right people.

Jason just so happened to be brought up to the north of Manchester, which in the mid-nineties happened to bid for a Commonwealth Games, and so had to build a velodrome, which then needed clubs and riders to fill it, one of which later happened to be his uncle, who decided to take Jason along. I was born needing to exercise because of my asthma. My mum needed to lose weight. She happened to meet someone who recommended a cycling club, and I happened to come up against bigger kids when we got there, fast-forwarding my development, and then just as I am approaching senior level, not only does an Olympics come around that is taking place fourteen miles from my front door, but they introduced a new event that suits almost everything about me as a rider. At the 2008 Olympics there was no omnium. In 2009 they announced that the individual pursuit was being dropped, and a multi-discipline competition was being brought in for London 2012. And Emma called it, even then. Laura will be champion.

We had ridden versions of the omnium throughout our junior careers. There were no individual events at British championships until we were sixteen, no specialization. I was practised in all disciplines and I was constantly improving. I raced a youth omnium in Portsmouth where I came into the home straight of the scratch race on my own with a decent lead, and I still lost. I had a tendency at that time to lose just a bit of concentration. Too off with the pixies. I might have appeared to have it sewn up, but you just didn't know.

It's why my dad doesn't remember me displaying that crazy instinctive mental strength that elite sportspeople are supposed to inherently have in their teens. Another weekend I was chasing points to qualify for a British Cycling talent team trial up in Manchester. I went to race in Cardiff knowing I needed a really good finish overall to secure my spot. Same thing happened. Into the home straight of the points race in control; completely lost the plot.

Dad took me to the little café in the foyer of the swimming pool next door. I knew what I'd done, but I didn't know why I'd done it. As we sat there, I got a little bit upset and a bit annoyed. I've blown this, I'm not going to win. Dad bought us a few drinks. We talked it over. I calmed down. We can do this. It's a speed bump, not a roadblock. I pulled it out of the fire.

So there was not yet the killer instinct, and there was not yet the unbroken concentration, but I was a girl in my teens. And what I did have was the ability to bounce back, to assimilate problems and solve them. Years later I'm still doing it. The World Championships in Paris, 2015. Disastrous scratch race, finished it in thirteenth, came back from nowhere for the silver medal. Yet in the Olympics in Rio a year later: lesson learned, no disastrous scratch race, finished it second, went on to take gold.

I remember always wanting to become an Olympic champion. My parents remember it more as an ambition to ride for Great Britain. Whichever, they never put any pressure on us, never pushed us too hard or tried to live out their own sporting dreams through their innocent daughters. After London won the Olympic bid they would always talk in terms of, 'You might go, you're probably too young for London but there's no reason why you shouldn't go to Rio.' They never thought they were producing two future professionals. There was never a master plan. There was a hope. All they wanted us to do – and it was always us, never me before Emma or Emma ahead of me – was for us to do it to the best of our abilities and as well as they thought we could. As long as we did that, nothing else really mattered to them.

We were lucky with our other great influences, Sophie Bruton and Simon Layfield, the husband and wife who were our original coaches at Welwyn. They treated each of their riders, no matter what their age or ability, like a mini professional. I mean that in the best possible way: not with pressure to get big results, but in terms of their preparation, their attitude and their skills. At the National Championships with Simon and Sophie, with the full range of kids from under-10s through to under-16s and maybe some juniors, each would be allowed one bag apiece so it would fit under the one chair each rider was given. 'This is what the pros do, and when we're at Manchester or Newport where the pros train and race, this is what we are going to do.' It looked impressive. More importantly, it worked. We got so used to it that when we made that step up ourselves to the top level we were already accustomed to the correct regime and a culture of professionalism. Packing light, being responsible for our own kit. Making sure your helmet and shoes were in the right bags so that if one case had gone on different transport, at least you could race.

We all owed Simon and Sophie a great deal. Others would come through under them too – Andy Fenn, who won the junior Paris-Roubaix and now rides with Team Sky; Pete

Bissell, who was the British under-23 road race champion; his sister Laura, who rode on British Cycling's development squad with Nicole Cooke, raced at the 2000 and 2001 junior Road World Championships and the junior Track World Championships in the latter year. Not all of us got to fulfil our true potential. Pete passed away horribly young, collapsing on a night out in December 2007. Laura, understandably, struggled with cycling for a long time afterwards. Simon passed away in 2014, aged just forty-nine. I will never forget them. I will always cherish the rides I did with them, and what those rides taught me.

Simon and Sophie understood the balance that a young athlete needs. Going in to big championships, they would never tell us that they thought we should win. Instead, like my parents, they would ask that we tried as hard as we could. They gave us confidence – 'You're good enough to finish top five, Laura' – but they made it about enjoyment, never expectation.

We were racers, but we weren't only racers. Sometimes having two daughters both doing well on a national level yet in different age groups and in contrasting disciplines put pressures on the family. I'd get in the car with Dad. Emma would get in the car with Mum. We would set off in convoy up the A10 and across to the A1 at Stevenage, drive a couple of hours north to Blyth services, have lunch at the Little Chef, and then a few miles on Dad would turn left to take me to my event in Rotherham and Mum would turn right to take Emma to a race in Scunthorpe. We made it work by being practical. Each weekend we'd swap over. Me with Dad one week, in with Mum the next.

Never was it just about the bike racing. There was a two-day event around Cardiff and Cwmbran, finishing up at lunchtime on the Sunday, when all the other girls and their parents would head back home across the country to London, Birmingham, Manchester. Long drives, long days. We would turn inland and go to the Big Pit, the national coal museum in Blaenavon. Or we might be racing at Heaton Park in Newcastle. We'd get up there early on the Saturday, take some pictures of the Tyne Bridge, and wander over the Millennium Bridge on Quayside. Eat fish and chips sitting on the steps leading out of St James's Park and then, after the event had finished, drive out past Gateshead Stadium, have a look at that, and drive on to the Stadium of Light in Sunderland.

We went through a phase that wherever we raced we would try to visit the highest-ranking football club in the area. Most of the time we couldn't get into the stadium, because we never knew when the official tours were. I remember Dad doubting, possibly unfairly, whether Preston North End even had stadium tours. One year, the National Road Race Championships were held just outside Burnley. Dad and Emma ticked off Accrington Stanley's home stadium.

I think they were more worried about us missing out on a normal childhood than we girls were, if normal is going to the Crown Ground when Accrington Stanley aren't even playing at home. We didn't feel we were missing out on anything. We had made the choice to ride and to race. But the racing didn't always go well, and having a daft adventure to go on that same weekend allowed us to step back from it all and realize that there were other things going on beyond the tracks and chequered flags. We saw the motorways and service stations but we also saw Legoland and Thorpe Park. Coach Simon had an obsession with rebuilding steam trains. There's a small railway museum up the A1 in Oakham where he and his old man Peter, an engineer, used to spend all the time Simon wasn't knee-deep in cycling. So whenever we rode the track in Newport, we would have to visit the Transporter Bridge across the Usk with him too. Drive down there, park up next to it, go across as foot passengers, get thrown off on the other side, line up and come back across. A hundred years of engineering history to soak up. Now, where's my track bike?

I think Mum and Dad find it strange now: four Olympic gold medals knocking around their house somewhere, world champions' rainbow jerseys in the cupboards, pots and trophies under the stairs. It's all a bit comic book to them. They know someone's got to do it, because those events are there to be won, but why us?

My dad is a rational man, and he's rationalized it with the help of Sammy Davis Jnr. Sammy called his autobiography *Why Me?* Dad heard him explaining it: 'You hear people exclaiming, "Why me?" when things go wrong. You're late for a meeting, now the train's been cancelled: why me?' Dad says Sammy saw his story the other way round. Why had this little black Jewish boy achieved all he did? Five Emmys, five Grammys, Hollywood films, one-man Broadway shows. Sammy would find himself in his later days sitting there, thinking, 'Why me?'

Dad has the same thought. Why me, and why not others? Sarah Hammer, seven world titles, world records … and four Olympic silvers. Me? Every Olympic final I've lined up in, I've won. Maybe it goes back to that old and simple idea: be the best you can. Another bit of advice from my parents: find something you're good at and enjoy doing. Emma went on to ride pro on the road for the Boels-Dolmans team. The minute she stopped enjoying it, just before her twenty-fifth birthday, she called it a day. We rode when we loved it. I still do. I am a rider. Pass me my helmet.

That was the growing girl, and that little spell of shyness is long gone. Now I can talk to anyone. My mum could make a wall talk; my sister has the same gift. Together we could chat for England and bring back all the major trophies.

These days Dad just lets us get on with it. He doesn't mind. It means he doesn't have to speak. He can take a step back. On a night out, I'm even more nuts. More out of control. I don't really care what I say or do; I'm here for a good night. Our chances to let the pigtails down are so few that we have to cash them in fully when we get the opportunity. We never go out for just one drink. It's to celebrate something, so we ride it hard.

**JASON:** As someone who struggles with small talk and frequently strikes new acquaintances as a man of few and downbeat words, I have always been impressed by Laura's ability to make a good first impression. People like her a lot straight away. She is easy to talk to, she's not intimidating, she is interested in who you are and how you're getting on.

At the Manchester velodrome I get on very well with the

mechanics. I get on well with the ones who do things that fascinate me, like the scientists. I will just walk through the office, not because I mean to be rude but because I'm not quite sure what to say. Laura will stop to talk to everyone, and make an effort when she does. She doesn't really care about the bikes, like I do. She's more interested in people's kids, their weekends, what gossip is going round.

It didn't surprise me to learn that she used to get kicked out of geography lessons at school for being too loud. Talk is good, but sometimes listening can be better.

Usually communication is a strong point for Laura. When I tell a story, I trip myself up. Halfway through an anecdote I feel like I'm losing my own interest, let alone that of the listener. When Laura tells a story she paints a picture. She uses a large canvas and an awful lot of paint, much of which misses the picture or fills in an entirely different one on the side, but she does it well.

She also has a talent for getting people to do things for her. At British Cycling she has half the team tripping over themselves to help her out, to do things that they would never dream about doing for anyone else. Maybe it's the difference between men and women. Maybe it's just the difference between this particular man and this particular woman. I don't like the idea of people doing stuff for me. I don't want to make anyone go out of their way.

She likes a plan, in her professional career and in her private life. We had been engaged for five minutes, the wedding a year and a half away, and Laura had already scoped out the venue and how she might want it decorated. She also likes a hissy fit, not that the rational part of her brain has anything to do with it. On the night of my twenty-fifth birthday she had bought us tickets to see *The Lion King* at the Palace Theatre in Manchester. Laura decided to wear a sandy-coloured dress. She selected shoes to go with it, and black tights to link it all up. All of which was fine, until we reached 6.45 p.m. and time to leave, and Laura could not find her tights.

I had got ready in just over four minutes. She went ballistic for at least twice as long. Right: no black tights, no night out. Nothing made it better – not a suggestion of a different outfit, not the idea that it wasn't that cold and it might not require tights, not the hint that, ahem, wasn't this my birthday, and shouldn't we have left by now?

My birthday bash was on the point of being cancelled when I offered to pop to the big Tesco just down the hill in Stockport. Pack of three pairs of opaque black tights, £4. Night saved. My own birthday treat rescued.

Quirky is not a word often associated with me. Laura is a series of interconnected and, to the unfamiliar observer, irrational idiosyncrasies. She is so sensitive to all that is around her on her bike that if her seat-post is half a millimetre too low or high she will instantly notice it and demand the mechanics explain why. I don't use that figure as a way of exaggerating for comic effect; she literally notices a half-millimetre difference. You'll know the story of the Princess and the Pea. Laura is the Dame of the Decimal Point.

She is sensitive and she is sideways. She had been wearing a pair of cycling shoes for a week when she noticed that the cleats on the soles were black, rather than grey as they had been for years. Her first reaction: how have these cleats changed colour? Her second: is this some sort of new design?

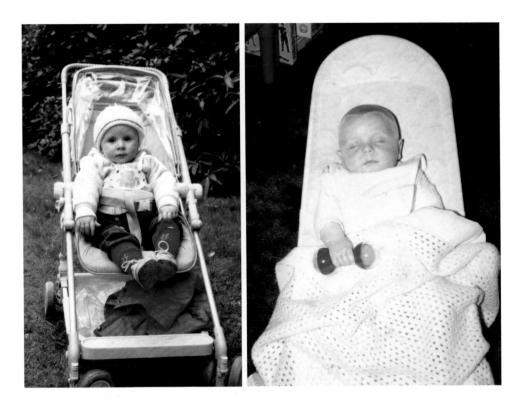

The adventure begins. Baby Jason (top left and right), calm as ever, and baby Laura (below left and below right, with sister Emma).

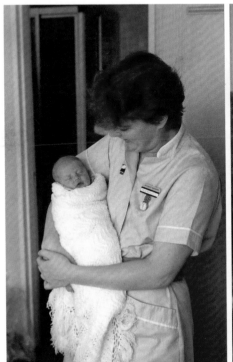

JASON: Always a sporty kid, it didn't take long before I found something to ride. Perhaps this is where my love of racing came from (top right).

LAURA: My first steps ... we Trott girls were always destined to become cyclists.

JASON: Ah, my beloved
Fort. I got quite
some use out of it!

JASON: You don't get far as a cyclist without the support of your family (top), and it paid off as I joined British Cycling a year early (with Vicky Pendleton, below).

LAURA: Here I am competing against the boys for Welwyn at the under-12 Nationals (top), racing on the road (middle) and lapping the field to win at the under-14 Nationals (bottom).

LAURA: Running must have helped my endurance on the bike – so did meeting Sir Brad, a true inspiration for a young cyclist.

Early trophies gave us the motivation to keep going – but little did we know bigger and better things awaited us.

Not until much later did she reach the rather more obvious conclusion that they weren't actually her shoes at all. They belonged to teammate Elinor Barker. Still, bits of toughened plastic that have looked the same for many years do frequently turn a radically different colour in seven days, don't they?

Laura is sentimental in a way I never would be. She still has the doll, Clumpy, that her nan gave her on her first birthday. Clumpy is a rag doll and was once torn apart. When reassembled she was all head and no torso. She is terrifying to look at. I lie awake at night, Clumpy on the shared pillow next to my face, and I fear opening my eyes in case Clumpy turns her head to stare at me with those unblinking dead eyes and starts tearing me apart, too.

Despite this, Clumpy is the first thing Laura intends to save in the event of a house fire. I'm to rescue the dogs. She will leave all our Olympic keepsakes and laptops and jewellery and car keys and carbon bikes, and instead concentrate solely on a patched-up rag doll that has also been taken to London, Rio, Colombia, Melbourne and many other places. Taken to hotels, but only once to the velodrome. Laura is obsessed with the idea of a rival getting into her kitbag and stealing Clumpy away. It's the only way another rider could make Laura turn bad.

Then there's a pillow, an ancient piece of Trott family bedding which Laura refuses to throw away. It has dark stains from historic nosebleeds across it. It has never been washed, and it lives on our bed. And to think she complains about my floordrobe.

**LAURA:** I am a woman with no hidden talents. I can't dance. Being asked to go on *Strictly Come Dancing* would be my worst nightmare. I can't cook. I've blown microwave doors off. I can't sing, I can't draw.

I'm glad I found cycling. Had I not, I would have been in big trouble. I stayed on at school into the sixth form, taking an A-Level in photography and two sport-related BTECs. I got a B in photography, and the other two – well, they were just BTECs. I didn't like school. I just wanted to cycle. I knew from Year 9 onwards that cycling was going to be my career, and if one teacher in particular mocked me for that ('Professional cyclist? That isn't even possible!') then I hope they remember now. I love dogs, I love animals. But I was never smart enough to be a vet. I would have been a housewife, a bored one who wanted to be out in the big wide world rather than sitting in front of the television. Out there taking people on, not indoors going slowly mad.

I am a terrible cook. Awful. I try to make good-looking, nice-tasting food, and I just can't. You can understand someone setting fire to the oven. Setting fire to the microwave takes real ability.

The most advanced thing I can make is scrambled egg. I'm good at opening packets of crisps. I don't eat fruit. Making toast is sometimes a challenge.

It's not just lost pairs of tights that make me flip. I'm a happy individual, but drivers who put my life at risk when I'm out riding turn Good Laura bad. I like to know what each day holds at least a week before I have to do it. If my coach tweaks my training on the morning of the session I'll be furious. 'Why would you do that? It made sense when you wrote it seven days ago, so why are you messing around with it two hours before I'm due to do it?'

It's not about control, but being organized. I'm uncomfortable with spontaneity. I dislike last-minute decisions. I hate change. I'm not keen on cleaning my bike, but Jason will look after the ones I've got at home, and if one ever gets in a terrible state I'll take it to the track, ask my mechanic Jordan in my nicest possible voice, and somehow, before I go home, the bike comes back as if it were new.

But let's not be negative. I'm not. Cycling makes me happy, Jason makes me happy. Our two dogs make me happy. I loved Rupert, our Shih Tzu puppy at my parents' home in Cheshunt, but Mum quite fairly insisted he stay with her. The day we visited Sprolo for the first time and put a reserve on him was almost as emotional as winning a medal.

I can feel helpless, sometimes, if people I care about are upset and there's nothing I can do about it. If Jason struggles in a race, I usually trust him to cope with it himself. He's strong like that. When he goes really quiet I know then that it's properly got to him. I'll try to text him, but we aren't allowed mobiles in the track centre, so I'll have to sneak off to the toilet and try to send some love from there. I'll still be racing, but I want to let him know that I'm there, although I'm desperate to tell him in person and a text will never feel enough.

My sister now lives in New Zealand. If she's ever upset, the feeling travels across from the other side of the world. After Rio she did a TV interview about me that was subsequently twisted badly in some of the newspapers. When told I had trained harder than anyone else, she pointed out that everyone at an Olympics is trying hard, that everyone has trained as smartly as they can. When told that Jason and

I were celebrities, she said that the family didn't put us on a pedestal. That I am the girl who used to pull her hair, and that we used to race each other up and down my nan's road on our scooters. To her we're clearly not huge stars, but when she tried to explain that, suddenly people decided she was slagging me off and was jealous and was the big bad sister. All of which is total nonsense, and is hugely upsetting. I know it's impossible, but I like to think that the lives of those in my family could somehow always be perfect. We grew up so close that those ties will never loosen.

Riding together, ticking off football grounds together, going to gigs together. My favourite musician even now is Bruce Springsteen, because my parents both love him and we grew up with the Boss blasting out of the living-room speakers. I went to my first Springsteen gig at the age of eight, all four of us Trotts off to Wembley together. Jason had never been to a single gig until I took him to see Adele at the Manchester Arena. I ticked off most of the big acts before I started my GCSEs: Elton, Meat Loaf, Take That, the Spice Girls. Only the last of those caused issues. Baby Spice was always my favourite. I was very jealous of sister Emma sharing a name with Ms Bunton. Sister Emma didn't even appreciate it: she wanted to be Sporty Spice. When a DVD box set featuring all of their videos came out, it was marketed in five different commemorative tins, each with the face of one of the five girls on the top. Evil marketing, and we were only allowed one tin between us. Which of us won out? Neither. We had to go for Victoria as the middle ground.

Some young girls might have been embarrassed going to these gigs with their dad. Not me. My dad is a sensational dancer. As a young boy he was put through dance lessons, and they really paid off. He can do it all: Latin, ballroom, rock 'n' roll, disco. Proper shapes, even now in his mid-fifties. If anything it's the daughter's dancing that shames the father. Another reason not to go on *Strictly*.

I'm still the girl who struggles to eat healthy food. Before the Olympics in Rio, to handle what they told us would be an epidemic of diarrhoea, we were given prebiotics and probiotics to protect our digestive systems. They made mine worse. I won't take energy drinks and I don't bother with protein shakes after training. Nesquik is fine for me, just as it was two decades ago, even if it's not technically a raw ingredient. It may not be all natural, but the taste of the powder in the Magic Straws range is clearly superior to anything that comes out of the ground.

I'm the same competitor on and off the track. Scrabble gets me every time. Jason refuses to accept my creative spelling skills or my ability to craft entirely new words. Apparently the official instructions don't favour the phonetic. Our house, my rules. I can get competitive about silly things – how many Twitter followers I have, how many followers I went up by during the London Olympics. (From something like 7,000 to over 200,000, if you're interested.) Jason couldn't care less about the number of his Twitter followers. He barely tweets. When he does, the number of people following him actually drops. Poor old Jason.

**JASON:** I love watching Laura race. I have none of the fears that my mother has watching me, nor the palpitations Laura gets when I'm in action. I have complete confidence in her.

In Rio I could see that Laura was enjoying herself in those critical gold medal moments. There was a freedom to her riding and tactics that was all about confidence and good form. In the elimination race she was doing what she wanted, not reacting to what others were doing. Riding at the front for a while, riding at the back, comfortable wherever she went, pure belief in herself.

The devil and the women is a much more thrilling spectacle than the devil and the men. The blokes ride it like blokes always want to ride – ballistic for the first half, all tactics and big moves in the second. Watching the women in that constantly shifting pack is like studying a living thing, all movement and late twitches. From the outside you can see someone blithely riding into trouble, not having the faintest idea about it, completely incapable of doing anything to respond when it suddenly happens. It's almost like watching a cross between a pantomime and a horror film: slow slow fast fast, the innocents caught out, a pause that lulls you into relaxation, and then another explosion – riders panicking, riders pulling shapes, others desperately hanging in there, throwing everything they have into the pan. I used to hate riding it: I would find myself in the first half in a strange position of not wanting to win but not wanting to go home. To watch Laura dominate it as she can just blows me away. I know secretly that I can do a lot on a track bike. But I can't do what Laura does, not even close.

She can fool the best. During the World Cup in London in late 2014, Chris Boardman – a brilliant commentator, a true track expert – saw Laura keep sitting at the back and only nicking through each time at the last minute, and described her as making it hard for herself. She was actually playing to her strengths. She didn't see the point of fighting to sit second wheel. I watch as a sprinter, and a sprinter never wants to be on the leader's shoulder. It means you're going the long way round them and not getting anywhere near as good a tow as you would be if you were tucked in cleanly behind. Laura is in tune with the devil. She knows that there is no safety in riding directly behind the leader. She will sit just over their back wheel and wait for some poor fool who hasn't thought it through to roll into that little space between her and the front rider, and when she does, Laura will glance to her left and think, 'Well, you're going home before I am ...'

**LAURA:** Sitting just on the outside of the leader's rear wheel. There's no safer spot. On the front you're always vulnerable to someone rolling you on your outside. When you're over-lapping in second, it's you who's going to be doing the rolling. Physically it's probably the hardest spot as you have no tow from the rider in front. But you are hunting the balance between being safe and being efficient. Seven might be my favourite number, but two can be beautiful too.

And the devil is my beautiful weapon. My win rate must be close to 80 per cent. Two days of competition in the omnium, me knowing that I'm likely to finish the first with an authoritative victory, the others going to bed wondering what else they might have done and how else they can rescue it now. At least one rival will always bomb out early, and they have to sleep on that too.

I like being ahead of the pack. On track, in my life. I bought Jason his wedding present months before the big day. Because I get too excited about things like that, I then had to tell him about it. Still months in advance.

But that's me. Get there first. Try not to let anyone beat you to it.

# Five: **Endurance**

**LAURA:** The change came, when I was aged fifteen, in 2007.

A few girls before me had been moved on to British Cycling's prestigious Olympic Development Programme a year early – Jess Varnish and Becky James were two, both sprinters. Jess would go on to win team sprint World silver in 2011, Becky the sprint and keirin World gold in 2013. At the National Track Championships in 2007 I had come second in the youth 500 metres, so I was being looked at as the next one off the rank and was duly moved up.

The problem was that I didn't think of myself as a sprinter. The second problem was that no one was allowed on to the endurance programme – which suited my attributes much more – a year early, at the age of fifteen. So I accepted my place on the sprint programme because I thought I had nothing to lose. I actually rather enjoyed the sprinting itself. Some of my times in practice were quite good. My quarter laps had made waves, and I was certainly improving. But I just never truly clicked with it. I stopped enjoying the training. It was all too short and sharp, and there were no races where I could test myself out. And I'm a racer. I couldn't go to the junior Worlds because I was too young. I couldn't go to the junior Europeans. It was as if I were on the squad just to make up numbers, and that was never going to work for my mentality.

It got to a point where I went to the Nationals and ended up riding everything, but everything badly. I didn't have the flat-out speed to compete with the sprinters, and because I'd been training as a sprinter I didn't have the endurance for a scratch or points race. Becky beat me. Jess beat me. At the end of 2008 head coach Iain Dyer sat me down at one of the Revolution track events and told me that I was going to be kicked off the programme.

There were no tears and no tantrums. I was actually glad he had made the decision. I knew it wasn't for me. I knew I wasn't going to make it. There were too many people ahead of me. It was a huge gap for me to jump, and I didn't have the raw power to make it.

What upset me was what they offered me in its place. Go and join the mountain-bike programme. I had never done mountain biking. Cruising round Lee Valley on a hardtail is not mountain biking. It is one of the flattest parts of the entire country. The world of berms, rock gardens and doubles was as foreign to me as a degree in fine art.

It made no sense to anyone. I had shown serious pedigree previously in endurance events. I had been circuit race champion for as long as I could remember. As an under-14 riding for Welwyn I lapped the entire field on a three-kilometre circuit. So I phoned Helen Mortimer, a former downhill mountain-biker herself, who was then looking after the whole of the ODP. A bold thing to do, but the stakes were high. I want a chance, I told her. I want a chance to show you what

I'm actually good at. She understood instantly. Within a day or two I was transferred to the endurance programme, and had a year to prove I was worth the gamble.

It caused a fair old stink. You were supposed to be tested for it to see if you were good enough to get on the squad. But there was no point in me testing because I had trained specifically as a sprinter, and so my chance arrived.

Still nothing came easy. The first camp that I could make happened to be doubling up as a trial for three new coaches. One was from Northern Ireland. I was straight out of Hertfordshire: I couldn't understand a word he was saying. I sat there, leaning forwards, straining my ears, trying to guess. Eventually I had to say something. 'I'm really sorry, coach, but I've got absolutely no idea what you're going on about.' The job went to former rider Rob Sharman. Not once did we see eye to eye. I was and still am bad at keeping my equipment clean and tidy. Those were the years when you were supposed to learn that your bike must be clean. And Rob was really picky. He would rub his finger under the brake calliper and even if he found only the tiniest speck of dirt, he would make you clean the whole thing.

Rob was there for us to learn from rather than to coach us directly. My actual training sessions were still coming from Nigel Hampton, my second coach, via my sister – carefully designed by one, tested out by the other. By 2009 I was travelling across to Belgium to race, and with a decent half-season in my jersey pockets this time I felt ready when the ODP testers came calling.

I learned something. I learned that static tests were never going to show me as any good. Some riders test brilliantly.

They hit all their numbers and do everything that is asked. They are a laptop's dream partner. They excel on Excel. I was useless, at least in that format. I was a Formula One car being asked to reverse park. I was a swift expected to fly in a cage.

It was a ramp test, done on a stationary trainer. You start off pedalling at ninety revolutions per minute. Every thirty seconds the resistance is increased. Harder and harder, incrementally more pain, until your legs seize up and it feels like cycling through quick-drying cement. As soon as you drop below 90 rpm you're done.

Emma told me in advance that anything between ten and twelve minutes was considered good. I lasted something like six and half minutes. Horrendous time, horrendous feeling, especially trudging back home to see Emma's expectant face and having to tell her that I'd barely lasted half as long as I was supposed to. 'Six and a half minutes? You're never going to get back on that programme in a million years.' Thankfully I was already on the endurance squad and the tests came partway through my year, but the coaches could always change their minds about me.

With reflection it made sense. I hated being on a static bike. It felt nothing like racing to me, and because it didn't feel like racing, my body and brain would not respond as they would if I were out on the track with a load of rivals coming over the top of me or trying to get a jump off the front. I could prove that, too.

At the Europeans in Minsk in July 2009 I got bronze medals in the junior individual pursuit and the points race. I had no idea what the British record was in the IP, but I broke it all the same, despite all that sprint training, despite what the ramp test had tried to tell everyone. I rode my first team pursuit there as well. Suddenly good endurance numbers were everywhere. Simon Cope, the British Cycling academy coach, came over to me with a funny look on his face. 'Did you know you've just smashed the British IP record?' It shocked me, because senior coach Shane Sutton had told me once that I would never make a decent pursuiter. Not strong enough, apparently, although I found myself thinking, 'But I'm fast enough, and isn't that all that matters?' Coming off after the points race, Copey took me aside again. 'The only reason you got a medal in that was because you were stronger than everybody else. You didn't actually have a clue what was going on, did you?' He was right both times. I was strong. I was fast. And I still had to learn how to utilize those gifts. But at last my foot was in the door.

I was still living at home while all this was going on, still at school, still in my first year of A-Levels. Normal at first glance, nothing like my contemporaries in any other way. By Year 10 the parties had started: venues hired out, discos, boys, dancing, and cheeky drinks when no one was looking. School trips came and went – an annual skiing one which I would have loved but couldn't risk for fear of mangling a knee or ankle, a one-off special to New York that I still pine for to this day. None of it mattered to me enough to stop cycling, though, and I never truly felt I was missing out. I had chosen what I wanted to do. No one was forcing me. My parents were supportive but never coercive. Taking cycling seriously wasn't even that serious. It was fun.

And so to that infamous teacher in the careers lesson at school. Early in that first term of the sixth form, the whole class sat down in our form room. The RE teacher takes to the floor. 'I'll come round to everybody in turn. I'd like to know, by the end of these two years, what everybody wants to be.' Round we go. Architect. Fashion designer. Dunno, sir. Dunno, sir. 'Laura Trott. How about you?'

'I'm going to be a professional cyclist.'

A pause and a face. 'Laura, that isn't even possible. That's not a proper job.'

Me, under my breath: 'If only you knew, if only you knew ...'

I'd actually got it wrong. I should have said 'already am' rather than 'going to be'. Being on the ODP meant that I was already being paid a little bit to ride my bike. The professional era had already begun.

Kristi, my best friend all through school, understood what I wanted. Things hadn't come easy for her. She struggled with the theory side of school. We would get asked to write essays and I would spend my time rewriting them for her or going round to her house to finish them off with her. The teacher would ask us to write an essay that covered both sides of a sheet of A4. You'd look at Kristi's. In her version all the writing would be huge. You'd come out of an easy exam and ask her how she had found it. You would have been sitting there all finished with half an hour still to go, and Kristi would still be staring at the first question.

Sport made sense for her. When asked that same question by the same teacher, she had answered 'stunt woman'. Imagine the face the RE teacher pulled on hearing that. Again, cruel misfortune intervened. She fractured her spine doing gymnastics. She is now training to be a firefighter, and is doing well.

In those sixth-form days it was Kristi who made sure I never felt excluded. She was quite the social bee. The morning after any school disco or big party at someone's house she would come round to ours and fill me in on all the gossip and scandal that I'd missed. She was also a butterfly, floating from group to group, never part of a clique, always ensuring that I wasn't left on my own either.

Kristi stuck up for me, and I stuck up for Kristi. She was there in the velodrome in Stratford in 2012 to see the second and deciding day of the omnium. It was her birthday. When I won, I took the flowers I'd been given on the podium and presented them to her. That's for us and all we did.

Other girls had boyfriends. It had never really bothered me. Not until later in the sixth form did I start seeing one who actually understood what I was doing. There were the ones you nominally dated for a month or so, more in theory than in action, and I felt like none of them got it. They would be going off to parties, say they would see me there later, and I would have to tell them that I wasn't coming. You can come round to my parents' house and sit on the sofa, or you can go by yourself: I'm racing tomorrow, I'm eating big, I'm drinking nothing and I'm going to bed before the first can of sweet cider is knocked over at that house party.

I wasn't an angel. I saw school as much about the social side of it as the education. During those long afternoon lessons I never thought I should probably concentrate, because it didn't matter to me. Others around me sat there twiddling their thumbs, but they had no thought as to what might come when we left. I had the most solid of end goals. I was working towards something else.

I was lucky in so many ways. Most people don't work out how they actually want to spend their lives for years, if they work it out at all. I had a passion for what I did, but I had also fallen into a sport that suited everything about me. I wasn't the fast winger in the school football team who didn't quite have the goal-scoring skills to cut it beyond county level, yet could have been a sensational long jumper had he ever trained for it. I wasn't the girl consistently finishing runner-up in south-east junior tennis championships whose hand–eye coordination was really best suited to golf. I wasn't even Emma, a brilliant road cyclist who, had she actually tried triathlon, could have been a world-beater.

And winning gave me such pleasure. A confidence, a kick. An identity, a future. I didn't like defeat, but I would never show it, not at the race. It would be on the way home in the car that it came out. Right, Dad, let's find a new football ground. Let's have a big tea at that Little Chef.

I could be angry with myself if I'd done something wrong. Other times there would be deep disappointment that I wasn't able to out-think someone. It was always easier to lose when the winner was clearly better. It was harder, much harder, when I knew that I could have won.

Boys would race girls, girls would not complain. No quarter was given or asked for. In one elimination race a boy swung past me and told me I was the one to go. Instead of arguing, I meekly rode off the track. A cunning psychological trick, and one I failed to spot. I lost all my points and all my hopes with it. A defeat where I could have done better with the physical resources I had was more painful than just being beaten outright. A quieter journey home, a better detour needed.

Each month brought fresh lessons. Each term brought me closer to physical maturity. That rogue RE teacher was not representative of the school's attitude towards me. I was allowed to complete my BTECs early, get the coursework done and dusted well in advance of the deadlines. One of the PE teachers, George Demetriou, was appointed as an unofficial mentor. I could go to him and ask for the next bit of reading or section of coursework. He would dig it out, I would complete it. By February 2010 I was done, weeks ahead of all the others, the grades mattering less than the freedom to focus on the examinations elsewhere.

That August, as others were awaiting their A-Level results, I was in Italy at the junior World Championships. For the first time at a global level the new format for the omnium was being tried. This was how it would be raced at the London Olympics two years later, not that this was anywhere close to my mind. I should only have been doing the team pursuit, but pursuiting talent was thin on the ground that summer. There were too few girls to make up a team. Instead I would try everything else: individual pursuit, points race, omnium.

Silver in the points race. Silver in the IP. Into the omnium, across two days for the first time in my career. On the first day it was another tough lesson from a bigger and tougher girl, Cuba's Marlies Mejias. She destroyed me in the 500 metre time trial and she put me away in the IP. She was hitting me hard in the devil, too, and then the devil got his own back on her. She rode inside the track on to the blue strip, the Côte d'Azur. She triggered a crash. Her foot came out of its pedal, and she carried on riding – through the warnings, through the shouts, through the two laps she had to get off the track. With that came disqualification, not just from the race but from the whole event. The field ahead of me was clear, and I took it. World junior champion. I could barely remember the BTECs.

Mejias is still riding. She was there in Rio. But she has never converted that junior promise, never kicked on after being kicked out. Eighth in the 2016 omnium. Maybe I should have thanked her. That world title set a fuse burning for what would end with me entering the nation's consciousness two summers later. Not that I knew. Not that I could guess.

Out of school and time to move on with my life: I was on to the senior squad. From the same bedroom I'd had at Mum and Dad's house since birth I was suddenly in the same set of British Cycling flats in Fallowfield in south Manchester that Jason had been through before. And the first week was hell.

I had never turned on a washing machine in my life. I'd never cooked a single meal. Mum had done everything for me. She would tell me to leave my washing outside my door. I would, and it would come back clean the next morning. On my very first day in Manchester I took a potato and stuck it in the oven to bake. Knowing nothing, I turned the grill on rather than the oven. Shortly afterwards the rock-hard spud went up in flames. Fire alarms across Fallowfield. Who is this new girl?

I had no friends up there. I was the only one who had moved up out of my age group. There was no one else but me and my overwhelming sense of loneliness. I hadn't even travelled up with anyone. Mum and Dad were at work, so I had packed my Mini full of a load of crap that I would never need and set off round the M25 and up the M1.

I was overwhelmed. On arrival I was given two skinsuits to train in at the velodrome. I wore one the first day and the other the next. The third morning I realized where I was going wrong. Leaving one of them outside my bedroom door had had no effect. The following day I needed another one. How did the washing machine work? What setting for a skinsuit? How to dry one properly so it didn't shrink in some places and go baggy in others?

I bought frozen chicken. I forgot to defrost it. I packed my one bag for the track, for Sophie Bruton and Simon Layfield had drilled me well, but somewhere between knowing I had to be out of the front door at 8 a.m. to get to the track and trying to tidy the place so it didn't look like an interrupted burglary I lost my way and lost the time.

At the track I was being coached by Paul Manning for the first time. For the first few days, I couldn't get on with him. I would ring Darren Tudor, who had coached me through 2010 up to that point, crying down the phone. Everything was new. I just wanted the security of the old.

Jacket potatoes, every evening. Tuna on it every time, because the chicken refused to get out of the freezer while I was away riding. The first time I wanted to cook tuna pasta bake, I had to get my mum on the phone to talk me through it step by step. Now grate the cheese, Laura. Now pick up the tin opener. Wherever you left it, Laura.

All the time tears, all the time regrets. 'Can you not just come up here, Mum?' I simply couldn't do it. I hated it.

In some ways I was experiencing what most people of my age were going through when they went away to college or university. The difference was that I was on my own. There were no equally struggling first-years in the rooms next door or freshers' events all week. There was no canteen as you have in halls, or bar promotions to break the ice. If students can't cook for themselves, at least eating McDonald's doesn't get them kicked off their course. About a month in I realized that there was actually a really nice stir-fry place downstairs. On that first day when I set fire to everything, I could have just gone down for noodles instead.

I did think about going home. I'm sure a lot of eighteen-year-old girls would have done so. I knew too that if I went then I would never come back. That would have been the end.

My mum has always been good at convincing me. She would phone me every day, email me little stories and jokes. I felt less lonely. She would send me little packages of stuff – treats, magazines, smellies. When she and Dad came north in person, as worried as they had ever been, they brought enough frozen meals to feed the squad. None of them featured jacket potatoes or tuna. At last a routine I could make work. Breakfast. Take out the frozen meal. Go training. Come back and cook the now-defrosted meal.

A month in, I got a flatmate. Katie Colclough, a talented track endurance rider, back from a spell living in Belgium. At last I had somebody to follow and help. I learned a few more of the basics: where the nearest supermarket was, where the cinema might be. Other girls closer to my age came round – Hannah Mayho, Anna Blyth. My initial reaction to Fallowfield ('I am never living here in a million years') began to dissolve in the face of local charm. People in Manchester seemed more laid back than down south. Everyone said hello to each other.

The drivers weren't all screaming at one another in a fuming traffic jam. The weather ... well, everyone who moves from south to north struggles with the weather. When I did go back to Hertfordshire it felt like I was going to Spain. I would drive down wearing trackie bottoms, a hoodie, thick socks and a waterproof coat, and arrive in 28 degrees. I would have to go through bags of old clothes in the attic to find something I could wear without melting.

In October, I was called up for my first major senior championships: the Commonwealth Games in Delhi. Emma – beautifully – was also selected, to ride the time trial and road race. There was no team pursuit so no chance to ride with Katie in that, but in the individual pursuit – only the second time I had ever raced over three kilometres – I knocked four seconds off my personal best to finish seventh. Or personal only, as it would have been at that stage. In the points race I rode to help Katie and came ninth. In the scratch I worked for Anna Blyth and came ninth again. Big sister rode well, eighth in the time trial and thirty-third in the road race behind the big stars, Lizzie Armitstead and Nicole Cooke.

I thought I'd made it. Proper nice kit. I couldn't imagine that anything could go wrong after that, didn't dream that Katie and Hannah would be long retired when I was defending two Olympic titles in Rio. I was naïve in so many ways. One afternoon I decided to explore the old part of Delhi. We had been warned not to wear our official England trainers in case we were kidnapped and held for ransom, but I had nothing else except cleats. The kidnap threat was laughable. So too was the mission I was sent on with Dave Daniell, one of my England teammates, to buy a Buddha clock. This in a city that is 80 per cent Hindu, 15 per cent Muslim and a little bit Christian. We didn't find one. Neither did we find the Eiffel Tower or Elvis.

As each training day passed by back in the north-west of England in those first few weeks, I grew to understand and appreciate Paul Manning more and more. One of the first things he had said to me had been congratulations on your junior world championship; you've got to forget about that now, it starts here. When you're eighteen, a World juniors feels huge, but I knew what he meant, and I understood how things would be. Paul would be straight talking. He would get to the point every time. Darren Tudor, who had also coached Geraint Thomas in his younger days, was wonderfully laid back. I would have to ring him every evening to ask him to send across the next day's training. Paul was a two-week-plan man. I had first met him when he came down to the velodrome in Newport, fresh from winning Olympic team pursuit gold himself. The first time I spoke to him – or at least was meant to speak to him – was in 2010 when he picked me up from a race in Belgium and drove me all the way back to London. I barely said a word. He kept trying to talk to me and all I could manage was, 'Yep.' 'Yep.' It was my shy phase. What to say to an Olympic hero who's now your personal trainer?

To a girl in her late teens he appeared strict. He had to be: he was trying to get a team that was still developing slowly to the top. When the immature part of you woke up you would think, 'Wow this man's horrible.' Two weeks in, finally feeling the benefit of his training, getting to know the man behind the stopwatch, I realized that I actually liked him a lot.

We would never look back, apart from a brief hiccup a few years later when the powers that be tried to take him away from me. After the World Championships in Minsk in 2013 he was suddenly moved across to the men's endurance programme and replaced by Chris Newton. He sat me down in Costa Coffee in Marple. 'Laura, I've got something to tell you.' I remember struggling to look at him. 'You're changing teams, aren't you? You couldn't just stay with us?'

I tore into Shane Sutton. 'You've taken my coach away from me!' I knew Paul wanted something new. He felt like he'd been with us a long time. Luckily for us, he would be back by December 2014. I needed him, and by then I knew it.

And so the journey continued. Into the Worlds in March 2011, selected for the team pursuit with my friend Dani King and Wendy Houvenaghel. It was a crazy mixed-up team: me exactly half Wendy's age, eighteen to her thirty-six; Wendy from the old school of cycling on the side, a military dentist before turning pro late in life and a military dentist once again afterwards; Dani and I both young kids through the ODP, me as man one, Dani in two, Wendy at the back.

It shouldn't have worked. We had only the most basic chemistry, and all of us were in strange slots in the team. Then we did qualifying and were out front by a mile, and I thought, 'Surely we're going to win this.' A couple of hours later we went up and sealed it, the USA trio in silver, Sarah Hammer little realizing how sick she would get of the sight of me one step further up the podium. It felt like the biggest thing ever. I was a first-year senior – that wasn't meant to happen in our first year. Now there were no thoughts of going home or tuna bakes. Instead, as we crossed the finish line: 'What on earth has just happened?'

My sister was there, commentating for television. I ran

straight over to her. Even then it felt like a turning point, the moment my solid certainties from school were starting to be borne out in a way that no one else could argue with. In the omnium I would finish eleventh, winning the time trial, coming fourth in the IP. I didn't care, because I had my first world champion's rainbow jersey and, for the first time, the London Olympics began to seem real rather than a distant illusion. It all seemed strangely smooth: do what I'm doing now, and I will make it.

The British Championships. Second in the IP, second in the points, second in the scratch, beaten only by Lizzie in the latter two. Shane's insistence that I would never have the endurance for team pursuit, and by extension the omnium, was still bouncing around in my head. I didn't think he was wrong. I imagined, because of who he was and all he had done, that he must know. I certainly wasn't training for it, and I'm pretty certain I was only selected to ride it at the European Championships in Apeldoorn that October because there was no one else. But I was flying now, and I had no fear. I won the devil. I won the IP, I won the 500 metres. I won the whole thing.

There could be no pressure, because I was doing all of this so far ahead of the projected curve. Cycling fanatics knew about me as the Olympic year began, but those from the wider sporting world had no idea who this fresh-faced assassin might be. I thought Rio. Everyone kept telling me Rio.

It helped that I hit the timing bang on. Elinor Barker came good the year after, so she had to wait the full four years to get to an Olympics. I just happened to start maturing eighteen months out and found a new peak six months before. But as soon as I came in to the senior programme I found I could keep up with everyone straight away. I don't ever remember going into Manchester for one of the team pursuit sessions thinking, I can't do this. There was never a session when I feared I wouldn't make the team, even from day one. I don't remember getting dropped in a single effort.

The standard at times was all over the place. The eleven women in the squad ranged from Rebecca Romero, who had won IP gold in Beijing and who had just come back from having her two-year break, to Nicole Cooke, who I worshipped as a rider but just wasn't well suited to the specific demands of the pursuit. Even when all were riding well I never doubted myself. I didn't even worry that I knew so few of them at the time. When I was on the bike I felt indestructible. In the saddle, helmet on, ready to race, that's where I was most confident and most comfortable. When I came off the track and was sitting in the seats recovering, I didn't mind just sitting there in silence. I never sit in silence. But I knew that in two minutes' time I would be back on the track. The track was my place. The track was where I felt most natural.

Mum and Dad, for so long the foundation stones that Emma and I had built our lives on, were no longer as central to all we did. All daughters must fly the nest. But they were still a huge part of all that success. When I went home we would talk of other things – we wouldn't sit on the sofa watching my races back or analysing my numbers. Yet they came to every World Championship except Colombia. Dad, his accountancy skills to the fore, always had input into any contracts that I signed. Mum still tried to wash my kit, at least when they came up to visit. Both of them cared only that I was happy, not that I was winning on the world stage. If I came off the track with a silver medal and had a massive grin on my face, Mum's day would have been made. Never did they moan about the sacrifices they had made. Dad used to love playing cricket. He was a decent spin bowler, and used to try to teach Emma to bowl off-breaks in the back garden. But he gave it all up for us two.

There was only one thing I couldn't share with him, not at that age, nor far younger. Athletes just didn't discuss menstruation, and very few do now, yet there are not many things that could have a bigger effect on your performance. Like all girls I can forever remember when mine started, on Halloween of all nights. That was okay: Mum and Emma had told me what would happen. Emma would never leave me to go through something like that alone. It was when I first came on before a race that trouble arrived.

I was thirteen, competing on the old circuit in Hillingdon, west London. At that age, under-14s, I was still racing against boys. There was a lad called Sam Fry who had never beaten me. He beat me that day. He actually lapped me.

Afterwards my dad couldn't hide his surprise. 'What is the matter with you?' Never in a million years could I have told him. It wasn't until I got home, sitting on the kitchen unit while my mum made tea, that I finally came out with it: 'Mum, I don't know what's wrong with me ...'

She told me about her own experiences, that it would be two days after she was on that she finally felt well again, how she would drop things, how her hands would shake. As a young girl you just don't realize. It was the first period that I'd raced on. You didn't realize because it was taboo, even among young sportswomen. I had close female friends in the cycling world, and I would never have spoken to them about it.

Even now, as a mature, confident woman, it can be difficult. There were no workshops on the ODP, no discussion on training camps. When you were on that talent team in your mid-teens and you were trying to train while on your period, there was no way you would have been able to go up to the coach and say, 'I'm going to go badly, this isn't a true reflection of how I'm performing.' I do tell my coach Paul everything now. I will quite happily write it in my training diary, but it's a horrible boundary to cross when you're growing up. Especially when I was going to races with my dad. As I've said, my mum would take me one weekend and my dad another, and it just had to be that the weekend I came on was while I was travelling with my dad: I am not going to tell him, it's just too awkward.

As I grew up and moved away from home I became braver. I recognized that if I were on my period at a World Championships, I may as well not start. I decided I wanted to control it, and so I went on the pill. It was my decision, nothing to do with coercion from coaches. It was just getting out of hand, and the pill helped straight away. I wouldn't come off it now. Neither have I had any side effects from it.

I do have my concerns. While it is a huge relief to have my periods under control, I do ask myself whether I want to interrupt what my body is trying to do, mess with the most natural of cycles. But big races just happen to come roughly a month apart. One year you could quite easily be on, or just recovering from your period, in every competition for which you've prepared so diligently.

British Cycling are more liberated in their thinking now than they perhaps were before. I don't know of any female cyclists, certainly in my generation, who were told to take noresthisterone, as some track runners were, to delay their periods in past major championships. Then, before the Rio Games, GB Cycling team's head physiotherapist, Phil Burt, put together an excellent initiative around saddle comfort. A couple of us were really struggling with pain at the contact points between body and saddle. At times it was horrendous. It was getting to a point where I was going to have to miss a session because I couldn't sit on the saddle any longer. I have had teammates who have had to have a week out and just spend time in the gym, because it was the only training they could do without being in severe discomfort. Phil, a brilliant physio, equally as exceptional in making sure that a rider's bike is set up to exactly suit their specific physiology, event and injury history, set up an app that allowed us to log how we felt. What were our symptoms? Were they affecting our ability to ride? When and where did we experience pain? It flagged up all the problems that had gone unspoken for so long. Phil pulled together a panel of experts – a friction specialist, reconstructive surgeons, a consultant in vulval health – and got everyone talking. I really opened up. I felt that the chamois we were using – the padded protection woven into our shorts – was failing us. It had gone unchanged since Jason had won his first Olympic gold almost eight years before.

They let us trial many different types of chamois. After testing out ten new designs, they then looked at the position the chamois sat in our racing skinsuits. I am small. Sometimes, when I stood on the pedals rather than sat on the saddle, the chamois would move position. Phil took all of this on board, and then put digital pressure pads on our saddles so he could calculate with total accuracy where more padding was needed and where issues would develop.

It worked. In the six months before Rio, not a single rider had a saddle sore. All that extra training, all that physical comfort instead of distress. I had gone through my whole career to that point not realizing that you didn't have to be in pain when you raced your bike. Phil understood. When I complained of numb hands he bought me gel gloves, gel handlebar tape, moved my bars up, tried me with narrower ones. He threw everything at it trying to fix the problem.

Then, at the Olympics themselves, numb hands. It turned out to be the new skinsuits. They were so skin-tight that they were cutting off the circulation under my arms. We worked that out too. That was our Olympic mentality: examine everything you do, stop at nothing to make it even better.

# Six: **Two Become One**

**LAURA:** It all began that Christmas after the Beijing Olympics, sitting at the dinner table in my parents' house in Cheshunt, flicking through that copy of my dad's *Cycling Weekly*, finding the riding rankings because Emma wanted to see how high they'd put her favourites, Nicole Cooke and Victoria Pendleton. And there was Jason, twenty years old. I looked at his picture and thought, that could be me come London. He's four years older, the London Olympics are four years away, things are starting to make sense.

And that was it really. I didn't fancy him. I didn't even ask myself if I fancied him, because he was nothing like my type, which, given I was sixteen, was all about boy bands – tall, skinny, big hair. Not massive legs and hair that his mum cut and a hairy chest poking through his jersey. I barely thought about him even when cycling was on television, except as a side-dish when something else was going on – watching Dave Daniell at the Manchester World Cup, Jason crashed across the line in the sprint, taking a big slice of skin off his back. That was hard to miss.

It wasn't until 2010 that I got on to the senior squad, and

it wasn't until the following year that I actually met him. I shouldn't have bothered. He was with the mechanics in the velodrome in Manchester. When they all said hello, it wasn't just that he didn't join in, he didn't even acknowledge I was there. On my part, there was no thought about anything at that point except being polite. I had moved up to the north-west from Hertfordshire without knowing anyone. Not the girls, not the lads, thrown in at the deep end. Just trying to make friends with everybody, with anybody who would speak to me.

Sir Chris managed to. He actually introduced himself to me, a man with four Olympic golds to his name and two more to come. From Jason I got nothing. I just assumed he was unsociable, because it wasn't only me he wouldn't speak to. None of the girls I ended up hanging around with spoke to him either. We would be sitting in a circle at the velodrome during training, all drained, all recovering, and it was as if I wasn't there. Okay, I thought. This must be the done thing in the big league.

It took until the European Championships in Apeldoorn, the Netherlands, in the autumn of 2011 for him finally to talk to me. Dani King and I had got into a habit of playing a word game against each other on our smartphones. We would take it in turns, putting in words, sending answers across, trying to stump the other one, trying to get the highest score. Jason happened to be sitting next to me in Costa when Dani went ahead. I nudged him, showed him the app and asked if he might be able to help me out. He could. A few nights later when the game had finished, I texted him. 'Jason. We won!'

**JASON:** British Cycling had given us all work phones. Each rider's number was preloaded. The first text I ever received from Laura arrived at 9 o'clock at night. 'You've won? I didn't even know you were racing today. Is there actually action at the velodrome tonight?'

**LAURA:** It was hardly the start of a whirlwind. We didn't speak again for months, because as an endurance rider you travel a lot during the summer, and I was in and out of the velodrome. We were on different training camps, different countries. Me in Mallorca, Jason in Germany. Me on the road, Jason in western Australia. Only when the World Championships came round in Melbourne in spring 2012 did we find ourselves staying in the same hotel again, racing on the same track, warming up on the same sets of rollers.

And the rollers were the problem. We all liked to listen to music as we loosened up, but I hadn't yet figured out that over-the-head headphones are likely to stay on better when you are pedalling hard and fast. I had the little in-ear ones. Predictably, as I sped up, they worked their way free and fell into the spokes of my front wheel. Wires and earpieces in different directions, a right mess. Fine. I could see another pair draped over the back of a chair. What, they're Jason Kenny's? Ah, he won't mind. Pass them over.

On they went. Round went my legs. Out fell the earphones. This time they disappeared into the rollers. They may as well have rolled under an elephant.

I didn't have the guts to tell him. I didn't even have the guts to find them and put them back myself – I left that to my swannie, my massage man, Luc.

Jason didn't even mention it. And then a little thought popped up in my head: he doesn't take himself or his headphones too seriously, and I like that. He's definitely not my type. I'm not telling anyone, and I'm not doing anything about it, but he's got something. And not just a set of broken headphones.

**JASON:** I wasn't actually a grumpy old man who people didn't talk to. I just came across that way and, to be honest, it rather suited me; it kept people away until I was ready to talk to them. As I'm a little shy, that can take quite some time.

The thing about broken headphones is that they inevitably also break the ice. Now we had a reason to talk, although it was probably only the third time we had done so, and when we talked, I realized I actually enjoyed it. It became natural to stop for a chat when we bumped into each other in the corridors at the velodrome; that sort of thing had never felt natural to me before. In the summer of 2012, with Laura training with the pursuit squad and for the omnium, we were both in Manchester at the same time a lot more of the time. When she went away we already had each other's numbers. It was easy to keep in touch, it became part of the day to drop each other a few texts. And then a lot of texts.

It was still Laura who was doing most of the running. It was certainly Laura who was doing the majority of the talking. She started ringing me up and talking for hours. We would talk cycling, we would talk shop, just in rather different ways. Once I'd had a 10,000-word breakdown about Laura's day, we would then have a ten-word breakdown on mine.

She was always laughing, and not only because of the ten

words I'd chosen. She made me laugh too, once I'd sifted through her thoughts and worked out the essential points she was attempting to make. It was easy. It was fun.

**LAURA:** I knew now that I liked Jason. It was so simple having a laugh with him. At the same time I really didn't think he was my type. I was still living in a flat in Fallowfield with Katie Colclough, and we talked about what he was like, how he looked, how he dressed. She had known a couple of Jason's past girlfriends, and the conversation made it clear that we weren't suited. Still the text messages went on, and I noticed him more and more, mostly because he was driving a very nice sporty white Jag and it was hard to miss. Not bad for a twenty-four-year-old, I thought. Then one night we bumped into each other at the academy flats, and I mentioned I didn't have anything in for dinner, and he said he was in the same boat. We looked at each other and said, 'Why don't we go to get something?'

Downstairs to the street, looking forward to my ride in the Jag. There is no Jag. Instead Jason gets into the worst car I've ever seen. It looked like something you'd see being towed to a scrap yard. And it stank. It stank of old men.

**JASON:** My brother and I had got into a habit of buying old bangers for about 600 quid, razzing them around for a bit and then getting rid of them for another. It was only in a moment of madness that I decided to lease a Jaguar, and only then because I thought, 'Hold on, I'm an Olympic champion, this is what Olympic champions do.' All the same, initially I was going to rent a sensible car. That was still going to set me back £350. Cogs turned. Why rent a diesel for £350 when I can get a five-litre V8 for £500?

I leased it for nine months. Laura didn't sit in it once; this meal fell on the first day of the tenth month. Instead it was the banger with its smell of old men and an engine that refused to start. Because I was away for months at a time, the battery kept going flat. I would jump-start it and allow it to recharge, until one day it had enough of that and died completely. I could have bought a new battery. I could have bought another banger. Instead I decided to carry a little booster pack around with me. When the car needed starting I would have to pop open the bonnet, stick on the booster and start her up that way. On my own around town that was fine. When it came to picking up Laura and chauffeuring her around central Manchester, it was somewhat lacking.

**LAURA:** We went to a little Italian in one of the arcades off Dean Street. I had pizza, and Jason paid. In fact he usually paid on those first nights, even if we always agreed it was my turn.

I was still doing most of the talking. I can talk to a brick wall. I can talk holes into a brick wall. Why use one word when you can use ten? If it went quiet I would just throw something in there. I told him about my sister. I told him about my mum and dad. I told him about my friends. It was more about getting to know each other than discussing teammates and tactics or who was doing what numbers down the velodrome but, in fairness, it was probably Jason getting to know me rather than me getting to know him. For quite a time I thought he was an only child. Then I thought he grew up only with his mum. He never mentioned a dad. Although maybe he tried, and a gap in the flow never opened up.

**JASON:** I took her back to my parents' house once or twice, because we were both sharing flats. We had nowhere else to go that was nice and quiet, and my mum and dad were both working, not that Laura knew more than one of them existed. I wasn't living there any more but I still had a key, so we would drift back there in the stinking non-starting banger and just hang around and have coffee. You know your mum's always going to have food in the fridge, no matter how long ago you and your brother moved out. One Sunday I phoned her up. 'Hi Mum. I'm bringing Trotty back for a bacon butty. Is that okay?'

When she asked – and they always ask, mums – I insisted we were just friends. In many ways we still were, but she sensed something was happening, as mums again always do. She knew of Laura already, having seen her riding the Revolution events as a junior, and she remembered her as a tiny little thing, bombing over the top of much bigger girls to take win after win.

On her first official visit Laura put her feet up on the sofa. Mum said she was pleased that Laura felt at home. She could see straight through me, I'm certain of it.

**LAURA:** Having never really spoken properly about Jason's parents, I then met them. I was surprised, and not only because he had a dad. And a brother. Lorraine and Michael were so loved-up it was unbelievable. It was like looking at a perfect couple. Maybe they did argue, but not when I was there. My family would have an argument no matter what company they were in. It wasn't a bad thing – it was just the way they operated, and I wouldn't have them any other way. Mum and Dad argue. If there wasn't an argument then something was wrong. If there wasn't an argument going on downstairs then I didn't want to go in that room because they wouldn't be talking. At the Kennys', Lorraine would shout for Michael to go in the kitchen, and he would go and help her do whatever she had asked for. At mine, Dad would get shouted at when he was sat on the sofa, trying desperately to pretend he hadn't heard the shouts.

It was fine. My parents have always been a team and a team I couldn't have lived without. Mum did all the housework, Dad worked non-stop to pay for everything. Despite all the knockabout arguing, they were the two people who made my cycling career happen.

I got on with Lorraine from the word go. With her having had two boys, having dreamed of having a girl around so she didn't have to stand in the rain watching them play football, or ferrying them about to cycling, or having a house full of mud and cap guns and spare bike parts, she said she was delighted to have someone to talk to at last about clothes and shoes. She loved the fact that suddenly her birthday and Christmas presents had some thought behind them, that when she made a casual remark about a Fortnum and Mason hamper she'd seen on the internet, one arrived for her from Jason that December. For me it became a home from home. I would get to see my own family once in a blue moon – once in a golden moon come Olympic year. I would make Christmas, I would make Mother's Day. But the three hours' drive on a good day could become five on a bad one. Jason's parents were half an hour away. He would go back every weekend. And so it became an easy habit to do bacon butties on a Saturday there and a full roast on the Sunday. I loved being part of my family, and I loved feeling part of Jason's. It was why I could put my feet up on the sofa. I felt part of it.

For a while we kept our relationship to ourselves. When something new starts like that you don't want it to get out. You're into it, and you just want to see if it can develop. Dani King was the first of the girls to know, and even then she took a while to work it out. As we were leaving the flat in Fallowfield, I took a deep breath and asked her what she thought of Jason. Pause. 'Yeah, he seems caring.' I tried again. 'Do you think he's the type of person who would look after you?' Dani, clueless. 'This is a bit random, Laura.' Another deep breath. 'We've been going out for some meals together.' Dani: 'What?!'

Dani liked Jason. So she thought about it, and she said, 'Yeah, I think he would look after you.'

**JASON:** How wrong can you be, hey? No, Dani had me right, and not only because I seemed to be paying every time we went to that Italian. I may have had a reputation for being socially backward, but I get on with most people. Dani was one of them. There was a little surprise around the velodrome as it gradually leaked out, and that made sense, because it was the track-squad version of an office romance, and office romances can be pressurized both for those in them and those watching on from the outside.

Some of the sprinters had guessed anyway. Chris knew,

because I shared a room with him on camps and at events during that time. When we were away in Mallorca I was on the phone to Laura the whole time. We would be lying on adjacent beds. There was no way he couldn't know. And he didn't mind, because as a sprint squad all of us were non-judgemental. Each of us was happy to mind our own business. If someone wanted to talk about a personal issue then we were there for each other, but we were British men. We just got on with it.

The only person who seemed to think it was an issue was Vicky Pendleton. When she had started a relationship with sports scientist Scott Gardner before London it had led to him losing his job, at least until he was later reinstated. But that was because our rider agreements stated explicitly that none of us could have relationships with staff members. Laura and I hadn't crossed any boundaries. Neither were we the first riders to date each other. It was a relatively common thing, for the simple reason that riders are the only people you spend any time with. And even Vicky apologized later for what she said, telling us that her comments – she was quoted as saying, 'Nobody seems to be bothered about them, but when it was me, it was a big issue' – had been misconstrued in the press. I actually felt sympathetic towards her and Scott. They couldn't help falling in love, and it was no short-term fling: they're married. And throughout the time he was in a position of responsibility, she was certain of selection for the team on her own merit. If it crossed lines they were only theoretical ones; as a rider I would actually have preferred if he had stayed throughout, because I really appreciated his expertise and input.

We understood there would be certain standards we would have to live by. There could be no holding hands walking through airports while on team trips. We would not be rooming together at championships. We would get no special treatment and no special time to ourselves in the velodrome or at London. I was fine with that. I knew why those rules were in place, and I understood them. We were professional athletes, and we had to behave professionally. We were part of a team, and the team had to come first. It may not have been what an ordinary couple would do in the early stages of their relationship, but our working lives were not ordinary, and London would be as far removed from the norm as any of us could imagine.

And so, as London got closer, the dates continued. The same Italian restaurant, another one in the middle of town. Making each other laugh, easy in each other's company, different characters but with the same lifestyles and aims. When I met her best mate from school I thought she was a little bit mad but in a good way. I could see why she and Laura got on. Laura then wanted to meet my mates, and I tried winding her up by telling her I didn't have any. That worked for a while. When we did bump into a couple of them, both working as cycle couriers in town, we went for coffee in the same café as I always went to with them. Tall Paul and Clodge were charmed. Laura was unintimidated and talked as happily as ever. When we went back to Bolton at weekends, I even felt my mum was forgiving me a little for not being born a daughter. It wasn't complicated, but it was working.

**LAURA:** The relationship was starting to really find its feet, which was critical, because the Olympics would require all the attention we had. This now had to be our main focus for the coming weeks.

All of us had raced the equivalent of omniums as kids. A pursuit, a time trial, a scratch race, the devil. Trying all the formats, seeing what worked for you. Testing out different strengths.

Then it became serious, having won the world title in Melbourne, four months before London. There had never been an Olympic omnium before, and suddenly being one of the contenders brought its own criticism. Omnium? That rewards the mediocre. It's an event for riders who aren't good enough to win an individual title. Jack of all, mistress of none.

I got called average. At those Worlds I won only two of the six disciplines. Second in the flying lap. Eighth in the points race. First in the elimination, because it's the elimination and I'm Laura Trott. Third in the pursuit, thirteenth in the scratch. First in the time trial, because a gold medal is on the line and I'm not letting anyone get to it ahead of me.

I could take the Little Miss Average jokes. I wasn't a pure sprinter. That had been proven by my not making it on the sprint programme back in 2008. I wasn't pure endurance either, because if you put me up against even the other British girls in an individual pursuit I'd get beaten by Katie Archibald. I was in the middle, and the middle was a very good place to be. I could do both. I could do almost all of it. That wasn't average. That was almost unique.

People close to me knew it. When the event was first unveiled, as part of the changes to the competitive track programme after the Beijing Olympics, my sister had said straight away that I would become Olympic champion. I couldn't see it. At the time I was so wrapped up in trying to be a sprinter that all I cared about was nailing the man one slot. Emma was so sure she posted it on Facebook.

Maybe there was some luck to it. Some riders spend their whole careers trying to find an event that defines them. There have been people in Jason's squad who would have been the best man four in the world if there were a four-man team sprint. But there isn't, and so their very specific physiological skills have never quite been put to best use. They were pretty good at what they did, but they were not outstanding in an event where you could win golds. The omnium may as well have been invented for me.

It isn't perfect. You get points for places rather than dominance. I could win the IP by two seconds, and I get exactly the same reward as if I'd won it by 0.1. Multi-events in the heptathlon allow you to cash in great performances; we're not compensated for excess speed.

But neither was I flawless. The points race used to scare the hell out of me. Twenty-five kilometres round the track, 100 laps, points awarded in descending order to the first four riders across the line in each of the intermediate sprints, and twenty points if you manage to lap the field. We all worked out before 2012 that if you finished top four or five in every single event then you'd be very likely to get on the podium, which was fine, except in the points race I would consistently be lower. One flaw could cost me an Olympic title.

I wouldn't always see eye to eye with Chris Newton, my coach from May 2013 to December 2014, due to the fact that he was much more focused on bunch races than I was used to. But partly because of that, and partly because he'd medalled in the points race itself when it had its last outing as an individual medal event in Beijing, he would be fantastic at teaching me how to ride a race I feared.

There were at least ten basic tricks and tactics that I had failed to grasp by London 2012. My main strategy had been to go to the top of the track. I thought being up there meant you could see everything going on, and react to all the moves that way. I was wrong. By riding at the front you've got the inbuilt leeway of being able to drop back down a little. If you're at the back, with everybody in front of you, you can do your own move without relying on anybody else to get out of your way, and without the fear of being at the back that the elimination race brings. Chris showed me that and much more. Lay off at times, leave gaps, let rivals go just a little bit in front, so you have the ability to go round. Make sure you score in the first set of points so that you're on the board, and being on the board early makes you feel more relaxed. Not just looking for the moves but also being aware of how they might develop. Swinging up the track looking the wrong way – down rather than up, as you usually would to see who's outside you. Look down and you can see what's coming underneath you.

As London approached I was still clueless about those old tricks, learned from long experience. And there were precious few opportunities for me to test myself. When we rode points in the Revolution series they would only be sixty laps long, and in sixty laps there's not a lot you can really do. So Chris and I would get on the track in Manchester, ride behind the derny, the electric motorbike used for pacing in the velodrome, and

Chris would pull a move and immediately ask me to explain what he'd done. Rather than looking down at my front wheel I would have to be looking up at the race and the riders in front of me. Rather than thinking about myself I would have to be thinking about what the time was and how many laps had gone. No more staring at his back wheel as I was used to from the team pursuit. No more waiting for others to take control. If there were tricks, I would be able to do them all. It would take a while before I mastered them, but master them I would. I just had to hope that, in the omnium, for now, my lack of knowledge wouldn't cost me.

**JASON:** I peak for the Olympics. The team peaks for the Olympics.

Having won that team sprint in Beijing, we would not take another title at any of the four World Championships that followed. Second in 2009, third in 2010, second again in 2011, disqualified in Melbourne in 2012. It made sense in practical terms: while Jamie Staff stuck around for another year after our gold at Laoshan, he was not the same Jamie we had raced with then. And so we were in a constant process of trying to find a new team, of trying to find a new balance that made us as fast and as impregnable as we had been before. I tried out as man one. Ross Edgar gave it a go. Our problem was that we had two natural man twos, the link rider, and two very natural man threes, the finisher. We would shuffle the order, rotate the cogs, but there would always be at least one of us battling our natural physiques. We were good, but we were never great.

Then along came Philip Hindes. He was a young lad, daft as

you liked, but he was freakishly fast at doing standing starts. He had only arrived from Germany in 2011, and it had taken him time to settle in to the academy programme, to life in a strange city and new sporting culture. When we first tried out he would be sensational in training yet not quite able to put it together in races. As a teenager you expect that. But it allowed Chris Hoy and me to slot back into our preferred positions at two and three, and while it all felt last minute, it was working. Being disqualified in Melbourne didn't change that; Phil and I just made a mess of the changeover, me coming underneath him much too early, just at a point when the commissaires were looking to crack down on that sort of thing. It was a shame, but nothing more. We had a team, and we would improve with every week.

In the individual event it was just as fraught. I had been upgraded to 2011 sprint world champion at the start of 2012, when Grégory Baugé was retrospectively banned for missing out-of-competition dope tests, but there had been nothing more. The same changes to the track programme that had brought in the omnium with perfect timing for Laura had also reduced the number of riders each nation could enter into the individual sprint at an Olympics from two to one. I was glad it hadn't happened four years earlier: with Chris Hoy the main man, there would have been no selection for me in the sprint, and no subsequent silver medal. It also left the selection panel with a headline-grabbing headache: pick me, the man in form, the man who had beaten Chris in the semis of the Worlds in both 2011 and 2012, or take Chris, reigning Olympic champion, figurehead for British track cycling, a proven winner when it mattered most.

I stripped it down, took away the emotion. I might have beaten Chris 2–0 in Australia, but he had won his bronze medal match as I had lost the gold medal match to the returning Baugé. He had won the keirin title as I came third. We could both race, so those results in April mattered less than the numbers we would produce in the final few months before selections had to be made in late July.

And I was training well, ridiculously well. I was going so fast we were getting nervous; it was almost too fast too early. I knew Chris was likely to get the nod for the keirin, for while we had both shown form, he was the consistent one. I could ride a stormer but I could also have an absolute stinker. He was already nailed on for the team sprint, so if he was chosen for both solo events too he would be doing three events at one Games. I would go on to do the same in Rio, but it's a far greater challenge than you might imagine. You think you will have plenty of recovery time between races because the schedule is spread out, except that also means you have more nights to sleep on it, more warm-ups and warm-downs to do, seldom a day where you can do nothing and think nothing but empty thoughts. Maybe with two on-form riders it made sense to do two each.

The papers saw it as the Olympic hero and household name versus the young pretender. I just saw my numbers in training. So too did the coaches. Selection in the end came with little drama: both of us in the team sprint with fast-twitch Phil, me for the individual sprint, Chris for the keirin. Chris was magnanimous; I was calm. I always am. Drama for many, day job for me.

# Seven: **London Calls**

**JASON:** That disqualification from the World Championships in Melbourne had probably been my fault. I knew that I wasn't allowed to overlap Phil's back wheel until the designated line on the straight, but I came out of his slipstream like a rocket. I was past his back wheel, I was pretty much off the track. It meant, as we moved from our holding camp in Newport to the athletes' village in London, that some people were putting a lot of pressure on us. A home Olympics, almost £10 billion to stage, hundreds of millions more poured into the preparations of the British team. A team that was supposed to be driven on by success in the velodrome, just as it had been four years earlier. A track cycling squad that was once again looking to the men's team sprinters to get the first day of competition off to the sort of start that would dismay our rivals and inspire those coming afterwards in the red, white and blue kit.

We kept our own expectations in check. Get a clean ride and a medal was there. But we were such a new trio that nothing amazing was predicted for us. Several of the other big nations had also started to ramp it up. We had a new lad at man one, so as we rolled out into the London velodrome for the qualifying round, everyone was watching everyone else. What do they have? How have they moved on? What exactly are they riding?

Philip Hindes was nervous. He was nineteen, he had been in the team for less than six months. We knew he was fast but we didn't really know how fast. He hadn't shown the form. He had shown that he was good, he had shown he was worthy of the spot. He was the fastest man we had, but could he find more at his first Olympics? Could I ride well enough to utilize that speed if it came? Could I hold Chris Hoy on, so he could do what he'd done so peerlessly in Beijing?

We barely knew Phil as a man. He was quiet with us, but he was young, and so you expected that. He was living in the old academy flats in Fallowfield that I had been in before my own debut Olympics four years before, and when I popped round to see the other lads still in there I would hang out with him as part of a wider group. He seemed a nice lad. All I really cared about was his speed.

Chris, a decade and a half older than Phil, assumed the role as the leader of the team. In Beijing I had been the young one, copying Chris and Jamie Staff as much as I could. Now it was Phil looking at Chris and soaking up all he did. I was only five years older, and Phil didn't regard me as that much his senior, and that was fine. Chris was a natural at taking the young ones under his muscled wings, and Phil needed that. He had immense power, but his bike handling still had some way to go. When he threw that power down coming out of the starting gate he always looked as though he was going to throw himself off the bike. It was strength rather than style, and that brought its own challenges. As I left the village that morning for qualification, Laura had asked how I thought he would go. I'd told her that we were either going to crash or win. In the end we did both.

The place was packed. Union flags, Union flag wigs, Union flag suit jackets. On the far side of the track I wondered how we would respond. The greatest fear at an Olympics is of going to pieces at the start. Then you spend the next six months picking the bones out of it – we should have done this, we should have done that, how the hell did that happen when we've been doing it in our sleep for years? Beep. Beep. Beep. Phil goes, those huge thighs contracting and pushing, and here he goes, except why is he all over the track, and why are we coming past him before we've even hit the first turn, and now he's down, he's down, he's down ...

Panic in the crowd. Pandemonium in the track centre. Chris and I throw our left arms in the air. Restart! Restart! For we knew the rules, vague though they were: if you suffered a mishap in the first half-lap you were entitled to start again. Not if you deliberately pulled your foot from its pedal, but if you fell. And Phil fell, and he had always looked like he was going to fall. A lot of conspiracy theories flew around at that time. We knew that Phil instinctively rode his bike like that, and we knew that risk was worth taking. So it proved, because when we did go again, the crowd still hooting in relief, we blew away the old Olympic record. Ahead of those arch-rivals France, and ahead of Australia, who had enjoyed such a spectacular haul at those Worlds in Melbourne just four months before.

There might have been nerves for others – you're now into

the first round, eight teams in it, fighting for a place in the gold medal match, and the crowd knows that you have Chris Hoy in the team, a man with four Olympic titles; a rider in man two fast enough to keep Hoy out of the individual sprint; and a kid in one who is so fast his bike crashes under the strain he forces through it. There were no nerves for me, because of my experience at one event. As a junior doing some stupid little race I had once felt sick on the start line. I thought at the time I'd eaten something. It wasn't until afterwards that I realized it was worry that was upsetting my stomach, and that annoyed me so much I decided I would never get nervous again. I wouldn't even let the nerves in.

That ability might strike some people as a gift. A lot of athletes spend a lot of time with some very expensive psychiatrists trying to get to that same point. Some never manage it, and it mangles their careers. To me, it was simple: it was all about performance. Everything in my head is about performance. Anything that gets in the way of that has to go. It's the same reason I don't sit on the chairs by the track before a final, jiggling my legs up and down. I knew a rival as a junior who used to do it, and it struck me that it was a waste of energy when you had finite resources to lay down in the duel to come; I wondered how I would feel if I lost a race by a thousandth of a second. It may have been nonsense, but as a junior that was how I used to think. So I never did it again. Forever onwards I would sit dead still. Let the man next to me jiggle. My battery is at 100 per cent.

Not everyone can do it. For Laura, for a lot of the team, the answer is to accept the fact that you're going to be nervous, rather than try to fight it. Accept it, let it come to you, let it go. I could just stop. And so, as we waited to be released in the first round, I wasn't nervous. My only thought was that I hoped Phil got off the line well.

He did: 42.747 seconds for us this time, a world record to blow away even our new Olympic record from qualification. France, with a national record, came second but still more than two tenths of a second off in an event usually decided by hundredths.

It put us into the final as clear favourites. Once again, after a relatively fallow period since the last Olympics, I was producing my best when it mattered. I don't like the idea that I need these great set pieces to ride so well. I never wanted to accept that what you think affects how you perform. I'm a logical man. I don't like unpredictability. I don't like someone trying to tell me that stress hormones are bad for muscle growth. I wanted to believe that if I completed the training and ate the right things then nothing external could stop me. As a youth I didn't want to accept that I should race better at my home track in Manchester than away from home. Then, as I matured, I realized that I was racing better at away meets. Something about the occasion, about the travelling, about the change in ambiance, would give me a little boost. I learned to accept that, and I tried to control it as much as I could.

Laura relished the noise in the London velodrome. She loved to be cheered, because she loves to feel loved. For me it made no difference at all. I know what it's like to fail; I've gone home in the first round of World Championships. I've not even qualified. I've been home before the finals have begun. So I felt no fear, and I also felt no need to seek assistance from something external that I could not control.

Chris? Chris was nervous. When you had raced with him for years you grew to understand the little signs. But he was very in control. He had done a lot of work with team psychiatrist Steve Peters before Beijing, and he had been the perfect pupil. That learning and all that experience meant I knew he would be fine. Maybe it helped me too. I had seen a lot of the senior riders work with Steve, and being the next generation down I had absorbed their good practice without also taking on the anxiety that had made it necessary. Those guys had built the team and built the culture. We had inherited it and the expectation of success that came with it. We were using tools forged in the heat of victory.

Phil's nerves were different. He had never worked with Steve, because it had been made known that Peters was moving on after 2012, and he wasn't going to take on anyone new only to have to abandon the project halfway through. I knew Phil had to be in his little bubble to perform. I had seen him in the gym, preparing for a key lift, when the rest of us would clap him to the weight stack as if he were a long jumper at the end of the runway. He would crack before even touching the bar. For an athlete so phenomenally strong he was also incredibly sensitive.

It could happen to anyone. Every team had their nervous riders, and many of them were the best in the world. It didn't always make sense; some had been fighting it for years. The French trio across the track from us that night were certainly intimidating. Grégory Baugé again, all that swagger that Laura dislikes so much. Kévin Sireau, back from Beijing on a revenge mission. Michaël D'Almeida, to bring home le bacon.

The start of a big sprint final can be the most macho of

moments. Slick suits, robots' visors. Huffing and puffing and chest beating. The camera at the bottom of the track looking up the line, and all three riders grabbing their handlebars and flexing and sticking their backsides out. I let it wash past me and silently rooted for Phil. You can do it, you can do it. Just don't do it too well.

In that first round Phil had gone off so fast that Chris had got really stretched. He had burned through so much gas hanging on to the back that he was in bits as we attempted to recover for the final. With just a forty-five-minute turnaround all I could think was, 'Get Chris on the back, you've got to get Chris on the back. He's the hero. These are his final Olympics. That bacon is ours.'

Away we go. Deafening noise. I take none of it in. Phil is out of the gate cleanly. Brilliant. Let the gap between his back wheel and me just play out a little, because then Chris can definitely get on the back, and if Chris isn't on the back then there's no point in me being right up Phil's arse, because it's Chris who's going to be the one crossing the finish line; I've got to protect him as much as possible. In that first round we had really hurt him. And I don't need to be that close to Phil to get the benefits of his slipstream, because a quarter of a lap in he's already doing 55 kilometres an hour, and by half a lap he's at 62; even if I'm 15 metres off him I'm still getting a massive tow. And when he delivers me into that second lap he's at 72 kph, and I'm going 2 or 3 kph quicker, and that is why the gap works. The hard work is done on Phil's lap. Now I'm just holding, holding what we already have, trying to deliver Chris as quickly as possible.

I'm desperately trying not to let my legs slow down. By

trying to protect Chris I have effectively made it more difficult for myself, having had to work really hard to close that gap, so now it's hurting. The qualification and first round had been like Beijing – really easy, floaty, dream-like. Because I can't leave Chris behind I'm in it deep now, down the back straight knowing that if I'm not floating then, crap, this is really going to hurt, this is already biting bad and I've still got six seconds of my lap to go.

Six seconds. Just six seconds. And yet it's brutal, the longest six seconds you can imagine. I'm trying to think about being smooth. Smoothness is speed. I don't want to slow down, but I'm at the point where I'm losing my coordination because we're pedalling at 155 revs a minute, and peaking at over 160 in the corners, and that blows your legs apart. Try it on your own bike on the road, in the easiest gear you can find. Now imagine doing it on a bigger gear than you will ever get to use.

When the coordination starts to fail, the flow goes. Your pedalling action goes stampy. You are fighting it rather than riding it. Let your legs follow the pedals rather than trying to smash the pedals apart. You're still pushing, but just try to relax. Everything I do in the team sprint is just relaxing. Relaxing in horrible pain.

In endurance events the lactic acid will slowly fill up your muscles. You can feel it making its way up your legs, into your arms, through your fingertips. Sprinting is different. It hits you like a hammer. It is as if someone has shot you with a lactic dart.

I come through the end of my lap. Chris is off me like a smooth pebble from a slingshot. A glance at the board. I see the time, I see Chris going away, and I know we have won. Chris is going to bring it home. Chris loses time to nobody.

We finish: 42.6 dead. Another world record. A hell of a time, a hell of a roar all around. Princes William and Harry in the crowd, reacting just like their subjects all around them. Prime Minister David Cameron, clapping slightly uncertainly, as if he's not quite sure what he's just seen. Me feeling so sick, me all on my own once again as Chris and Phil link up naturally on the far side. I've got Sireau inside me offering his hand, and I attempt no words of consolation in French because my French is terrible.

I love winning in a team. You're winning with your mates. But I was on my own, and I'm not very good at celebrating, so I climbed off at the back straight and clattered straight into the track centre. The boys were both waving their arms in the air and blowing kisses to the crowd, and I just walked off. Phil looked as if he was going to crash again. Chris was lapping it up, looking properly done in and properly relieved as well. When eventually they left their bikes – and Chris did at least four victory laps – they both grabbed flags, put their arms round another, got ready to pose, and ... hang on ...

You can watch it back on YouTube. Chris, ready to hold the flag out for the photographers with his teammates on either side, and then suddenly stopping, frowning and looking round. 'Where's Jason?'

**LAURA:** I was watching it all in the athletes' village with the girls. Screaming, definitely. Tears at the end. I loved it for Jason and I loved it for what it meant for the rest of us. We knew now that the team was bang on it again. The wheels were turning. And they were better than the wheels anyone else had.

I already felt as if it were all coming together. I'm obsessed with that number seven. Our team pursuit qualification was on 3 August. The first round and final were on the 4th. You might think this was bad news. Why not 7 August? I was delighted. Three plus four is seven. Jason may have raised an eyebrow at my logic, but it was my logic and it worked for me.

We knew what was ahead. In the first day's qualification round you had to finish in the top four to have a chance of gold. On the second day, first would race fourth and second race third for a place in the final. We had left the holding camp in Newport aiming to hit three minutes fifteen seconds as our peak around those three kilometres and twelve laps in London. Instead we hit it in that first outing in qualification. Four seconds clear of the US in second. We'd had four races together as a trio up to that point: four victories, four world records.

I wasn't scared. I wasn't intimidated. I trusted those two girls, and they trusted me. We liked each other and we rated each other. Into the first round the next day and we clocked 3:14.682. Another world record. Another step closer.

Into what we called the golden hour. We had trained for this, the fifty-five-minute turnaround from first round to final. We knew how it felt to race like that and we knew how best to recover. Strap-on hot pants, like electric sleeping bags for your legs. Drink. Sit still. Get back on the rollers and find your tune – 'Lose Yourself' by Eminem for me – no thought of losing anywhere in my mind. My own headphones this time, not Jason's, not the little in-ear ones but proper over-the-head, safe ones.

A word from our coach Paul Manning, a glance around at the packed stands. I knew my mum and dad were there, and Emma. Mum had the flag: 'Go Trotty Go'. A nation behind us, the US against us. Sarah Hammer, my own omnium rival, Dotsie Bausch, Lauren Tamayo. Us in navy and white skinsuits with red helmets, them in paler blue with white flashes.

Go, Trotty, go. Cameras on me at the start, all wrong; they should be on Jo Rowsell. Please don't start like a rocket, Jo, because sometimes she listens to the crowd, as she did at the World Cup in London the February before this, and the rest of us were useless because we started too hard in an attempt to keep up.

First lap in and we're fine. I'm thinking, 'We're on, we're all together, and we're a step up.' We don't want to look up at the scoreboard because it will break the airflow, so coach Paul shows us instead. For every tenth of a second we might be up he will take a pace away from the centre line. For every tenth we are down he will step towards us. We're up, and it's time for me to come through for my first turn. Jo swings up, Jo swings down on to Dani's back wheel. First turns are easy. First turns are just about holding pace – they should be settled, should be fine.

I'm riding round knowing the pain is still to come. I'm thinking, 'Hold pace, Trotty,' because if man two goes too fast then man one, on the back and needing a breather, doesn't stand a chance at all of feeling good, and Jo will need to feel good because the pain is still to come.

You want even turns. Same pace and the same form. Hold

whatever Jo's given me because we're already a step up.

I can feel it, even after the first lap, that this is going to be fast. Everything just feels smooth. After my changes I always glance over to see where the other team are, and the US are already down. It feels perfect, it feels seamless. It feels like we are one; it doesn't feel like we are separate riders.

I'm in second again. Jo's last turn was a lap. I go to the front and on a lap and a half. Keep the pace. Keep the form.

We're already in the Americans' slipstream. We're already getting a drag. As soon as you're in front you start getting it. This had been our big fear: what if the US came out as fast as they could, knowing it was their only chance, and got into our wake? You don't need to be that close: get a second on the trio in front and you're already in their slipstream benefiting from that precious tow. When you're being towed you're being dragged to victory.

But it still feels easy. It feels slightly mad. Just like Jason in Beijing, I'm floating. Your gear goes light, your legs go light. You can feel the catch from the US ahead. You're trying really hard but you don't feel like you are. You don't realize how fast you're actually going.

Swinging up and down and to the back again. This is my hardest point. Dani comes through. Now I'm in pain all right, and there is no escape. There are three of us, and all three must cross the line. All three have to stay upright. No one can drop off the back. It's a whole world of leg pain. It's like somebody has tied an elastic band around the top of my leg and you want to stop peddling but you can't stop and now the band is getting tighter still. I never really get it in my chest – that doesn't bother me at all. My heart rate is stupid anyway. The way I used to ride time trials was by listening to my breathing. Unless I was breathing heavily I knew I wasn't trying hard enough. So it's definitely my legs that crack me first, and when the legs start to go there's nothing you can do about it. The band getting tighter, the pain growing. I have to finish. We all have to finish. But once it snaps, it snaps. There's no getting it back, not with mental effort, not with a second charge, not with love for the girls in front of you.

Now Jo goes a half-lap longer, which we didn't expect. She's feeling good. She is flying along. This is the best I have ever seen Jo ride – her line, her pace, her changes.

We are ready to carry one another. If I think Dani can't hit the front again after watching her turn I will just carry on. You sometimes get a good feeling in the line. In the Worlds before this, we'd qualified two tenths of a second quicker than the Aussies. We'd broken the world record so we were pretty chuffed, and then came the final, and Dani went half a lap shorter than she was supposed to. I didn't know what to do. Paul could see what was unfolding behind me, and he was screaming at me to stay on the front. One lap on the front, two laps on the front. Paul on the floor, screaming, Dani hanging on, us just beating the Aussies. When you're ahead in the line you can't physically see it. You can't see that the rider you're about to deliver to the front is struggling. Everyone watching at home knows: that rider is all over the place, they have nothing left. You are one bike length away from them and you have no idea.

Four laps to go. We're so far up we only need to stay upright and pedalling. Two and a half laps to go, we can see them in front of us as we come off the curve. We only have to finish. It's almost a lap of honour, but you don't feel like you're about to vomit on a lap of honour. From a hips-moving World-Championships Dani to a confident, together Dani in London. Holding it together, coming round the last bend, fanning out from our loosening line, one last dip and we push the bikes out in front of us.

The time: 3 minutes 14.051 seconds. Gold medal. World record. Another world record. I never thought we'd do a 3.14, even though I knew we were on it and that we were tight.

And then all I knew was the noise, and how totally sick I felt. Dani was suddenly a new Dani, riding round almost without decelerating, going crazy with her celebrations. I thought I was going to be sick inside my helmet. Only when I stopped did I begin to start recovering. Only when the three of us finally found ourselves in the same place on the track did it all feel real. Mark Cavendish said he had a tear in his eye when the three of us started hugging, because he could tell how much it all meant to us. There were lots of 'I can't believe this!' and 'Did this really happen?' and then just lots of laughing. Real and unreal, a familiar feeling of victory yet on an unimaginable scale.

Up on the banking to find my parents. My dad took hold of my helmet, which was fine, and he brandished it to the crowd as though we were gladiators coming out of the coliseum, and that was just fine too, except he then forgot to give it back. Later we would be in the track centre, starting to calm down, and the worried shout went up: 'We're a helmet short! We've lost a lid!'

Dad crying his eyes out. Emma next to him. Mum next along. The 'Go Trotty Go' flag being shaken and flapped.

Dani trying to find her own mum and dad, hanging on to the railings at the top of the track so she didn't cap her moment of triumph by falling on her backside and sliding down into the photographers. Jo spotting hers on the opposite side. Jason watching on back in the village, watching with the rest of the team. Being Jason, not stressed at all.

Paul McCartney was there. Paul McCartney conducting the crowd in 'Hey Jude'. More weirdness. Time for the podium, and none of us had any make-up, because we hadn't wanted to jinx it by taking some down with us. Even our official podium outfits were taken down by someone else. The Americans, delighted with their silver, Dotsie Bausch pulling out a huge make-up bag of her own that she'd brought with her and handing bits out and sticking it on our faces and I was thinking, 'I'm glad someone's prepared.'

There was no complications with the feeling on the podium. I was going nuts with happiness. I was laughing the whole time. I looked up and saw Dad still bawling his eyes out. So much happiness inside me that it was almost overwhelming.

I don't want to be clichéd about it, but it had always been my dream to win an Olympic gold medal, and it had just happened. Jason may have been calm and in control when he won his first in Beijing. I'm not like that. I was an emotional wreck. Nothing had ever had a bigger impact on me. On that day, in that moment, not even Jason. Not yet.

# Eight: **Everything Changes**

**JASON:** You stay calm when all around you are losing their minds. Medals everywhere, a relentless deluge for Team GB, we cyclists conjuring up golds in almost every final – that team sprint, Laura's team pursuit, Brad Wiggins in the time trial out at Hampton Court, the old bankers of the men's team pursuit quartet bringing it home once again.

I might have been the calmest man in London. I had to be. I had another final to come, if I raced as I should in the rounds scheduled over three days to get there. Ten a.m. on Saturday 4 August, back into the velodrome for qualification for the first round, Laura's pursuit final to come that evening, the Games a week old and holding everyone in the country in a happy headlock. A flying 200 metres, and I really was flying too – an Olympic record of 9.713 seconds, an average speed of almost 75 kph, ahead of Baugé by more than two tenths of a second, ahead of powerful Aussie Shane Perkins, too.

From a start like that the draw opens up. A first-round bye, a second round against nineteen-year-old South African

Bernard Esterhuizen that did nothing to upset my equanimity. Past Malaysia's Azizulhasni Awang the following afternoon, winning again the first two races of the best of three, and then straight sets again in the next day's semi-final against Trinidad's Njisane Phillip, in my wake and on my wheel but never past me on the line.

And so to Baugé again. Always Baugé.

When he had beaten me to the world title in Melbourne that spring he had been untouchable. I thought I was riding well in the first race, and he came past me like I'd thrown out a parachute. Totally smoked me. Cruised it. The French coaches were celebrating as if they'd already won gold, and when your man rides like that, you pretty much have.

My coach Iain Dyer and I had exchanged words before the second heat in that final. There's nothing we can do, so let's hit the emergency button. On with a smaller gear, out with the cunning plan. Usually in sprinting you play cat and mouse before switching to greyhounds. This time I smashed it from the gun. Iain gave me a cheeky little push, and I launched away. Baugé caught by surprise, a look squeezing out from under his helmet that said, 'Oh shit ...', a huge gap opening up, the rest of the British team watching back at the hotel going crazy, Geraint Thomas shouting the corridors down.

Feeling him closing on me all the time, coming down the back straight like a runaway TGV. I didn't know he'd blown his own doors off. I thought he was going to go straight past me. So just as we came round the final bend, I gave him the tiniest little hook. Just the slightest deviation from my line, just to kill his flow, just to take him a fraction wider. I knew it was marginal, that I had nibbled outside the red line when officially you're not allowed to change your racing position.

The effort had almost finished him. I think I would have won anyway, but I had no idea his engine had nearly died. I had looked up at the board and saw him cruising behind me. I hadn't seen the desperation. So I took the race and the crowd loved it, only for the commissaires to watch it back and spot exactly what I'd done. Disqualification and my win reduced to a silver, the cheers suddenly turned to cartoon boos, Baugé's gold. He deserved it. He had been phenomenal at those Worlds.

As he was pushed out on to the track in London for the first of our three heats, not a seat spare in the velodrome, barely a place to stand, the attempt at intimidation was an impressive one.

Baugé is a big man. He's bigger than Chris Hoy. He may be the most powerful man I've ever raced against. He had qualified impressively, shown me several little signs that he was going into this final as dangerous as he could ever be. Take his visor and helmet off and he's human again, and he's a friendly guy too, smiles and handshakes. On the start line it's all about bullying and fear.

That's fine. To me it's all a calculation. I'm trying to figure out what his worst-case scenario is and then deliver it. I want to make him think and I want to make him worry. I want to show him nothing, which is why my poker face never shifts, not now, not in the final desperate seconds. You don't pedal with your face. Give him nothing. Keep everything back.

**LAURA:** I'm watching it all unfold. I'm on the rollers in the track centre, warming up for the elimination race in my own second showdown, the omnium. Warming up but not warming up, watching it on the big screen but not really watching it. I can feel myself getting emotional. Concentrate, Laura. My carer comes over to reinforce it. Each minute of your warm-up is carefully calculated. This power, then this effort, then this recovery. It can't go out of the window now.

**JASON:** I am pushed out on to the start line by Iain as the home support roars again. There's never any chat from Iain at this point, not unless he thinks my opponent is going to try something clever, not unless he thinks the other man might launch a long one like I did in Melbourne. Iain's quite matter-of-fact, very monosyllabic, not over-emotional. He has been my coach for eight years at this point and we have grown to be the same in these moments. The turbulence all around will do nothing to either of us.

I rest my arm on his shoulder as he holds the seat-post and handlebars. It looks an oddly reassuring gesture, as if I am casually leaning on him, as if I trust him completely. I do, but it's entirely a practical thing. It's just where my arm needs to be when I'm sitting up in the saddle with my hands off the bars. To my left, Baugé is being hugged by his coach. At least that's what it looks like. It's just his coach trying to hold his great weight upright, but each of these little actions become part of the show.

As a junior you are taught to look at your opponent on the start line. It's to make sure they don't surprise you at the whistle. When you do it as an adult – and we all do – it takes on a more confrontational air. Some riders will get as close to you as they can. Staring without seeing, because we all have mirrored visors on, and you can't tell if your rival has held your gaze or blinked or even bothered staring back at you. It doesn't happen in the endurance events; you won't see Laura giving Sarah Hammer some chat as they walk to their bikes, or stare her down as they line up for the points race. Sprinters like to be pumped, and although I am the exception – I beat them with composure, meet testosterone with tranquillity – I will still look across on the line. You've got to watch them anyway. You've got to watch them all the way. You're watching for the long one, for the twitch, for the jump. You never take your eyes off them.

Baugé leads it out. Calculations. He's man one for the French team sprint, one of the most explosive athletes in the world. You don't want to take him on at his great strength, accelerating over short distances. I was first in qualification, which means I'm faster, certainly over the course of the whole race, so I'm not going to want to let him come into the last lap and then just do a 250-metre drag race because of that dangerous acceleration. A long, fast race is good for me. Keep it fast, I tell myself. Stay high so you can get extra speed dropping down when you need it, trust that you will have the legs to get round.

Baugé in front, creeping round. Three laps, the first a game of chess, the second all feints and ducking, the third going at each other and knockout punches. Baugé is trying to watch me, looking back under his right armpit when I'm further up the banking and twisting round to look past his left elbow when I flick down the other way. He's wobbly when he looks round, but he's very good at looking at the right times. You can look forward all you want as long as you're watching when it matters. I just look all the way. Never let them out of your sight.

He doesn't really want to be on the front – I suspect he would be quite happy to let me past. He tries to take me high, tries to invite me through, and as the second lap unfolds he stays up by the blue line, me higher still. We wind it up. I fake a dip back down, sending him low, and then switch back high, and as we come into a lap and a half left I go, give it the full beans.

Through the line for the final 250 metres. I go high again to swoop down with the extra speed. It's a long fast race, just as I wanted, and I've stolen as much height as I dare.

Two hundred metres to go, and there's just a little gap between him in front and me, but I know I've won it. The gap will suck me in. The gap gives me space to accelerate into. I'm travelling faster than him, and unless my legs abandon me – and it can happen, it has happened to me – that speed is an unanswerable physical law that he cannot break.

The gap is gone. Halfway down the back straight my front wheel is level with his back one. On to the curve we're level. Even if my legs go now on this final bend his may be going too. He may have given up because I'm all over him and coming past.

My legs stay strong. 1–0. Crowd roars.

I need one win from the remaining two heats for my first individual Olympic gold. There are ten minutes before the second race, so it's on to the rollers to ride out the lactic from that first battle and prepare for the next. Water is fine. Nothing special is needed unless the weather is scorching hot, when you might have an electrolyte drink instead, but just because it is an Olympic final it doesn't mean you should do anything differently to what you have done before. Don't start taking supplements in the last four weeks before the Games simply because some people will be panicking about being in the best possible shape. Don't start adding new vitamins or probiotics. And certainly don't use a recovery drink you've never previously used, right in the middle of the two biggest races you've experienced.

As I pedal slowly I think about the mentality of being one up. Should I think: 'That first one means nothing; we start again here'? Or should my thinking be: 'I'm halfway there; all the pressure is now on him'? My strategy is always to see the second race as the critical one. If you have won the first, the second one puts it to bed; if you've lost the first, you've just switched all the momentum and pressure.

This time I will be man one, the first rider to be pushed away. Each rider has their own favoured position, depending on their physical skills. Often it's the same for both of you, and it is for Baugé and me – we both prefer man two. I've just won the one that I should win. If we were playing tennis, I've just held serve. Now he's going to be in two, which is where he wants to be, and I have to win the one that he's supposed to win. He's serving, but I've got him at break point.

Rhythmic clapping as we pedal back out. Silence as we are held on the start line. A nervous explosion of noise as Iain pushes me away.

Baugé is happier now. I can tell. He is the hunter. I want to go fast enough to keep some control, without going too fast. I'm not trying to lead him out. In some ways it has become more straightforward. I know he's not going to do anything.

His best chance is in the last lap. He doesn't want the front, he's just trying to get me moving.

A lap and a half in, watching him all the way, I need to start taking control. A big stamp on the pedals, bring him down off the high part of the track with 300 metres to go, and at this point he's having a nightmare. The gap between me and his front wheel is about right for him but I'm higher than he is, which means I've got more potential and he's not getting any pull off me. He has come lower to try to get on terms, but he's not close enough to me to get down the inside, and now we're going faster. He can't physically get round. I've ignited all I have. For once my mouth is open and my teeth bared. Final bend. On my shoulder. I know he's there, but he's not in my peripheral vision let alone my sight. Thirty metres: holding. Twenty metres: sensing he is close now, really close. Ten metres: clear. Clear to the line, clear all the way.

Clear to my third Olympic gold. Inside the track, Iain – unemotional Iain, keep-a-lid-on-it Iain – is jumping about with all the easy grace of a man who doesn't jump about very much. My arms are out and my fingers are pointing to the roof. I have no idea where my parents are, which will upset my mum, although since she finds my races too tense to watch she's probably only just taken her hands away from her face. My eyes aren't the best, and even though I've got contact lenses in I still struggle to pick people out. Down the track to Iain, bouncing about, big hugs from men who have always kept it reined in.

Two events, two golds. Laura on the rollers, being told not to cry. No McCartney this time, but I can handle it. I rather like these Olympics just as they are.

**LAURA:** Remember my lucky number? It's amazing how you can get to seven if you try. The night before my omnium began, my coach Paul Manning brought the start sheet into the food hall at the athletes' village. For the first event, the flying lap, which got underway the next morning, I was in heat 16. Problem? Not at all. One plus six equals seven. Perfect.

But it meant a long wait the next day for me to restart the engines. My flying lap – a solo time trial over 250 metres, coming in as fast as you could manage – didn't get underway until just after 4 p.m. I had to watch girl after girl go out while I warmed up and then stayed warm. Something on that start list jumped out. The French had pulled their usual omnium selection and stuck in a pure sprinter, Clara Sanchez. Straight away I felt the nerves rise. She would be in bits in the endurance disciplines – what if she got in my way on the final lap of the pursuit? She's going to beat me in the sprint events. She's going to get in the way of me and my main rivals ...

Sanchez goes in the fourteenth heat. Two times seven. Maybe that's even luckier. Maybe it's twice as lucky. She posts 14.058 seconds. The fastest I'd ever gone was a 14.2. Shock and fear. I can't do that, I can't go that fast.

Cue Paul, the calm one, with the experience of becoming Olympic champion as the favourite four years before now showing through. He keeps it simple and positive and motivational all at the same time. 'Now we will see how good Laura Trott really is ...'

We do. The bike is going so fast I can't really handle it. I get shocked coming out of the bend because I've never travelled this fast before. This is all new. This is all wonderful. I come across the line and the crowd are going nuts, and now I look up and I see why: 14.057 secs. I've beaten her by a thousandth of a second. I punch the air, and as the time sinks in I put my hand up to grab my helmet, which has come loose with the effort. Sanchez hasn't ruined me. She's done me a huge favour. I'm delighted she's riding. Vive la France!

Now I'm nervous no more. I've worked really hard, and that lap has set me up for all that is to follow. An hour later it's the second of my six events, the points race: twenty kilometres around the track, points on offer at each intermediate sprint. At this stage I'm still in my points apprenticeship. I hate these races because I'm rubbish at them. It won't be until the Commonwealth Games in Glasgow two summers later that I feel as if I've cracked it. I barely have the endurance to get round. All I can think about is limiting my losses. I'd made a horrible mess of it at the World Cup in Cali the previous December, finishing second to last. A repeat of that calamity in Colombia and my medal hopes would be in pieces.

I'm lucky. It's a soft race. Sarah Hammer doesn't take a lap on the field and all the points that go with it, even if many of the outsiders for the overall title do, and she finishes down in fifth. The other big danger is Australia's Annette Edmondson. She's even further down, so while my tenth place isn't pretty, it's not game over either. In the overall standings I'm third behind Hammer by a single point. Fine. On we roll.

On we roll to my banker. The elimination race. The devil. The devil in me says I'm not being beaten, not in my race, not in my home Olympics. Every two laps the last-placed girl will drop out. I will not be that last-placed girl.

There is expectation in the air. As I am on the rollers Jason is going for sprint gold. All that emotion waiting for him to ride, watching the massive bulk of Baugé going round slowly like an angry bear. Me trying to keep it in check, watching but not watching, celebrating but not celebrating, because now the crowd is even louder, and the pressure is switching to me, because I haven't lost an elimination race all year. Here we go, into the deep end. Everyone wants a show. Another thrill to match what has come before.

Confidence, Laura. We start, I feel okay. First sprint, second sprint, fine and easy. The third sprint is a shaky one. I'm in trouble and heading backwards when a gap just opens up, and I think, 'Go for it,' clattering off the Russian Evgenia Romanyuta to squeeze through the narrowing space and into the next skirmish. Okay. Let's ride on the front for a while. Let's stay out of danger.

I'm watching Hammer, I'm watching Nettie Edmondson. Other girls keep dropping, surprised by the late speed of a rider outside them or being swept up as three come fighting past on the outside as the line flashes under our front wheels. Six left. Five.

A second scare. I'm coming over the top of Hammer, ready to nick ahead and drop another, and Hammer comes out and rides me off the line. In that fraction of a second I'm convinced I'm going to crash. Handlebars flick right and I stay upright, and I stay in the contest by the width of a rear tyre.

With every elimination the noise rises yet another level. Now Romanyuta goes. Three of us left: me, Hammer and Edmondson. Great Britain, USA, Australia.

Australia leads it out. USA lurks on her hip. I sit deeper still. When Hammer makes her move and slingshots past

Edmondson, I go with her, and now it is two, fighting it out over the last two laps.

I know I can beat her in a one-on-one sprint. She must know that. No one has ever, to this day, just gone for it – crossed the line and carried on going, tried to get the jump on me and then hold it until the end. Everyone takes me up to the top of the track and waits. Most can't beat me in a 500 metre time trial, so why slow me down?

Hammer falls into the same trap. She keeps it slow. Sarah, you either want to keep it fast or you want to go for a long one.

She keeps it slow, and I go fast. I eat her up on the back straight and blow her away in my wake. She is gone, and she knows it. She gives it up, and I canter down the home straight waving to the ecstatic crowd. We will be level on points overnight.

**JASON:** Laura was nervous that night and the next morning. Off the back of my sprint gold I had to do press conferences, television interviews, shaking hands and waving. Five rings to jump through. In separate apartments, in separate bubbles, we said a little goodnight and then went in our different directions. The usual breakfast routine was to pedal over to the food hall in the village. I was supposed to be doing a breakfast routine reserved for British Olympic medallists – back to the Olympic Park to appear on BBC TV again. I sacked it off to start my day with Laura instead. Not in the food hall, because there were so many faces in there and so much background static. We went to the carers' room, where the massages were done and where all the spare food was kept. Breakfast there, low-key and chilled, at last able to chat properly, attempting to talk Laura down from some of those nerves.

**LAURA:** I couldn't think about what I was eating. I couldn't stop thinking about the race ahead. The individual pursuit, three kilometres round the track and against the clock.

Me against Hammer again, the top two off last. So much crowd noise as we wait on the line but I don't react at all, not on the outside at least. Hammer is on the far side of the track. Behind her clear visor she is all huffs and puffed cheeks. Behind my mirrored visor I have borrowed Jason's poker face.

She gets out well. She keeps going well. This time, unlike in the team pursuit, it is the US that gets up and holds it.

She finishes a second ahead of me. It's okay. It's not as fast as I went in the Worlds, and there's a little sting of disappointment about that, but it's not a disaster. Edmondson comes fourth, so the top three overall stays the same.

Now for the long wait. Two events left, and most of the day back in the village to obsess about them.

Ed Clancy came into my room. Ed could understand what I was going through: he'd finished the men's omnium the day before and done it well, winning the bronze. Ed felt nerves too. He was the most anxious of the quartet that had just won team pursuit gold in consecutive Games. Ed could talk me down. 'Don't be so worried. You're in great shape. You've got a couple of good events coming up. Go and do what's going to want to happen naturally.'

All afternoon waiting. Back across to the velodrome for the 4 p.m. scratch race. Simplest of the lot: forty laps, all of us in together, first one across the line winning. Hammer is a point clear in the gold medal spot. I'm in silver.

And I mess it up. The plan is to make sure that if anyone makes a move then I follow them, regardless if it's somebody way down the standings. That way I can try to keep the thing together and then win the sprint that ends it all. Only I get stuck in the middle. It gets to the sprint and I don't know what to do.

Two laps to go, Hammer hits the front. I try to follow, Edmondson moves into second. I'm really high, too high to take control. Down on the back straight, Hammer and her pale blue skinsuit and white helmet leading, Edmondson all in Aussie yellow on her wheel, me fighting for third. Coming on to their shoulders off the final bend, but whoa, Nettie Edmondson squeezes me out, and now I'm up high by the blue line, all momentum gone, all chance of rolling past gone too.

I come off the track and I am gutted. I finished third. The amount of times I've beaten Hammer in a sprint and in a scratch race. I thought this was going to be fine – not easy, it's the Olympics, she's a world champion, but fine, I could do it. There is only one silver lining. Edmondson has squeezed past Hammer too. That not only makes her comfortable in bronze but keeps my own fight alive. If Nettie had just got past me but Hammer had held on for another win, then we would have gone into the final event with me needing Hammer to finish fifth in the time trial.

Even now, if I beat her only by two places, it means a tie at the top of the overall standings. And if it's a tie, the gold medal is decided by the cumulative total of our three timed rides: the 250 metre flying lap, the 3,000 metre individual pursuit and the 500 metre time trial. That gives Hammer a 0.681-second advantage going into this time trial. Just over half a second, gone faster than I can think these words, a great chasm in this sport of decimal places, shaved forearms and aero lids.

I speak to no one. I know Hammer has 15 points, me 17, Edmondson 22. You want the lowest total possible, because you get one point for coming first, two for second, three for third. To beat Hammer overall I'll need three clear places between us. Even if I win the time trial, I need her to be down in fourth.

The aero helmet goes on early. I get on the rollers and listen to 'Lose Yourself' on repeat. One shot. One opportunity. Will I capture it, or just let it slip?

Rider goes after rider. Two by two, one on each side of the track, flat-out weary now but flat out too in the final push. My new friend Clara Sanchez lays down a lovely marker – 35.451 seconds, hard for Hammer to beat but tough for me too. Edmondson up now, focused on that podium: 35.140 seconds. Nice one, girls. Two big rides. If I can get on the right side of them and Hammer can fall the other way, this might just happen. It might.

Paul comes up to me as I am about to get on the track. There's a photo of me that I found later, and you can see us head to head, his face reflected in the visor of my helmet. Paul keeps it simple. You can do this. A support. A statement.

I'm not nervous now, not in this moment. I know that if I ride to my very best I can get past Edmondson and I can get past Sanchez. This is the omnium, the truest test of all your riding skills. I am neither pure sprinter nor only endurance, but I can do them both. I am Little Miss Average.

The noise from the crowd, though muffled by my helmet, still hurts my ears. Hammer is across the track. How does she feel – comfortable? In control? Or rattled, pressurized, worried about what Clara and Nettie have done and terrified about what I might be about to do?

I come out of the gate so clean. It's one of the best starts I've ever had, even to this day. I've got to be on for a good time. Hands on to the tri-bars at 200 metres, flashing past Paul, all his restraint gone, his eyes out, his arms and hands everywhere. Flashing flags and rolling noise. Float, don't fight. Smoothness is speed.

Gone. Over. I look up at the board. There is the numeral one next to my name. I've gone fastest. I look for the number next to Hammer's. Nothing. Nothing.

And then it lights up. Four.

I don't swear, I don't lose it. I just say, 'Oh!' in shock, in disbelief. The magic number is not my time of 35.110. That's not the only number that matters. One and four are the key. One add four equals gold.

I cried after that. Victory by a single point. I couldn't believe I had done it, even though I was already world champion and had already proven I could. Never in a million years did I think I would win.

I still felt like a kid. To me the Olympics always seemed as if you would have to be at your very best, at the peak of your career. In London I didn't feel like that. I was twenty years old. I was doing it because it was fun.

That must have helped. By the time Rio came round four years later, I felt like I had the weight of the world on my shoulders. It was my own pressure. I put it on myself because

I didn't want to let myself down. In London I was a newbie. No one really knew me. It was fun. I simply rode round.

The celebrations from our coaches and support team were almost bigger than mine. Watch the video back and you can see team psychiatrist Steve Peters jumping around like he's on a trampoline. That worked for me. I felt it was a victory for us, not me on my own.

Round I went, gradually slowing down, in that messy place between laughter and tears. I undid my red helmet, balanced it carefully on my tri-bars, and waved and waved. No unzipping the skinsuits as Jason had done in Beijing, because these ones were so tight we were terrified about tearing them, even if we could have got out of them. I was actually in the wrong kit. I had the long-sleeved one on when it should have been the short. Once you've got your race numbers pinned on just so, you sometimes don't want to switch them over to a new suit. It might be a little damp and a little smelly, but it's yours and it'll do.

I could see my parents up in the first row of seats along the back straight, and I decelerated into their arms. Clinging on to the railing, my feet attached to the pedals by toe-straps under my overshoes, so I was unable to pull them out and balance. Dad had lost it. He was all over the place. Emma was there with the biggest hug of all. Dani King next to her, also in that 'I'm not crying I'm laughing with happiness but yes there are tears and oh my God I can't believe it' state of wild emotion. Mum gave me the 'Go Trotty Go' flag, and as I brandished it at the crowd the chant went up: 'LAURA! LAURA! LAURA!'

Me? I was all pigtails and wearing the world's biggest grin. Eight gold medals from eight opportunities at the three major championships I had been to. And to think, had France gone for Pascale Jeuland rather than Clara Sanchez, then Jeuland wouldn't have kept Hammer out of one of the top slots in the flying lap, and she definitely wouldn't have pushed her out of the top three in the time trial. She might have scared me when I saw her name on the start sheet, but Sanchez actually did me a huge favour. Without her I might not have won.

**JASON:** I watched it all unfold from the ramp leading up from the track centre to the boards. Just. I had been sat with my parents in the Westfield shopping centre by Stratford International, thinking I had all the time in the world to get there, and then suddenly noticed that the 500 metres was about to start. I legged it all the way through the village, on to the Olympic Park and up to the velodrome. I got there just in time.

You'd hope that by Rio I would have learned my lesson. In Brazil, come the finale of the omnium, I was on the toilet. It's not good to have a habit of missing Laura's crucial moments, and it's really not good to be missing them because you're in the smallest room in the arena. I could have sworn I had plenty of time. And in Rio I couldn't run, because I still had races to win. Cyclists don't run, not when there are still medals to be won, not even when their partner has just achieved something truly remarkable.

# Nine: **Shifting Gear**

**LAURA:** You think it will be all glamour when you've just won four Olympic golds between you at your home Olympics. Yes and no. We met up with our parents for some food. Normal. My feet hurt. Normal. You could get free entry to a club in the West End if you took along your medal – not normal – and if it was a gold one you could reportedly drink for free. But it wasn't a great club, and it wasn't as fun as the Olympics, so instead we used our success to catch as much of the other action as we could. The diving was an early winner for Jason. As with lots of Olympic sports you walked into the venue knowing nothing about it, and five minutes later you were discussing the merits of risking a high-tariff effort and shaking your head at someone's entry off the ten-metre board as if you'd been watching it all your life. Jason had been convinced it wasn't really a spectator sport. By the end of the session he was ready to argue the toss with the judges. 'Oh no! What was that?'

People can assume that all Olympic athletes know everything about all other Olympic sports. Often it's the opposite. You spend so much time dedicated to your own that you don't have enough energy or opportunity to get into anything else. We tried watching hockey. Not so good this time. The Kenny verdict was that the ball is quite small compared to the playing area, and that the rules were a little hard to understand. Lots of whistles, lots of balls going out of play.

The beach volleyball? That was different. Horse Guards Parade, a proper party atmosphere, under the lights, drinks and a lot of cheering. It also got surreal, and rather glamorous. While Jason was floating round the village, he was asked if he wanted to go with Prince Harry, who was attending anyway and wanted to sit with some British gold medallists.

He did rather get given the impression that there would be twenty or so of us there. Instead it was just Jason and me and a rower. A very, very posh rower. We walked to our seats. There were bodyguards everywhere. They didn't introduce themselves as bodyguards, but you could tell. The build, the suits, the way they carried themselves. One of them came down, checked the area and then disappeared again.

And suddenly Prince Harry was there. He just sat down and introduced himself to us. 'Hello, I'm Harry.' It probably wasn't strictly necessary, but he was so normal that it seemed perfectly natural. Both Jason and I were drinking. We offered him a beer, but he pointed out a row of photographers down the front who had their lenses pointed back at the stands rather than at the court and explained that he couldn't. He also warned us that we should be careful, which was when I handed him a beer I couldn't open and asked him if he could sort it out. No problem. He held the bottle by the back of the chair in front and slammed it down. Off flew the lid, straight at a woman sitting a few seats along. That was the point all the camera shutters sounded. We tried to keep a straight face, but we all knew what had happened. Sorry, Harry.

We were certainly enjoying ourselves. Jason asked me if I knew how the scoring worked. 'Not a clue. Jason, I wonder if the old prince will know.' The old prince. He heard me, too; of course he did. 'You two are hilarious. And you're a nightmare ...'

Harry said his farewells, still without a beer. Probably enough drama for us for one night, certainly when you've barely been out for the last eight weeks, definitely when you haven't had a beer for a long, long time. That was when David Beckham walked in. Okay. Play it cool. David Beckham's sitting on the row in front of us. A chap nearby asked us if we would like our photos taken with him. We could see he was there with his sons, so we turned it down. He insisted that we should. Why not? A sandwich suddenly appears from somewhere. Would we like it? We're professional athletes. We've just won a load of Olympic gold medals. We can't go eating food we can't trust; anything could be in it. We put the sandwich down.

David Beckham turned around. 'My security guard has just bought it,' he said. Right, it's had the Beckham seal of approval, we've been riding our backsides off for the last few days, we've had some beers, the sandwich gets it. That was the moment the shutters went again. Beckham looked at us. When he turned back, we polished off the sandwich and saw off the beers. Under the lights, Olympic champions, so happy to be together. A kiss, a cuddle, a bigger kiss.

We should have listened to Prince Harry. Take one member of the British royal family, a global sporting icon and two

Olympic gold medallists when all anyone in the country wants to talk about is the Olympics, and the tabloids have got photos that are going to make them a whole heap of money.

The game ended. We walked down towards the River Thames and sat on a bench, trying to spot a taxi. It's a long way from Horse Guards Parade back to Stratford, and Stratford had changed a lot in a very short space of time. The cabby duly dropped us off by an old run-down pub at the wrong corner of the athletes' village to get back in. My feet, unused to walking, unused to even standing, were by now in agony. Jason, being Jason, put me on his back and piggybacked me home.

**JASON:** As I carried her, Laura asked me a question. 'Am I actually your girlfriend now?' I looked back over my shoulder. 'Well, do you want to be?'

I thought we already were boyfriend and girlfriend. I thought the reality of how much time we spent together was what decided it, rather than it needing to be formalized. I didn't realize we had to put it down in writing.

I didn't think that the world was shortly going to find out either. The next morning Laura woke up to a series of texts from her agent. 'Laura, what the hell?' 'Laura, Google yourself.' In all the newspapers were half-page photos of the two of us kissing away like teenagers at a bus stop, David Beckham in the foreground.

The photographs were the least of my worries. In the accompanying reports, full of detail about our courtship, none of which was based on the reality of it, I was described as having a child from a previous relationship. I was reported as having celebrated my sprint gold medal by going to my kid in the stands and embracing them. If I did a web search on myself, my wife came up as Julie Manning, the partner of Laura's coach.

Laura was the main story, that was clear. Maybe the papers felt they had to give a bit of background. But the background was not just out of focus, it was the wrong picture entirely. I recalled Chris Hoy, years ago on a training camp in Perth, telling me he had signed up to Twitter not to tell the world all the ordinary things he was up to, but to get his side of the story out there when things were printed that simply weren't true. That day I did the same. I knew we had to tell the world that we were together. We also felt that it wasn't anything to do with anyone else. But we definitely wanted to make it clear that no, I didn't have a child, and no, I wasn't married to someone who was already married to someone else I knew very well.

It was the strangest couple of weeks, and neither of us were quite prepared for it. Track cyclists had always had such low profiles that I could walk down Plodder Lane in Farnworth and not be recognized, as long as I wasn't riding a fixed-gear bike with a disc wheel and wearing full Great Britain kit. I had seen what had happened to Chris, but it had come to him relatively late in his career. In your thirties you have the experience and nous to handle it. Almost overnight Laura appeared to have turned into a celebrity, and neither of us even liked the word. People were pushing her into events and appearances and deals, not all of which she wanted to do. I just wanted to go home and be together on our own.

**LAURA:** I couldn't even leave the athletes' village. I had planned to go back to my parents' house before the closing ceremony. It's only fifteen minutes on the train: Stratford station, straight out over the M25 and into Cheshunt. I wanted to go home, but I was warned in advance by my mum: don't bother, there are media camped outside our house. Photographers, reporters, presenters, presenters' producers. I spent the whole of that week in the village. What solved the problem was a street party being organized for me back home. I went, of course, because it was a lovely thing to have done for you. The photographers all got their photos, and the police gave them twenty minutes to do so. They were then asked to leave. The worst of it was over.

**JASON:** In the aftermath of all that had happened in the velodrome, everyone you met wanted to see your medals. It was a very natural thing for supporters and spectators to do. They saw them as something very special. Never before had a British team won sixty-five medals at a modern Olympics. Twenty-nine golds was almost impossible for lots of people to imagine: only sixteen years before, the team had brought only one home. We had five just in our burgeoning relationship.

We felt differently about them. It wasn't about the medals for us. It was what they represented: all the hundreds of hours of training, the thousands of hours of work from the coaches and support staff, the tens of thousands of laps of velodromes across the world. If you were to ask us, in a parallel universe, if we would ever give up one of our medals so the other could win one, it wouldn't really work. It's not the medal itself that matters. We have had the police round asking about how we store them, telling us how valuable they are. I thought, 'Well, they are valuable, but only to us.' It's not the kind of thing that's going on eBay, because if John Smith tries selling a gold medal, it'll be obvious where it came from – the medals have the competition they were won in on the edge. An Olympic gold medal hasn't been made of solid gold for more than a hundred years; there are only about six grams of actual gold in each one. To be made only of gold they would have to be the size of the smallest chocolate coin you get in your stocking at Christmas. Ours were a symbol of so much more, rather than something to be carried and cherished for their own sake.

**LAURA:** It didn't take long until we weren't even looking at our medals any more. Mine were given to my mum. Although they were safe, she soon didn't have a clue where they were either. It wasn't as if you wanted to take them out at Christmas and stare at them. Only when we have kids can I imagine taking them out of storage.

We still got asked to show people them at events. We started to pretend we had forgotten to bring them with us. I loved the first sight of them – when I initially got that team pursuit one in London I couldn't take my eyes off it. I had an hour of that, and then I had to prepare for the omnium, so straight away the practicality took over from the emotion. Medal back in its box, racing back out to the fore.

The two of them meant a lot to me. But it was the effort, not the bling, the 24/7 for eighteen months that we went through that I cared about. It's not like wearing a crown. You don't need to do it to show who you are. And you will always be Olympic champion, regardless of whether you keep them in your pants drawer or if you have them stolen. The title matters. The medal does not.

**JASON:** Ours was still far from a normal relationship. There could be no holding hands while on the open-top parade that followed those Olympics, or when doing anything in an official capacity, while in private we were still getting to know each other properly, despite what some rather public displays of affection might suggest. Yet it did develop.

There was the point when I realized that calling her Trotty was probably a little impersonal, even if everyone at the velodrome did and it had been fine when we first started going out. There was the point also when I realized my usual forms of communication – ideally very short phone conversations, limited texting on a phone so old its screen could hold a couple of lines of text but no more – were no longer going to cut it. Laura was all smartphones and WhatsApp. While she loved the Trotty nickname when she was racing, it was made clear that what works painted on a Union flag does not work on an iMessage surrounded by emojis. No longer could I tell my mum that I was bringing Trotty round for a bacon butty. No longer could old nicknames of mine also be used. At school everyone had called me Kenny. That was fine until a girl I was going out with was speaking to her mates as I stood there, and I twigged that she actually thought she was going out with somebody named Kenny rather than a boy called Jason. Had she not wondered why anyone would be christened Kenny Kenny? In retrospect, perhaps it is clear why she was not the girl for me.

**LAURA:** As the relationship gradually found room to grow, I began to really appreciate how easy it was to spend so much time together. I never had to push the conversation. I never wanted to spend more time by myself. Time together was always fun. No one understood better what the other had just experienced. We started doing everything together.

The next stage might have been too soon for some. It began as a practical solution, but it equally felt quite instinctive. I was at my parents' house, speaking to Jason on the phone, explaining that I was going to spend the next week looking at houses in the north-west because I felt too old for the British Cycling academy flats in Fallowfield and had nowhere to live.

Jason didn't mess around. 'Just stay at mine.'

'But I'll need to be there for at least a couple of months, I can't just rock up at yours.'

'Of course you can. Don't worry about it, just do it.'

He was almost offended by the suggestion that I should get a hotel instead. 'Do you not want to stay, or what?'

**JASON:** My thinking was relaxed. If Laura came to stay for a couple of months and we couldn't stand the sight of each other by the end of it, then we could move on instead of riding it out for a few years and then realizing we couldn't live together. Why not crack on? It wasn't like I was giving her half the flat. I was giving her half my bed on loan.

That was the theory. Then, in September, Laura arrived, and she seemed to have brought everything she owned along with her. I had been envisioning a holdall, maybe a single suitcase. At that point I didn't even own a wardrobe, just a rail held up at either end with a couple of hangers on it. I didn't even keep any cycling kit there, which was a good thing, because when Laura moved in I went from thinking that I might need a real cupboard to thinking I might need more actual rooms.

It was a chilled-out vibe I had there with my flatmate Lewis: playing guitar until two in the morning, messing about on a set of electric drums that you could play wearing headphones so as not to disturb the neighbours' enjoyment of the late-night guitar sessions. I really liked living there. It was one of the favourite set-ups I've had. It just needed some adjusting to the presence of a young woman.

**LAURA:** That place was fine, once we'd established that a girl cannot live like a boy, and certainly can't live out of a single bag. You can learn a great deal about someone when you first move in with them – the habits they'd previously kept private from you, how they dress when you're not on a date, what their levels of hygiene are like on a normal Tuesday evening.

It was the house Jason owned in Bolton that was the shocker. The first time I went round there you couldn't even see the floor in his bedroom. He didn't have a set of drawers. He had one bit of furniture next to his bed and a box, but he preferred something else – something I would become intimately familiar with – his floordrobe. Sounds like a great invention, looks like a big pile of random clothes on the floor. Even then, some of them washed, some of them dirty, some of them somewhere in between. I cracked and just piled it up and put it in a box.

**JASON:** I had bought the place in Bolton as my first ever property, after coming back from Beijing. I lived there on my own for ages, and to be honest I found it a really lonely experience. I should have rented the spare room out so I had someone to hang around with in the evenings.

About the same time as I decided I could afford to lease that Jaguar in 2012, I decided I could also afford to buy a flat closer to the velodrome in Manchester. I rented out a room in the Bolton one; I rented out a room in the Manchester one. I was emotionally and financially sorted. The flaw in the plan was that, while I thought I would live between the two, I spent most of my time at the much more convenient Manchester one. It meant that Bolton became first a place for storage, and then a place for dumping. You accumulate a vast amount of kit as a professional cyclist. Every year you get the same thing again in slightly different fabrics and colours. I like to use stuff until it's worn out, but you can't wear kit out in twelve months, so the new kit is piling up in cardboard boxes and the old kit is piling up in multiple floordrobes. Even though my mum cleaned the house while I was away, I didn't feel like I could throw any of it out.

Laura had other issues with the Bolton place when we did occasionally stay there: the bed was never made, the bed only occasionally had a sheet on it. She came from a house where her mum had made her bed every morning. She was barely out of it and it was being re-made. She thought my place was freezing cold, and she hates the cold. The shower there, which to me was acceptable because at least the water was warm, was another black mark against me because the water pressure was insufficiently robust to be able to wash long hair properly. It had never mattered to me because I used to shave my head. Around the same moment as Laura was accusing me of not caring about plumbing or hot water, I was coming to the realization that I preferred to have a partner not sporting a number two buzz-cut – someone who might require good enough water pressure to wash their hair properly. Something had to change.

**LAURA:** I had no problem with Bolton itself. As a teenager I loved Cheshunt so much that I vowed never to leave. Even living in the Fallowfield academy flats I didn't consider myself as having moved permanently to the north. I came to love it, and Jason was a huge part of that, even though the learning curve was steep. The portions of chips you get with fish are larger than down south. A scallop in the north is not a shellfish. The Chinese restaurants are greasier in Hertfordshire, and I see that as a good thing. A good Chinese to me is a bad Chinese to everyone else.

The sort of Chinese I had grown up with was one where you could get an all-you-can-eat deal for £16, and that included items from the menu, too. Jason's mistake was to take me to a series of nice Chineses. I wanted a dirty Chinese, not a fancy-pants one with meals they might actually eat in China. When I took him to a dirty Chinese down south he walked in telling me there was nothing there that he would ever eat. We ordered. When it came out, extremely rapidly, of course, he was adamant. 'Even though I've ordered it and paid for it I don't want to eat it.'

My mum came up to visit us soon after London and asked Jason, when he went to the chippy, if he could bring her back a saveloy. He looked baffled.

Jason: 'What the bloody hell is a saveloy?'

Me, witheringly: 'A saveloy, Jason. It's a saveloy. Like a giant red sausage.'

Jason, still baffled. 'I can get you a puddin' if you want.'

Glenda, even more baffled: 'A "puddin'"? What's a "puddin'"?'

Nothing but a few teething troubles. I knew I liked the north and I knew I was staying. I knew, too, that I wasn't staying with the floordrobes and the terrible plumbing in Bolton, or the Manchester lads' pad. I started looking for my own house.

My funds weren't great. I was still only twenty years old, my money coming mainly from the Olympic programme and my sponsors. My mum giving her inheritance to my sister and me provided me with much-needed additional cash. I could just about afford a deposit, but I couldn't afford anything to actually put in a house. My dad, an accountant, came up with the financial solution. I found a show-home among some new-builds in the village of Marple, just on the Peak District side of Stockport. Dad phoned up. 'We'll have it. We'll pay what you're asking, but we want everything in it.' They left the lot. Curtains. Carpets. Kettle. Toaster. By October of 2012 I was into my instant house. And Jason came too, although we didn't officially announce it as the two of us settling down together, and he was technically still in his flat, technically just staying over for lots of successive nights. Because he's Jason, he brought all his stuff in one box. I thought, 'Thank God, because I need all this room ...'

With the serious stuff, even if it was dressed up in casual clothing, came the first sign that not everyone approved of all we did. We realized we had moved from me and you to us and we. Some of our friends liked that, some found it strange.

With the big stuff also came the little changes. For some couples it's the point she stops wearing make-up when they're together. Jason was familiar with me looking pretty bad at the track so that was never an issue for me. That's one of the silver linings about being a professional athlete: he had already seen me red-faced and sweaty with my hair glued to my head and me being sick in a bucket. What can be worse than that? We hadn't met with me all dressed up and we hadn't fallen in love in nice tops and smart shoes. Wet Lycra, skinsuits that needed a wash, helmet hair. When that's the daily reality, it can only get better when you actually go out together.

**JASON:** I think most men remember the point when their girlfriend feels relaxed enough in their company to start breaking wind in front of them.

In Laura's defence, I'd always done it in front of her. You can call it managing expectations, you can call it being yourself, but I'd also never done my hair, often not had a shave and sometimes not even bothered with a shower. Maybe it's more about standards.

There was no recognizable turning point when we got down to breakfast one morning to find that we were both dressed in identical free kit from British Cycling's sponsors. That was an everyday occurrence from the start. More of an issue for me was when Laura started borrowing my clothes. I had one expensive t-shirt that I cherished so much that I barely wore it myself. One day it randomly went missing. It wasn't until months later that I realized that she had been taking it away with her to training camps and races to use as a pyjama top.

She claimed she took it because it was the only clean one, and that it's a nice thing for girls to borrow their partner's clothes. Comfy, affectionate, sharing. Except the reason it was clean was because I was saving it for special occasions. I must have had a hundred t-shirts. She could have had any one of them, but she had to choose the favourite.

It was only the start. I soon discovered my socks were fair game too, despite the fact that my feet are considerably larger than hers. I had just about reconciled myself to the fact that she was borrowing them when I found a couple of pairs with her name actually written on them. She had labelled them for when she went away.

Move it on another step. Because her friends on the team pursuit squad share the same attitudes as her, then they start stealing my socks that had become Laura's socks. Now half the female riders at British Cycling are walking about in my socks. How did that happen?

**LAURA:** London 2012 didn't change how we were together. Our relationship just became more of what it already was. In some ways we had gone past several big landmarks so fast. I don't regret any of it, because moving into Jason's flat in Manchester that September meant we got used to each other more quickly. You test each other out, you discover both what they are like and what you are like together. You know when you are ready, and we were.

And then we got the dog, and the dog decided to ruin our lovely new shared house. Jason was away for the first week that Sprolo was around, which is why I feel entirely justified in having made him clean up every other thing that's come out of Sprolo's back or front in the subsequent years.

We dealt with the other staple disputes in young relationships by arguing about them until I won. Let's say I asked Jason, out of the blue, if we could get an elephant. Being calm and logical he would reply, 'No we can't have an elephant, that's stupid.' The next day I would corner him again. 'Can we have an elephant now?' Three hundred days later, probably a fair few middle-of-the-night questions too, every one of them the same: 'Jason, can we have an elephant?' 'Just do what you bloody want, Laura ...' By which time I've ordered it online. It's already in the basket. A patient victory.

I suggest we should move the table to a different part of the room. Jason disagrees. When he's out I move the table. We have curtains up that don't work – stylistically, that is. They function in terms of blocking light. Jason hasn't noticed an issue. He notices when he gets back one night to find a new set of curtains up, but by then it's too late.

Jason would never do something without talking about it first. I don't think I've ever got back to the house and been surprised by a dramatic change in the decoration or layout. He would still be recovering from one set of new curtains when he'll come home to find that the new curtains that replaced the old curtains he didn't think needed replacing have now been replaced by even newer curtains, because I've decided overnight that I didn't like the first new pair that replaced the old ones that worked just fine anyway.

He once walked into our bedroom to find I'd moved the entire bed. There was almost admiration mixed in with the confusion, because being an ottoman design with storage underneath, it took a lot of shifting for anyone, let alone a girl of 5 foot 4 inches.

I'm not a dictator. I wasn't keen on Jason's motorbikes because motorbikes are so dangerous. But I understood that he loved them, and I understood they were the fastest and most efficient way for him to commute in to the velodrome.

But he would give in far more easily than I ever would. Four years later, when we had moved on to the moment of getting married, I asked Jason if we should have a videographer to record it all. I wanted to be able to show our kids the big day. His was the same logical response you'd expect: 'We'll never watch it back; my parents never watched theirs back. Even if you wanted to watch it with our kids, the technology will have moved on and rendered it obsolete. "Hey kids, we used to use something called a USB. That's right. U.S.B. They weren't very good, but at the time we thought they were amazing, because until then we had been using DVDs. Eh? I can't even remember what it stands for, that's how old they are."'

We got a videographer. That's how you manage a relationship. Make decisions, don't sit on the fence.

JASON: I never felt the pressure, even at my first Olympics in Beijing, as I joked around with Chris Hoy, who beat me to gold in the individual sprint. It would be gold for me, and him, along with Jamie Staff (bottom, left) in the team sprint, though.

LAURA: The dream team of me, Dani King and Jo Rowsell Shand in the team pursuit at London. Winning that, and the omnium (top right, with Sarah Hammer of USA and Annette Edmondson of Australia), was more than I could have hoped for from my own Olympic debut. Below, a congratulations from British Cycling Director Dave Brailsford.

JASON: Beating my old foe Grégory Baugé in the sprint (left) made victory so much sweeter, especially as it followed hot on the heels of Chris Hoy and I, with Philip Hindes, retaining our team sprint title.

Oops, outed: Harry had warned us about the photographers. This is the day our relationship was revealed to the world, as we watched the beach volleyball in London, David Beckham an unknowing witness.

Things quickly moved on for us as a couple and, soon after we moved in together, we welcomed Sprolo and Pringle into our home (above).

In December 2014, we got engaged (Laura showing off the engagement ring bought from Prestons of Bolton, left), but before that happy occasion came round in September 2016, there was the small matter of the Rio Olympics to attend to.

Wonderful Rio: Laura celebrating gold with the team pursuit girls (*l–r* Jo Rowsell Shand, Katie Archibald and Elinor Barker) and her mum (middle left), with that famous flag; Jason beating roommate Callum Skinner to the sprint title, and celebrating with coaches Jan van Eijden and Justin Grace after a memorable keirin gold.

Professional cycling can be tough, but it becomes a lot easier when you have your best friend and your partner beside you all of the way ...

# Ten: **Growing Up Together**

**LAURA:** You don't realize at the time, and you certainly don't spot it coming when you are only just out of your teens. But an Olympics drains your batteries – physically, mentally, emotionally. After a little time off, after winning those medals through hard work in the velodrome, you feel as if you should get back to training. You feel as if you should be supercharged. You're a double Olympic champion. This is what champions do.

So I rushed back into it, and I was terrible. The Glasgow leg of the World Cup came round at the end of October 2012. I was ill. I went so badly that I confessed in a post-race interview that I didn't even know why I was there. Some people got the hump after I said it. Who does she think she is? It's gone to her head. Doesn't she realize the Olympics only comes round every four years? This is the bread and butter. This is where you earn your crust.

When I look back now, I wonder what on earth I was thinking even competing. I suppose I felt I had to because it was the first home competition after the Games, and maybe there was a little chasing that 2012 buzz too. But I was exhausted. I couldn't race, as my results illustrated, and I couldn't think straight, or otherwise I wouldn't have made such a private confession so publicly.

Things had changed, but not as we had hoped. Our team pursuit was disappointing. We were almost seven seconds slower than in the Olympics. I normally get a buzz off the team event. It sets you up for your individual event. It's the one that you focus on: if you've got it out of the way, it's going to plan. Not this time.

You could dig down and uncover the reasons pretty quickly. Dani King and I had enjoyed ourselves immensely after London. We had partied and drunk and stayed out and done all the things we had denied ourselves for so long. Alongside us we had young Elinor Barker, super keen to make a good impression and get on the team, and she had two Olympic champions going worse than they probably ever had since making the squad. With those ingredients it could only go one way. Until then we had been so solid and successful as a team that it seemed improbable we could ever struggle. That performance made us fully aware that unless you've got all your girls going really well at the same time, you struggle to go fast.

Although qualifying at that World Cup was terrible, by our standards, we managed to turn it back around and win the event, holding off the Australian trio to claim victory by just over a second. But we knew we could do better.

The need to all pull in the same direction at the same time was illustrated again when we failed to win gold at the 2015

Worlds, which was a shock to people outside the team because they had become so accustomed to us being the bankers in the British squad. Stick your house on those girls, they always bring it home. And it was a shock to us as well. I didn't feel that we ever took anything for granted, but we must have.

Those years between Olympics were up and down. Three times I would win silver medals in the omnium at the Worlds, twice behind Sarah Hammer, once behind Annette Edmondson. Not until Rio was closing in would I take an individual world title back. A reshaped and remotivated team pursuit quartet – after that dreadful World Cup performance – would win the world title again in 2013 and 2014, but we would drop away to that second-placed finish a year out from Rio. Jason found it even more difficult to maintain that champion's form. While he would win the world keirin title in 2013, he would not win either the team or individual sprints at the three World Championships between Olympic years. At the Commonwealths in 2014 he would have to settle for silver in both.

It left me confused and upset. There was the expectation I was putting on myself, both because I wanted to win and because I felt, as Olympic champion, that I should be doing better. Then there was the other side of the coin. Sometimes I felt like I had fluked the Olympics. Where did that form and speed come from? Why can't I do that again?

London had been wonderful, a fantastic surprise, the greatest experience of my life. But it set the standard so high. It might be the individual pursuit where the difference shows the most. You go up and do your efforts, and you throw everything at it, and yet the numbers don't come. Why can't

I physically go that fast? I did it once. I am clearly capable of doing it.

You spend three years locked into a spiral of negative thought. I am fast, faster than all these times show, and I've beaten all these people before, so why is it taking me so long? You start to lose faith. I've sent crisis emails to my physiologist Len Parker Simpson. I would hammer my worries to him: I'm losing trust in the training because I am not getting any kind of results, or the times I want to do. They're just not there, and I can't push on the pedals any harder. I am trying my best, but the times aren't there ...

It changed my idea of success. When I won omnium silver at the Worlds in Minsk in 2013, four points off Hammer in gold only six months after pipping her in London, I was perversely quite happy with the result. While my form made me miserable, what I could achieve with that form lifted my mood. I wasn't fit enough and was nowhere close to being in World Championship-winning shape to do brilliantly in my solo races. Hammer came into those Worlds flying. She had looked at what went so badly in London and worked on her weaknesses, and it paid off. She stormed it. It's probably the best I've ever seen her go.

All that, I could rationalize. So I finished, and thought, 'Yup, I'll take that.' It became much harder to deal with when I started to go better but couldn't make it count in the same way that Hammer had in Belarus. In Paris two years later I was able to deal relatively well with the fact that the Aussies beat us in the team pursuit. Not every one of the four girls was fit. Without four girls pulling, you can't go fast. Others might try to compensate by doing more work, but the sums don't add up. I felt in good form, and so I thought, 'Forget about that one for now, we can speak about that one when we get back to training; let's move on to the omnium.' But it went wrong. That first scratch race on the track, I just didn't know what to do. I felt as if I wasn't thinking, as if I wasn't capable of getting my racing brain into gear. I ended up almost just riding round. Came home thirteenth, a lap down on the first four riders. Everything else after that went fine – won the individual pursuit, won the elimination, even second in the points race. Hammer was ill and off form. It should have been between me and Nettie Edmondson, and it felt like it should have been me on top.

It wasn't. I missed out on gold by the exact number of points I had ceded to Nettie in the scratch race. I had thrown the whole thing away with one bad race. Silver? It felt much worse. I went up to my mum and dad at the end and I burst out crying. Dad was as dads should be. 'What's the matter? You've just won a silver at the World Championships. You did brilliantly in race after race.' But I knew I had failed to do myself justice. In training, all had gone well. I had set a personal best in the flying lap. A lack of focus in one race had rendered all that meaningless. I was genuinely gutted. Never waste form. Always cash in those chips, because what happens if the form drops away again, and it's all out of your hands the next time?

Hammer was the constant. I beat her in London; she beats me at the next two Worlds. She's under the weather for the next; I get back on top in 2016. The rivalry is undeniable, and it changes the way you behave towards the other. We don't talk to each other between events, we don't talk before finals.

The only conversations come on the podium, and even then not always. I'll spend time with the Aussie Mel Hoskins, particularly when we're in Perth, and I'll sit there at races chatting quite happily with Nettie or with Holland's Kirsten Wild, who is extremely nice, but Sarah and I have never given each other the time of day. Maybe that makes sense. She's a different generation, significantly older than me. We want to beat each other. If it's not one of us with gold it's the other. And it's not as fierce as it was between Victoria Pendleton and Anna Mears, it's just that we don't give each other the chance to get on.

**JASON:** My rivalries in those fallow years were all with the stopwatch. I've seen Australians go fast, I've seen Germans go past me, I've seen New Zealanders go faster still. The French have always been there, and Baugé has felt permanently on my shoulder at times, but if you looked at the top step of the podium at each World Championship from 2013 onwards there was a different man there each time: Germany's Stefan Bötticher in 2013, France's François Pervis in Cali the year after, Baugé back for home-town hero status in Paris 2015. After a period when Theo Bos won everything, and then Chris Hoy took over, sprinting has now become much harder to predict. In part that is down to changing technology: some riders are more suited to bigger gears than others. Some of it is just the event. It's always been about fast guys and tiny margins.

And sprint form is hard to find and tougher still to hold. Endurance riders on the track – the pursuit specialists, the points riders – can feel it coming on slowly. You can watch them training and see it coming through the season. Sprint form comes all at once. Not until the last moment before competition do you get all your form. You have to be fresh. Undercook it by a week and you'll be in perfect shape at the airport for your flight home. Squeeze in the wrong big session at the wrong time and you'll tip too far the other way.

It's one of the reasons my results have varied so much between Olympic Games. It looks from the outside as if I've smashed it out of the park in 2008, fallen back, won everything in 2012, seen loads of other riders come past me, and then hit it again perfectly in 2016. But the whole of British Cycling is geared to those four-year milestones. That's when jobs are decided and budgets set. It's the only time as riders we do a full taper, coming right off everything else for the one big shot. World Cups you train through. World Championships are subsumed beneath the relentless push for success at the Games. And there are random little things too, lifestyle changes that you don't think will impact at the time but with hindsight may just have knocked you fractionally off that fine line between perfection and second place – moving house and spending a week at the wrong point in the training cycle humping boxes around and shifting sofas, getting a dog and having two weeks of broken sleep as it howls the house down every night.

Losing is not good. It feels awful. At the time you don't find yourself thinking, 'What the hell, it's only 2014, I'll be unbeatable again when it matters.' It is difficult getting your head kicked in.

I had times between Beijing and London when I thought I was struggling. In reality we were still roughly on the podium or thereabouts. The real bad days came after 2012. Going home in the first round is horrible. The only real way I found of dealing with it was to relax and accept it all. Accept that everyone wants to win, everyone is trying really hard. If it so happens that someone has trained better, and that they are better than you on that day, then you just have to admit it. The gaps are so tiny sometimes that there may be twenty riders who go faster. The changes in the way qualification for the sprint works means that what used to be a fairly easy first ride can now be significantly tougher. There was a learning curve with that new system, and maybe we were slow to react. Only by 2016 did we really start playing it right.

You would like to think that experiences of 2012 bolstered my self-belief in the years before 2016: I improved when I needed to for that Olympics, I'll do so again this time. Actually you forget. I was worried, seriously worried. Only when you see unarguable signs in training do you start to have faith again. For all the hoping and wishing – it's got to be there somewhere, it's got to be there – it took the large and unmissable figure of Philip Hindes to finally convince me. When Phil starts travelling, you know about it. In the weeks around the track in Manchester before the Worlds in Olympic year, Phil was clearly back to his bull-like best. By the time of the Worlds he was on fire, and when you have Phil on fire in man one, the whole team knows that we're probably going to be the fastest team there after the first of the three laps. When you're the fastest a third of the way through, the other two of you are left with a straightforward and pleasing scenario: we're in the race, we might as well get our act together and stay in the race. It gives you that added motivation.

I could feel my own form moving in the right direction too. I never really set personal bests in Manchester, but we were okay with that; we had climbed such an enormous peak in London that our personal bests had been set miles out of reach. But every now and then I would chuck in a really good session, and as I started creeping back up towards those PBs, nudging the odd one or two, I began feeling the excitement. When you see promising times, you want to build on it. You want to build on that momentum, because so much of success in sport is about momentum. Belief flows from that. Confidence to ride the way you should. Confidence to take on those men who have been winning while you were down, and dictate to them the way a big showdown will go.

**LAURA:** I'm not sure whether people actually expected me to win everything in those years, or whether I just thought they did. But I certainly felt that was the case. It didn't matter that my original development pathway was meant to bypass London and treat even Rio as a staging post towards the Games of 2020. Three silver medals in the omnium at the Worlds at the ages of twenty-one, twenty-two and twenty-three would ordinarily have been seen as spot-on for where I was in my physical development and tactical maturity.

I worried. I worried about what the coaches were doing. I worried about how my body was responding. They would be firm with me. 'Stop losing the faith in it, just stop. It's going to work.' Jason would try to tell me too, with his experience of going through the same thing after Beijing 2008. I couldn't listen to him either. When I sat down with the coaches and I was thinking rationally, sitting in the meeting when it was all fresh and I was all fine, I could believe it would come good. Yup, that sounds exactly like what I should do. But once the doubt was in there it was horribly hard to shift. I couldn't change my mind on it.

It's different for Jason. He helps put together his own training programme. If he isn't happy with an element of it or doesn't believe in something he's been given, then he will change it. I get told my programme. Jason would joke with me to try to lift the mood. 'If your programme said get up at one o'clock in the morning and put your underpants on your head and do star jumps, you would do it. That's how blindly you follow your programme.'

**JASON:** What helped us through all those misgivings and paranoias was our relationship. Had one of us not been a track cyclist we would have had to explain all those issues in great depth before the other could grasp what we were going through. So specific are the demands and responses in track cycling that even if they had been an Olympic athlete from another sport it may have been impossible. We instinctively understood. We knew the characters each other were talking about; we appreciated tiny nuances of things like form and confidence, the balance in a track cyclist's life between past results and future fears. We realized that there would be flashpoints triggered not by each other but by the pressures we were under – a timed effort that had gone badly, an issue with a new test one of the physiologists might have brought in. We grasped that there would be days when ordinary household tasks like mowing the lawn, doing the ironing or washing the car would not happen, because a crucial race was coming and one of us couldn't afford to waste that energy.

We knew that together we would have to be different. When we went to a World Championship we could not expect to sit together on the plane. We could not hold hands by the luggage carousel. We could not sleep in the same bed; we couldn't even spend the night in the same apartment. At those big competitions you live your courtship like first-year students in single-sex dorms, or second-years going round to each other's shared houses. One of us will knock on the other's door. If their teammates aren't about, or if they've finished racing already, we might pop in and watch a bit of telly. No staying over.

Those pressures did not in any way freeze the relationship. They strengthened the bond and speeded us up through the ensuing stages. Another commitment cliché to tick off: buying Laura our springer-poodle cross Sprolo, not only because she had been moaning at me in classic Laura fashion about getting a dog, but because I had always been around them as a kid and loved them. Welcome to the family. In 2013, a year after she had bought her show-home in Marple, the next big decision: shouldn't we buy a place together?

Farewell Bolton bolthole, farewell the young-man-about-town flat in the middle of Manchester. I would sell and rent those, respectively, Laura would sell Marple but keep all the show-home accessories that had come with it. We found a property between Knutsford and Altrincham that we could afford but which failed the survey pretty catastrophically. Happily so, as it turned out, since we then found a cottage deeper in the Cheshire countryside that I loved as soon as we saw it. Laura would take longer to be convinced, but for once it was me with the pester-power and my choice that won through. It would make the commute to the velodrome on the east side of Manchester a long one, but I had my motorbikes, and I saw riding these as good fun and a bit of quiet time. Zipping through the Manchester rush-hour traffic would also keep my brain sharp, even if I did occasionally find myself glancing in non-existent wing mirrors while on the track bike an hour or two later.

We fell into the sort of efficient, intuitive division of labour that makes partnerships work. I would do 80 per cent of the cooking; Laura would do 20 per cent of the washing-up. She would use every pan and utensil in the kitchen to produce the most basic of dishes; I would do a full Sunday roast and have it all cleared away before the gravy went cold. At meal times Laura is a fussy sod. She won't eat fruit. She is obsessed with crisps – the naming of our second dog as Pringle was not intended as a tribute to the shape of the velodrome roof in London. She would agree to eat chicken fajitas if they were cooked for her, so too the ginger stir-fry from our local butchers. But her favourite was bangers and mash – loads of butter and full cream milk in the potatoes, plenty of salt, the whole plate dripping in gravy, with some big fat sausages wedged on the side. It's not the ideal dish for Olympic athletes, and we had to rein it in at one point after realizing it was becoming a staple rather than a treat, and possibly in danger of affecting our on-track performance.

There were fewer bacon butties than back home in Bolton, because I had a new home now, with Laura. Another step into adulthood: our parents would come round to stay with us, rather than vice versa. Mum loved the dogs, she loved my roasts. They surprised her – how many sons learn to cook when they still live with their parents? – but they were better than Laura's famous Exploding Baked Potatoes, and less dangerous to prepare in a house you've just bought.

And so to the biggest step of all. December 2014, two years on from London, with Rio on the distant horizon and those wonderful Games of 2012 in our wake. Time to look to the future rather than back.

After coming through the hurricane that was London, after the hard times and happiness that had followed it, we both knew we wanted to get married. We hadn't discussed when, and we hadn't talked about the how, but we knew we worked together, so the idea was there. One Saturday afternoon, on a rare solo flight to my parents', I told my mum I was thinking of popping into Prestons of Bolton, and would she like to come? Now, Prestons – recently closed, sadly – had a reputation. It had been on the corner of Deansgate and Bank Street for more than a hundred years. In its day it had been the biggest jewellers outside London. Four floors of expensive shiny stuff. A man from Bolton doesn't pop into Prestons just to admire its history. He goes there on a mission, and my mother understood that.

It was the first time I'd ever looked at a ring. So much choice. Far too much choice. If Laura hadn't given me an incredibly detailed description of exactly the sort of thing she wanted I might have been in trouble. Instead I was able stroll in and be specific: 'A halo engagement ring, please, with a circle of little diamonds around a larger one in the middle.'

Ah, the innocence of a young man on his first visit to Prestons of Bolton. I had walked in thinking there would be one of them. There were about 25,000. Bloody hell, they all look very similar.

This is where mums come in very handy. From the baffling thousands of alternatives, she was able to pick out the special one. Suddenly there was a glass of champagne in my hand, which by the time it had been drunk had exactly the effect the Prestons staff had been hoping for: 'Sod it, I'll buy it.'

I genuinely believed I was still hedging my bets. The bubbles wore off. I hadn't signed anything. 'There's nothing to say that I have to ask her if I don't feel like it, I could probably just bring it back ...'

Two issues to deal with. Number one: Mum. She loves to talk. On this occasion she promised not to, not until the deed had been done. Number two: Laura. She has an uncanny nose for these things. I knew that if she got the slightest whiff of anything, she would search high and low. I would be interrogated, and no matter how robust my resolve, no man could withstand the relentless questioning of Laura at her most insistent.

Where to hide the box and receipt? Not my pants drawer, because that was too obvious, and she would find it – not when putting my pants away, but when she was shoving something else in there that shouldn't have been in the drawer in the first place. As a typical male I have a very strict drawer system. Pants in one. Socks in another. Cycling socks in the next one down. Laura's was a slightly more relaxed system: if it fitted, it was probably where it belonged. Even if it was her socks in my pants drawer, or her socks that were actually my socks before she secreted them back in the drawer from which she had first stolen them. Instead I went for the big pile of soft toys and race mascots that sat on a shelf above the television. They were seldom disturbed and never dusted.

There it sat until an episode of *EastEnders* one night that, as usual, was failing to grip me as much as Laura. I was passing the time by winding her up, showing her £30 engagement rings on eBay, and passing comments like, 'This one's just as good as any expensive ring', and 'What about this one? It's even cheaper.' And then I suddenly decided that this was the moment: a dark December night, on the sofa, a soap opera in the background and the dogs at our feet. 'Will you marry me?'

She barely paused. 'Yes.' She certainly didn't believe I had a ring, so when I fished it out from the toys and presented it to her, at last *EastEnders* was put on pause. And the tears began to flow.

Such happiness. Lots of phone calls. Lots of photos with the ring on her finger so she could send it to friends and family so they could say, 'Ahh ...'

It was quite a while until *EastEnders* went back on after that. Unfortunately, unbeknown to me, the ring didn't fit. An hour before, Laura hadn't known she had a ring. The day before, it hadn't mattered. Now it was the most important thing in the world. She was engaged. She wanted to wear a ring. So the following day it was back to Prestons of Bolton to get it resized, and while it was being resized apparently I had to buy another ring as a stand-in. That was fifty quid extra, which enabled me to reflect that it's a bloody expensive business getting engaged if you don't know someone's ring size.

In fairness, I thought I was spending quite a lot on the actual ring, but it turned out it was one of the cheapest in the shop. In some ways it's a shame I had to take it back, because no one needed to know where it was in the ranking. But it was a beauty, and more importantly, it was the one she wanted. Well played, Jason.

**LAURA:** I know some people get engaged to be engaged, but we got engaged to get married. Jason hadn't asked me so we could sit in a holding pattern. We wanted to push on. We were ready. Our biggest issue was keeping it quiet from the paparazzi. There would be no Prince Harry when we kissed each other this time, not unless he asked to come, but we still wanted our special moment to ourselves.

As 2014 became 2015, the concerns were all about my form and how I could improve. I had no doubts I could get to the church on time. It was the Worlds and Olympics in the sort of times that could beat Sarah Hammer that were my focus now.

Jason had always had much more input into his training than I had. It was true for most of the sprinters. It went back to the time of Chris Hoy and Craig MacLean. The two of them had so much experience, and had had so many different coaches, that a new guy would come in to something of a negotiation. But me? Following was the only thing I'd ever known to do. I wouldn't have known how to coach myself if I tried, which is why my relationship with Paul Manning was going to be so critical to getting me back on top of the world.

Paul understood me. As importantly, he understood what it was like to step out for an Olympic final. That was huge for me. Jason had earlier had a coach at British Cycling he considered a very smart man, an excellent coach, but who had never been a rider himself. It meant that he had all the theory but not always an understanding of its best application. Someone who has raced on the boards might have less of the science, but they will be really good at translating the science into actions.

And Paul got me as a person. It hadn't always worked for me, following blindly. With Chris Newton, neither of us were tuned in to the other. His training wasn't the same as Paul's – he was much more tactically focused rather than timed event based. I still owe Chris a lot. He's the reason I won gold at the Commonwealth Games and won the 2014 National road race. He managed to teach me how to ride a bunch race where so many people had failed. But I felt incredibly fortunate to end up with someone like Paul. There are riders who wouldn't like to be coached by him. For me, I will always trust him completely because I know that come that day's session or race, he's gone through every possible aspect of it.

As a former rider he likes to push, push and keep pushing. I can't always do that. Leading into a competition I will change some small details. By that point it's about me knowing myself, filtering out how he's been influenced by what he knew of himself. Doing a three-hour road ride two weeks out from the Olympics would have made his legs feel better. It's not going to help me. If I think it's wrong at that late stage, I'm not doing it.

It doesn't weaken our bond. It is a sign of a great coach that they can take that on board and yet don't see it as you threatening their authority, that they genuinely want detailed feedback from their athletes about how they're feeling rather than dumb acceptance of everything they say. It is why I want

Paul as my coach forever. He's not allowed to leave me. He knows this.

You can't be friends with your coach. That's the boundary. You're part of a larger team. But you can trust them with the most personal information. British Cycling brought in a strange online system for rider feedback. The idea was that if you'd had an issue with something that might affect your performance – your physio, your nutrition – then your coach would know about it. I never bothered. If I had an issue, I would ring Paul and pass the problem on direct. He would sort it out. I would ring him at least twice a week, if not every day.

The system had a section where you could type in any personal issues that might be affecting your performance. There was no need to specify what it was. Privacy was respected and protected. Well, I never had an issue with just going up to Paul and saying, 'Jason and I had a blazing argument last night, so this session isn't going to go well.'

If I hadn't told him, he would have looked at the times I was recording in that day's training and assumed it was something to do with his programme. That's why it is so important for a coach to be the kind of person who isn't going to judge you, and for the rider to feel comfortable telling the coach.

I can be demanding. I can be hard. I don't think there are many coaches I could have that kind of relationship with. And that is why I consider myself lucky. I have no idea how long Paul will coach me but so far he's never let me down.

**JASON:** I saw my coaches Jan van Eijden and Justin Grace, as well as Iain Dyer in the past, as helpers rather than teachers. I respected their credentials immensely – Jan had been a world champion at both sprint and team sprint, Justin rebuilt track cycling in his native New Zealand and then coached François Pervis to three world titles – but I saw them as having both strengths and weaknesses, just as I did. My aim was to make the most of their expertise, so my training schedule was the result of negotiation and a real brain trust. When it came to selection, they had the final say. When it came to my personal training plan, the buck stopped with me.

I did see them as friends. We would go for coffee, and we would talk about things away from track cycling. But my idea of friendship tends to be different. I don't do that much socializing with anyone in cycling. To me they were like friends, but then maybe because I'm not that overly friendly with anyone else. I was happy with a professional relationship that left me in charge, because if my career blew up in my face, I was going to be the one to get dropped. I would be the one visibly failing. It would be no good pointing the finger at Jan and Justin and saying, 'Well, you gave me a rubbish programme.' It was my responsibility, and I should have done something about it. There must be trust there. Everything you do as rider and coach must be about making you as fast as possible. I have seen riders not being frank enough with their coach, and their results have suffered for it. If you don't like something, you have to trust that they will listen to you, and that when they hear what you have to say they will not get the hump.

The Commonwealth Games in Glasgow would go okay for Laura. She didn't qualify for the medal races in the individual pursuit, but won gold in the points race. I found it a much more testing summer, an illustration both of the importance of that honesty with your coaches and how the Olympics dominated our professional aims even midway through the four-year cycle.

Because, for a track cyclist, there is always a conflict with the Commonwealths. You want to go well, but the only thing on the line is pride. Our funding for the Olympics begins two years out from the next Games. So does the start of the Olympic qualification. You want to do well because you want to race for England, and the kit is cool too; there's something about that white, and it's a rare privilege to wear it. The problem is how much training and emotion you invest into those races. Results at the Commonwealths do not reduce or extend coaches' contracts. It's different for the New Zealand and Australia teams. Their programme is partly dependent on their results there. As a team they are bang up for it; as individuals, they throw more at it. You know what you're up against. You know, too, what you have to lose: a key block of training in the Olympic cycle by tapering for these races, thus having a knock-on effect on a key period of qualifying for the next Games through your performances at the European Championships and World Cup series.

This time it was further complicated by how wide open the team sprint qualification for the 2016 Olympics was. We knew we needed to be in the top five European teams to get a place in Rio, and that meant beating one of Russia, Poland or the Netherlands even if we couldn't match the French and Germans. The coaches and riders debated it among ourselves: should we actually go to Glasgow?

From that reduced level of commitment, a pair of silvers felt like a great result. My qualification for the individual sprint was a timely reminder of how important it was to be bang on it from the start; having clocked the second-slowest time, I then had to race the first seed, second seed, third seed and fourth to fight my way through to silver. I was throwing up all over the place. Best of three, the third race needing to be run almost every time, scrape after scrape. Even with three Olympic golds to my name, that long day taught me an awful lot about sprinting and even more about myself.

**LAURA:** You mature as a rider in different ways. I had seen the role Chris Hoy had played within the squad, and I noticed how a few of us younger ones had subconsciously taken on some of his unspoken leadership roles. You start to realize that somewhere out there there's possibly an eight-year-old Laura Trott who idolizes you. That means you have to act in a certain way. Simple stuff. Wearing the right kit on the right days. Being on time for private track sessions. Standing up for younger riders coming through.

I can be feisty. Even as a relatively young presence in the squad I would be happy to stand up to the bosses if anyone in the team had any issues. If I got my head bitten off, so be it. At least I had tried.

Before London, I certainly wouldn't have been that person. I would have been scared that I was going to lose my spot on the squad. Now I would wade in for the rest of the team pursuit girls, for the lads on the development squads below us, if I felt the coaches and performance directors were treating them unfairly or letting them down.

I wasn't being deliberately argumentative. It was all about getting the best possible performance out of myself and those around me. When we raced at the World Championships in 2014, 2015 and 2016, we still had our SRM power-meters on our bikes. That meant that each of the pedal cranks weighed 400 grams more than a proper racing set. That might not sound very much to you. To us it was worth 0.1 seconds in a standing start. That again may sound like nothing. To us it could be the difference between gold and forgotten about. I felt we shouldn't be using them at a Worlds. The bosses said they wanted our power data to use at the Olympics. I couldn't see how that data would ever be used. They won that one, but that was the level of detail I felt I had to care about.

**JASON:** The frustrations could be huge. As a rider you live to win. As soon as you pin on your race number and pull on your helmet then you want to race and you want a victory. That attitude could sometimes feel as though it was wasted on a management team on consistent wages for the whole four-year Olympic cycle. We were the ones dying on our arses at the Worlds, getting our heads kicked in by nations and riders we would then have to take on again in Rio. One time I glanced at my cranks and saw the date 2008 engraved upon them. I was riding equipment that was seven years out of date. I agreed entirely that the Olympics had to be our main target, and that we should thus save our best kit for that peak, but there were times when it went too far – we riders still wanted to be in as good shape as possible at the intervening races. You would be sat there before a race, you look at your bike and it would have Dura-Ace cranks on, which were good, but designed before I was born. You would look down to see standard handlebars when the rider you were racing had all carbon cranks, carbon bars and everything else moulded to perfection.

A lot of the British team, Laura and me included, were Lottery funded through UK Sport. Our funding was calculated on our performances at the Worlds. It didn't stay at the same level for the four years after London, no matter how many Olympic medals you had taken home. You were guaranteed that for two years only. After that, it came off your display at the subsequent Worlds.

It could be a big percentage drop if you didn't perform well. It might be from £27,000 a year to £18,000. That's a good chunk if it's your only income. You weren't riding for the money, but ultimately you still had to make ends meet. I was slightly luckier than some of the other guys. I was Olympic champion so I had a bit of money to fall back on. Lots of my teammates were just racing, the same as I had been back in the day. Displays at the World Championships meant more to the riders than the staff, and that was wrong.

It made it all the more welcome when 2016 finally came round, and everyone pulled in the same direction. Head coach Iain Dyer would warn us: there is no magic wand we will be waving at the holding camp in Newport. Just because we came out of there in 2008 and 2012 and won pretty much everything in sight doesn't mean it will miraculously happen again. You will have to work for it. We will need to make sure we do everything right.

We knew that. We knew too that the Olympics were how the wider world would see us, and how history would define our careers. If someone said to you, you can have those four world titles but you won't win the Olympics, you would choose the Olympics every day over the four world titles. Four world titles or an Olympic silver? You can keep the silver.

I liked to look at it another way, too. You want to win all the time. There's nothing to say you can't have both.

# Eleven: **Comeback Kids**

**LAURA:** Olympic years bring doubts as well as excitement. I worried about Jason as 2016 began, because I hadn't seen the dominant rider of old at any of the big championships since London. Even his keirin triumph at the Worlds in 2013 felt a bit of a fluke. His finding the form to win sprint gold at the London Worlds in March, less than five months before we were due to fly out to Brazil, meant that I could share the happiness of my own gold medals in the scratch and omnium. It was the first time we'd ever won an individual world title in the same year. For a partnership like ours, that mattered.

**JASON:** I remembered years ago the GB team psychiatrist Steve Peters saying that, when you're on the start line, if you ask yourself whether you have done everything you can and the answer is yes, then it doesn't matter whether you win or lose. After the Worlds in 2015, I realized that my answer was no. I thought I had pushed myself to the limit, but I couldn't have done. I was the perfect athlete for the six-week build up to the Worlds, but only six weeks; from that would come a vow that I would be perfect for a whole year in 2016.

In the team event I had just felt flat. That was the moment I started to wonder whether the spark would ever come back. Winning the world sprint title in 2016 was wonderful. It was a real fight. But the solo event is different. You can get round it, you can gear up – put a bigger gear on to generate more power with each pedal stroke. In the team sprint, your gears are governed by how you intend to start. You have to be able to turn that gear really quickly, and I was starting to wonder whether I could still do that any more. Maybe I had changed as a person. Maybe now I was just stronger rather than as fast as I had been. Was that the reason I was only winning on bigger gears? I felt in the team event that it was my responsibility to ride the best lap out of any man two in the competition. If Philip Hindes did the fastest opener and Callum Skinner the fastest third, then I thought I would be letting them down if I too wasn't the quickest of all.

Faced with those misgivings, Laura and I stripped every-thing else in our lives back. All our food shopping was done online. When we cooked there was no standing over a hot stove for an hour. We needed to save every fibre in our legs, and that simplified our culinary tactics: get it fried, get it eaten. While sitting down. Don't stand there forever mashing something by hand or adding a protein-free garnish. Don't think about the pleasure of preparing a special meal over a number of hours. Find something nutritious. Put it in your mouth. Send it to your muscles.

As the weeks ticked down we moved temporarily into a new little house we had bought in Cheadle, much closer to the velodrome. In fact, everything was closer – the nearest garage, the nearest supermarket, the nearest Italian restaurant (which helped, because if you can get someone else to do the standing and frying before you do the eating, that's even better). Even walking the dogs had to be streamlined. I would wake up, make a smoothie, take it with me as I set Sprolo and Pringle loose in the field behind the house and sit on a bench motionless while they chased invisible enemies. They would wear themselves out, I would wear myself in. Laura and I would still sleep in the same bed; we knew cycling couples who didn't because they felt that they slept better alone, but even after a crash in training that left me with deep abrasions across my body, we felt that the advantages of being together outweighed the occasional 3 a.m. elbow in the ribs or tug-of-war over the duvet.

A lot of riders would never have had dogs in the first place. Shane Sutton told Laura in strong terms that he disapproved. Pets are not the done thing in the cycling world, because what happens if one gets ill, or needs more exercise than you do, or licks your face after licking another dog's unmentionables? The two of us were different. We always said that cycling would never take us over so completely that we had nothing else in our lives. It wouldn't dictate us. Cycling isn't life; it's part of our life. We wanted a dog. He turned out to be a little terror, so we had to get another one.

Sprolo and Pringle certainly made things more testing for us. When we were away training or racing and my mum was looking after them, we told her not to contact us if one ran away or fell sick. We couldn't fly back, so why find out? When we were at home, Pringle went through a spell of waking us up at 5 o'clock every morning. Waking me up, at least. Laura bought and erected a small fence on her side of the bedroom floor so he couldn't get close to her. Instead he would come round to my side of the bed, wake me up, wait until I went to use the toilet and then jump into the warm spot I had just vacated. Cheeky thing.

Your relationship becomes both your great rock and your go-to stress-ball as an Olympics draws closer. When we argued, I knew that Laura didn't really mean half the things she would say; I had experienced precisely those pressures and disappointments. Had I been a plumber rather than a track rider, if I were just sat at home getting that abuse all the time, I'd be thinking, 'This is not the kind of relationship I want to be in.' Instead I would try to listen, knowing that having each other was so much better than going through it alone. If one of us was training or racing better than the other, it didn't matter. We had both been successful and we both had natural dips.

We had to learn how to argue. That might sound strange, but the rows in my family were always big and loud and then done. I would get big and loud with Laura, but rather than the instant resolution I'd been brought up with, she would hide away and brood. Simmer for a while, write me an essay on text message or WhatsApp and keep it going. Think of it as sprint versus endurance once again. Alternatively she could just cry, and I would instantly crack. The trump card that every girl has.

**LAURA:** It takes a lot for Jason to properly blow. I do a lot of grumping but I never really lose my temper. With an Olympics on our minds it was good we understood that, because there was suddenly tinder for rows everywhere. It's always the small things, in every relationship: me never hanging my bike up on the hooks on the garage wall, me using the garage floor as an extended cupboard rather than as a macho working environment as Jason believes it is. One of my sponsors was round at the house doing some filming. I let them leave their gear in the garage, and there was a lot of it. Cameras, furniture, lights. Jason went out for a ride, being shy, planning to hide in the garage when he got back so he didn't have to try to make small talk and fail with a group of strangers. He opened the door and found a woman standing on the only square foot of floor that wasn't already piled high. 'My garage! What are you doing in my garage?' The poor woman was terrified. Jason went to the bedroom and sulked.

Small things that everyone can relate to. Olympic gold medallists also argue about whose turn it is to do the washing-up. Jason will crack first. I wash the clothes, Jason hangs them up afterwards. Or rather, I'll put the clothes in, not tell Jason, forget they're in there and leave him to discover them going mouldy. Frequently I'll use the tumble-dryer, shrink his favourite clothes and then take them as my own since they now fit nicely.

In the last few weeks before we left for Rio, the tension would erupt in fresh ways. Out on a road ride together, me having to do a certain number of faster reps, Jason on an easy spin so as to not strain himself.

Me, angrily: 'For God's sake, just push on!'

Jason, sighing: 'Stop half-wheeling me.'

Me, trying to ride off: 'Yeah, I am half-wheeling you, because we need to go faster ...'

Normally, cycling manners would dictate you stay together,

not force the pace up to something one rider doesn't like. When the pressure builds, manners can go out of the window.

Take evening meals. 'Well, I can't do it because I'm doing my packing.'

'Well, I can't do it.'

'Well, we just won't eat then, will we?'

My teammates had partners who were happy to sacrifice their own summers for them. Making tea, cleaning up, kipping in the spare room. With only one cyclist in the family I guess it's easier for the other one to be more of a carer. Unlike us. Neither of us could give. At one point I needed my turbo-trainer putting in the boot of the car.

'Jason, I can't lift it. Do it for us, would you?'

'I'm not putting that in the car. If my back goes then I'm out of the Olympics.'

Marginal gains, marginal losses. You think about everything and anything, and anything that is going to injure you isn't happening. In the end I bought a second turbo-trainer so I could leave one at home and one at the track. It was worth the couple of hundred quid rather than risk a pinged muscle or tweaked fiancé.

**JASON:** My build-up for Rio had started early, ten weeks out. As always, I tried to peak slowly, but as always there was the worry that you've peaked too soon. I tried to take comfort from the memory of being exactly the same before London 2012: three weeks out, setting new PBs, thinking, 'Isn't this too early?' An Olympics can turn every normal emotion back to front. If you were going slowly you would have every right to be anxious. Instead you start cracking out great sessions and it's almost worse. People are so scared of going well that they end up doing some hard sessions to knock their fitness back down, tire themselves out and get hurt. I had to keep referring back to our training programme and trust that when we wrote it, it made sense, so it still made sense now.

In our last week in Manchester I did one epic flying 200 metres that felt fantastic. Then we went to Newport for our usual holding camp, and I had a tiny dip – a few more worms wriggling in the mind. Then a couple more great flying 200 metres, even without full new Olympic kit, which was expressly designed to make you go faster still. When I put the kit on, no further improvement. Hmm. But I knew the form was there, and I knew my team sprint partners felt they had it too.

It was a new trio, and not much was expected. Still Phil in man one, the strongest man in Britain, me in two, and then – after years of trying to find a replacement for the retired and now knighted Chris Hoy – young Callum Skinner as man three. At our try-out at the Worlds in March in London we had finished sixth in qualifying, outside the medal races and almost half a second down on eventual champions New Zealand. Callum had failed to make the medal races in the solo sprint. It made some suspicious souls wonder post-Rio how we could have improved so much in just a few months. Well, we did: we were learning how each other rode. And Callum was quick, even in spring: fifth in the sprint qualifying, only two paces back in flying 200 metres terms of what he would later hit. Within the team, we knew he was on an upward curve. More of the coaches were worried about Phil, although Phil was never worried about himself. He has unflappable self-belief, possibly more than any other rider in that track centre. Everyone would take the mick out of him for it ('Three tenths quicker on race day!'), but he always would find that form at the last minute.

A week until departure. I still didn't think I was going as well as I was before London, but I wasn't really worried about it. By that time you have done 99 per cent of the work. If it hasn't come off, it's not going to change. There's nothing you can do at that point to win the race; all you can do is lose it by messing up.

**LAURA:** I was worried all right. There was my form, and then there were our bikes. The development team would ideally like to give you your new kit the day before competition. That way they have the longest possible time to develop it. But we want it as early as possible so we can get used to it. This time, our Cervelo track bikes arrived with Rio only a few weeks away and then had to be sent back. When the second lot came, I was adamant that something was wrong with the front end. It was the Princess and Pea again. The engineers insisted the front end was in the right place, so I tried moving everything else around. By which point I'd lost sight of what my riding position was supposed to be, so I went back to my old bike. More doubts, just when I least needed them. I was going badly, and I couldn't tell whether it was the bike or my form. The one good session I had was on my old bike.

In the final week of the holding camp they finally got the set-up feeling good. I went out, rode the fastest two laps I'd ever ridden with the girls ... and the handlebar snapped. So too did I. I had already been teetering. I shouted at Paul, I shouted at head coach Iain Dyer. He was on the track, holding Callum as he and Jason and Phil put in a key effort. Pretty good test of focus, watching through your visor as your fiancée has a public hissy fit and starts shouting at the highest-ranking coach in the building.

That night I sent an email round to the whole team – riders, coaches, mechanics – to apologize. But I was at breaking point. Momentum is important in those last few weeks, and I felt I'd already missed sessions by going to race in Poland, crashing during a training session on the road, travelling all the way to Valencia from there, only to find Lufthansa had lost my bikes and then couldn't find them. And my outburst worked. Loads of all-nighters were pulled to get it right. When it came back for the third time it was perfect. If only my form had been too.

The team pursuit was always the one in which I was most confident, the one I was most comfortable with. In Newport I lay awake with one thought banging around my head: it's abandoned me. There were three or four efforts on the track that I couldn't even finish. I always finish. Am I sick? Have I eaten something weird, or changed something critical that I haven't spotted?

I was the only one of the squad going through it. Jo Rowsell Shand had two bad days when she got sick but then went well again. Katie Archibald was flying. Ciara Horne is always rock-steady. Elinor Barker is the most consistent rider and was already in race form. Even now, I don't know how my Rio form happened.

**JASON:** And then it was upon us. Rio, loud and lively, sweaty and dangerous, quiet and a little bit like a school dormitory

225

in the British section of the athletes' village. Men and women were not allowed to share apartments, no matter if they had been going out for four years, no matter if they were getting married a month after getting back to Britain. Instead, Laura and I had apartments opposite each other, me sharing with Callum and Phil, Laura with the team pursuit girls. It's not glamorous at an Olympics. Single beds, shared bathrooms. Secretly, neither of us minded. We were now ready for our own beds, and with Laura's penchant for talking in her sleep when anxious, I was sparing myself considerable earache. Her language during nightmares could be atrocious. She would suddenly sit bolt upright and shout, 'I don't want to paint the f***ing ceiling!' That was one of the more specific ones. 'F***ing Chris!' Which Chris? In the morning she would never know. Her dreams were tangentially related to cycling, but only in an unusual brain – once she woke up convinced she and Dani King were trapped in the cab of a campervan, claiming, even on being reassured to the contrary, that she could still feel the motion of the van. When she was younger she had shouted for her sister. In the absence of Emma in Brazil, I wasn't entirely upset there were a few thick walls between us.

It could still be sociable. We could pop round to each other's apartments during the day, sit on the sofa watching TV, eat each other's food. The girls were tidier. Callum and I shared a bedroom and were horrendous. A bed against either wall, a no-man's land in the middle with kit and bags everywhere. You inevitably take more to an Olympics than you actually need. You were also warned not to leave anything expensive lying around in case it got nicked, so you were always shoving stuff under the bed. I could tell the difference, even without a quick smell, between which piles were clean kit and which dirty, but to those walking in at a glance, all they saw were the piles.

**LAURA:** The village was a group of concrete apartment blocks right on the western edge of the city, a long way from the thrills of Copacabana and the iconic beach at Ipanema. Functional, clean, not feeling that Brazilian, but just fine. British flags hanging over balconies to mark our patch. The usual vast dining hall. A cycle path to take us cyclists from living quarters to velodrome.

The bathroom in Jason's apartment was between his room and the adjoining one. Three men and one bathroom is a bad sum. Phil had the other bedroom to himself because Jason and Callum would still be competing when he was done. The same thinking saw me get a room – an en suite – all to myself, across the corridor.

I kept mine like an icebox, partly because I could sleep better wrapped up in a duvet and partly because I was so terrified of catching the Zika virus. Because of that I also put up a mosquito net in a dome over the bed. It was over the top in more ways than one. No wonder Jason didn't want to stay over. As much as we're a couple, as much as you're in the GB team, when you're away your first priority is to look after yourself. I would tend to go over to the lads' apartment. I knew them well. Callum had been on the same Geoff Cooke sprint camp as me when we were fifteen. And we team pursuit girls weren't quite as welcoming to visitors, a team off the track as well as on it. We preferred to eat all our meals together, and were happy to spend our spare hours catching up and talking ourselves through any anxieties and issues.

The doubts were still there. Two days before team pursuit qualifying I still wasn't going well. Even coach Paul was starting to panic. We were doing a standing 2,000 metres, and I hit the front for my first turn and I couldn't do it. Literally 500 metres in, only a fraction of the distance we would be racing over. I bailed, the girls didn't finish. I came off and said to Paul, 'I'm knackered. I can't train tomorrow.' I was scared but I was also phlegmatic. Nothing I can do about it. It if comes, it comes. If it doesn't, who knows where it went?

One day to go. Paul persuaded me to train. A standing start, just as we would have to do on race day, just one turn on the front each. That didn't go great for us either, although I finished and felt a lot better than I had on the previous day. Katie came off the track and told us that if she felt like that the next day she wouldn't want to be in the team. Some of that was venting, some of it was genuine. She is naturally inconsistent and she knows she is. Her trend was to have a couple of bad sessions before race day then blow it out of the park on the big day. But because it was the Olympics, she couldn't see that this was her. Deep down we knew she would pull it out of the bag, and Paul made it clear to her. He sat us down and told us that he was not changing the line-up. What we had was what we would use.

**JASON:** They did love to wind themselves up.

On Wednesday 10 August, one day before the team sprint would kick the whole thing off, we sprinters just spun out our legs on the rollers. Anything more, anything approaching peak power, and we would risk taking too much out of the tank.

Our expectations were still kept in check. We had clocked 42.9 seconds across our three laps in training, which we didn't think would win it but knew was good. We were happy with that. I was just worried about hanging on to Phil. The start of a team sprint is all about your power to weight ratio, and I became obsessed with it. Everything had to be as light as possible; I even took the rubber grips off the back of my race shoes and replaced them with the thinnest strips I could find. Man one does the time everyone obsesses about. Man three finishes it. Man two is the glue that holds it all together, and at those Worlds in March I had let us split.

I didn't tell a soul about my doubts, certainly not Phil. When anyone asked me how we would do, I was bullish. 'We'll be fine, don't worry about it.' I was the most experienced one there, but I didn't see myself as a father figure, the way Chris Hoy had been for Phil in London. We all treated each other the same. I didn't feel that the other two needed any kind of guidance, even though this was Callum's first Olympics.

The final night: Laura with team pursuit qualifying the next afternoon, we three with our full team sprint competition. Laura's team loves a meeting. Paul Manning loves a meeting. She had priorities other than me.

**LAURA:** I popped round to Jason's, not just to say goodnight and good luck but also to tell him I was actually in the team. Between us girls we had always had a shared understanding that if you thought you couldn't play your part in the team, you had to forget about the medal and forget about being an Olympic champion. We had to be completely honest with each other: if by being in that team you were going to ruin the chances of everyone else, you had to pull yourself out. Had my scare come one day out rather than two, there is no way in hell that I would have ridden. Jason had been telling me not to worry, that he had a feel for how I was going. And that final day had gone better, for me at least. It was coming, however late. I could feel it.

I lay in bed. I was still far more worried about my race than Jason's. You put all the hard work into your own race, you want it to go well. The little secret that kept me cool was that we had already broken the world record in a session in Newport. The question was whether the track in Rio was a fast one. Nobody knew, because there had been no test event. In the few training sessions we had been allowed, the air was cold. Cold air is slower; it's harder to move through, more dense. Your legs feel crap. Then there were the dimensions. All tracks have their idiosyncrasies. If the air-con was on, it could feel like a tail wind on the back straight and a head wind on the home straight. What was the best line for us to hold?

**JASON:** The first morning of track racing at the Rio Olympics. The start of Laura's campaign to defend her team pursuit and omnium titles, the beginning of my attempt to win three golds in six days.

It all felt remarkably normal. A normal breakfast, a GB tracksuit, the usual early start because a sprinter's warm-up always takes so long. Keep the team together, Jason.

I didn't waste any thought on the New Zealand team: Eddie Dawkins, Ethan Mitchell and Sam Webster, the reigning world champions, the favourites for gold. Nor was I distracted by the amount of bike porn on display at an Olympics: new bikes, lighter wheels, new shapes of helmet. The mechanics love it, and ordinarily so would I. But at an Olympics you learn to ignore everything that isn't about you and your own speed.

Into qualification. Let's hit roughly what we were doing in training, plus maybe a little bit extra. And it worked. Form peaking, bikes working, the team one smooth unit rather than a splintering machine. We clocked 42.562 seconds, cleaning up our own Olympic record from London.

New Zealand were a tenth of a second down. Over three balls-out laps, that's significant enough to change all our thinking instantly. We're going to do what we did in London – we're going to run away with it.

We got ahead of ourselves. In the first round they turned the tables on us. This time it was the Kiwis who nicked three hundredths off our new Olympic record. That didn't last long.

We stayed calm; we were still into the final as second quickest. We had held it back a fraction in that second outing, and we got the sense that they had really gone for it, stretching things out as far as they could. I still wasn't totally sure that we could beat them. Three nice guys: Sam quite intense and a real top rider, maybe not yet with the results that his abilities deserved; Eddie, a big strong lad, all the horsepower in the world; Ethan, starting them off. Phil was angry, because Ethan had become the first man one to ride a 16.9-second opening lap at sea level; we all knew Phil could have done it, but there was no point, because the other two of us couldn't have stuck with him.

Ahead of that evening's final we sat down with coaches Justin Grace and Jan van Eijden. We decided not to change anything. New Zealand had looked to be at their limits, but they might have more left for the gold medal match. We decided we had no option but to go all-out. Although I again kept it to myself, at that point I feared we were relying on them falling to bits for us to win.

**LAURA:** In that gap between Jason's first round and final came our team pursuit qualification. I was really nervous. I threw up before the start – sat in the chairs waiting, threw up into my mouth, swallowed it, had no choice.

Our psychologist called us together for a pep talk. 'Everybody looks really relaxed, ready to go.' I sat there thinking, 'I've already thrown up.' As we waited to be called out I told Jo. She is always good. If there are nerves she hides them brilliantly. Whenever I've felt the butterflies start to kick I've called on her. She told me I'd be fine. It felt good to hear it.

I'd said to the girls at the start of the day: 'Don't make this an occasion. This is just another team pursuit. We do this day in, day out.' I felt like we were getting worked up about it not going right, just because it was the Olympics. Girls, we do this all the time. Then all of a sudden I wasn't listening to my own advice. It felt that if somebody had said, 'Laura, there's an escape hatch', I would have jumped down it in a flash. Which was madness. That's not me. Offer me an easy exit any other time before a race and my reaction would be the opposite: 'Why are you taking this away from me?'

I watched Jason's qualification from the track centre. I was less surprised than some others by how fast they went. I knew they had stepped up from the Worlds, and I was surprised no other team matched them. It also gave me a little kick: okay, this kit does work. Our taper looks good.

Qualification made me feel better. The form wasn't just there; it was fizzing through us. Every turn on the front perfect, every change textbook. Four minutes 13.260 seconds. Jason, we see you boys setting your Olympic record, we'll go one better with a new world record. A second quicker than the US quartet a place behind us, almost six seconds up on the Aussies in third.

Back to the sprint boys, expecting big things: despite the Kiwi comeback, their own qualification had convinced me they would bring it home.

**JASON:** Fifty minutes between first round and final. A warm-down, a process you are familiar with from so many other races, so many other training sessions. Clicking into our pedals, being pushed on to the track. Who's holding us today? Okay, that seems fine. A glance to my left at Phil, who had said after the previous round that he hadn't gone 100 per cent, and that now he was going to go 100 per cent. Thinking, 'Here we go, I'm going to have to turn myself inside out to keep up with him if he goes as hard as he can, but if I'm going that hard, Callum is not going to be at the back ...'

Waiting on the far side of the track, visors down, dark blue skinsuits with red cuffs, darker crest on our chests. Phil and I in white helmets with red and blue decals, Callum not matching, in a black one, because his head's too big and the white ones don't fit him; Phil on a different bike. Normally the lack of synchronicity would upset me. Not now.

We get away cleanly. First sensation: the gaps between us are perfect. I have to let Phil go as far as I dare to give Callum as much leeway as possible, but Phil has come good – he's going a fraction steadier, so we are links in a chain rather than in danger of rupturing apart, and if the Kiwis are up by a fraction, that's good because Sam may have gone too fast and left his teammates stretched and struggling.

We slingshot round the fourth turn, and I'm catching Phil at a rate of knots. My best lap of all, keeping it as smooth as always but turning myself inside out at the same time. I can hear the crowd noise echoing off the sides of the velodrome, as deafening with British support as if we were riding at home, but you know from the noise it's tight. Coming past the Kiwi coaches, halfway through my lap, halfway through the race, keeping the poker face so they get nothing from me except for, 'Us lot are smashing this, by the way ...'

Coming round my last corner, wanting to deliver Callum into his finale as quickly as possible, making sure I drive straight through the line. They've really tightened up on where we are allowed to change. I have to go right to the line before swinging out, so there's no more changing early if you've blown and no coming through early if you're feeling on fire in man three. All the way through the line and not showing Callum the inside, because I don't want to tempt him and get disqualified. Stay right on the black line and drive it straight through.

I come past our coach Justin as I change up the track and let Callum rip past. I am looking at Justin but I can't read Justin as well as I used to be able to read Iain Dyer – I could see in Iain's eyes if it was going well or not, but with Justin I'm in the dark, and then I look up at the board and I read it the wrong way and I think we're down. We're down.

**LAURA:** I'm back in the village. I'm watching it with the girls. I'm going mad. There's no point them trying to calm me down, because they're going mad too.

**JASON:** I still think we're down. In that adrenalized moment I can't make sense of the scoreboard. I haven't considered that we were starting on the back straight and so were the team at the bottom. I'm not looking at the GB or NZ next to the names, or the national flags, I'm looking at the time and I think we're down.

Up the top of the track, screaming swear words at Callum. It's pointless. He's a ball of exploding energy going away from me. My words are going nowhere but into my helmet. I'll be hoarse that night for no reason. I'm shouting for him to catch them, not knowing that we had delivered him slightly ahead, not realizing yet that, because we had been so tight all the way round, he was gaining even more time. Eddie Dawkins trying to pull it back, but he has had to work harder on that first lap, and here comes Callum again, and this time there's no getting that board wrong.

Great Britain: 42.440. OR. Olympic record. New Zealand + 0.102.

**LAURA:** A few miles west of the velodrome, a tidy apartment in the village goes nuts. And I burst out crying.

**JASON:** The celebrations at the track told their own tale: physio Phil Burt grabbing Iain Dyer in a bear-hug – and Phil Burt is built for giving bear-hugs; Justin bouncing, Callum thrusting his fist forwards as if jabbing an invisible opponent on the chin. Neither he nor Phil Hindes could get the Union flags that they'd grabbed from the stands open as they rode round. I was floating, across the track as always for man two, feeling the blow of the air-con so strongly that I didn't want to take both hands off the bars, floating along with one arm up in the air.

It felt like one of the great turnarounds. We had been on the ropes for so long, and we had come off them together in the one fight that mattered more than any other. Winning as a team, Phil reining in his first lap to get Callum on the back. And I can't tell you how much it would have hurt Phil not to have done his fastest lap when he knew he had it in him, having to forgo the one-man world record despite having the legs to do it. We were never the bankers for the British squad; we were the comeback kids, the trumpets to sound another British Olympic advance. After the first round I hadn't been at all sure we could find that extra little bit, and that was why this was a proper celebration, less a 'Thank God, we've done it' than 'God, we've done it!'

Up to the stands to see my mum, crying her eyes out as always. My brother there with his girlfriend, an actual cuddle from my dad, which happens about as frequently as the Olympics themselves. Gold medals bring a lot of man-hugs down upon you, a lot of backslapping. They also bring the risk of being handed a Union flag the wrong way up. Laura's okay: she can tell from the 'Go Trotty Go' painted across it. I ask my parents to make sure they deliver it properly. By your third Olympic Games you've worked these sort of small details out.

And that was the end of the celebrations. One gold medal

attempt down, two to go. Phil could go out to party, but with Callum and me going again in the individual sprint one day on, recovery took precedence over rock 'n' roll.

**LAURA:** When the tears had dried it was time to push Jason's gold to one side. When a team that's just done so well comes back to the village it lifts the whole team, staff as well as riders. The buzz is there. But you have to focus on yourself. Your fiancé has just won his fourth Olympic gold medal, but you greet him with a wave rather than a bottle of champagne. Had they lost that final instead of winning I would have been gutted, but I couldn't have let that leak into my own mood. Steve Peters always used to say you shouldn't use emotions. Well, if a positive emotion is there, then that's a good thing and you can let yourself get a bit caught up in it, for a little while at least. But if a team comes off the track that's not gone so well, you have to put your guard up. There'll be time to kick back later.

One day for us between qualification and the heats and final. Never before had we had a day off between rides, and it was a little unsettling. Our physiologist Len wanted us to do a hard turbo session. I hadn't totally bought into the idea before Brazil, but after a few days there I'd realized that the only thing that made me feel good was to keep pushing on the pedals. Len's sessions had been great all through our months of hard work, but the one he suggested this time was just too hard.

It wasn't easy to convince him, but I knew I was right. Instead I did two fifteen-second sprints and one minute at power. That was it. Paul, as a former rider, understood. There is training protocol and there is listening to your body. His only question was whether we tweaked our line-up for the final. Was one second a big enough margin? There was enough evidence in our training data to suggest Ciara could have stepped in for someone if needed. Equally there was enough to suggest we didn't need to change. What would our rivals least like us to do? Stick with a quartet that had just broken their own world record in getting to the final, that's what. So that was what we would do. It worked in the semi-final, when we took more than a second off our qualification time, and we had to believe in it again.

It would be the US up against us once more in the final. Sarah Hammer, Kelly Catlin, Chloe Dygert, Jennifer Valente. I felt it was going to be close. There were no mouth vomits as we went on our turbos in the track centre to warm up, but you are suddenly aware that this is the last connection you will have with your riding legs before the gun. We had decided: no matter what happened, if you couldn't stay on the front, if you were going to slow the team down, just get out of the way. Forget the pre-planned strategy of who should be on the start for how long. If you couldn't handle it, let someone else through.

Helmets on, out in the bright lights. Pale brown track, yellow and green stage dressing all around the arena. All that frantic activity in the centre of the track, the mechanics and coaches, the television interview points, all suddenly quiet.

No thought of, Oh my God this is the Olympic final. Just the sensation: my hands have gone numb. Oh. Now? No looking round for my parents, although I do know where they are, because this settles me down.

Another thought: we've a little energy left in the bag here. We had benefited from getting in the slipstream of the opposing quartet in the qualification, but the time had still felt easier than it should have done. If our line and changes were perfect it would take something beyond perfection to beat us.

Jo leads it out. I get on her wheel. It's up to me and Jo to set it up, because by the time man three hits the front, we're already a kilometre in. Past Paul, and he has stepped away from the centre line. We're up. On Katie's first turn it feels really light, and that can only mean we are shifting. There are other little clues – the sensation as you flash past Paul, the feeling that your legs are flying beneath you. The noise from the crowd rising and rising, the track commentator shouting. You learn to watch out, too, for the false leads. Sometimes the other coach will start walking up to fool you into thinking his team are up. I've had Sarah Hammer's husband, one of the US coaches, actually shout, 'Go on Sarah!' into the space behind my rear wheel as we flash past, trying to get me to think she is behind me getting ready to catch me. I've had him look at my bike as I go past him on the track and mutter, 'That's a big chain ring for a little girl ...'

Save it. We're riding a little bit up the banking, not the absolute shortest route around the track but it doesn't matter so long as everybody follows. This way you travel fractionally further but the superior drag you receive saves you so much more in the legs.

The US have started fast. Dygert, their man three, has been a heroine in the first two rides. As a junior she won the world road race and time trial in the same year, and she has pulled huge turns to get them this far. Trouble is, they've burned her. She's got nothing left.

They had to go out hard. It was their big gamble. Get out hard, try to get a slipstream, hang on to it. It had paid off at the Worlds and it could have paid off here if the effort of chasing them down had broken us. With Dygert at the front in qualifying they had surged every time she took a turn, and it had only been in the final two laps that we pulled away. So this is brave. It's not settling for silver. It's death or glory.

They've gone out hard, but we're in front. Now their turn lengths at the front are getting shorter. They're going half-lap, half, half. We are keeping it together. I do a lap and a half, but more important is that we're keeping pace. None of us is dropping off.

A glance over, and I can see them. I know we are winning, but not for a second do I think it's over. It only takes Elinor not to get back on the line after a change or Jo to be thinking, I can't hold the wheel, and that would be it. Jo could drop, and that would leave us with three, which is all we need: your time is taken from the moment your third rider crosses the line. But if she goes and El is suffering and we split to a two and a one, it's gone.

Instead El brings it home. Two laps to go, and I know we've won it. Keep it light. Stay together. Push push push.

A roar from all around. Another world record: 4:10.236.

The emotion hits you straight away. I just scream. I deafen myself by screaming, because the helmet is so tight it's pushing against my forehead and giving me a headache.

It has come together. After the disaster at the Worlds, where we only got bronze. After all the rides we have done that have gone crap. I knew we had it in us, but for the first time in two and a half years, one has gone perfectly.

I went straight over to my parents. I just remember my mum screaming in my ear. My dad was crying his eyes out. They always grab me really hard as well. Paul, so relieved, because he had seen all the bad days. He would put on a confident exterior, but I am close to him and I would speak to him, and I know that there is doubt there sometimes.

I loved winning with those three girls and seeing their faces in our moment of triumph. Such joy and happiness. I get asked which Olympics means more. They are so different and I guess there's only one first time. I also missed having Dani there – we had lived together, the two of us both new to the programme. We did silly things together. Now I was twenty-four, living with Jason, living out in the sticks. I had done a lot of training on my own, and both those inside and outside of the team looked to me to be the leader. I was a different woman.

But it still felt golden. That scream echoed on. We had done it again, despite it all, despite all the fears and panics and what ifs. And I had more to come.

# Twelve: **Together But Apart**

**JASON:** I had watched Laura and the girls, but not as most fiancés would. While she had been trying to get that rest day right between team pursuit qualifying and her first round, I had been back on the track for the flying 200-metre qualification of the sprint competition.

Now I was certain the form had come. You couldn't ride the way we had in that showdown against New Zealand and then lose it overnight, and with that form came confidence. There was no tiredness in my legs, no pressure in my mind. It was as if those intervening four years of near misses and big defeats had never happened: the fastest man in the field, 9.551 seconds, an average speed of more than 75 kph. It was an Olympic record, which was a pleasant surprise to me but no shock at all for Chris Hoy, watching it all for BBC Television, who had seen the first run-out in the team competition and declared off-air to one lucky cameraman that he should put serious money on a Kenny clean sweep.

Callum too was carrying that speed into his next challenge

– second fastest in qualifying, ahead of Australia's Matthew Glaetzer, ahead of old campaigners like Russia's Denis Dmitriev and good old Grégory Baugé.

After that the first and second rounds just flowed: past Germany's Maximilian Levy, past Colombia's Fabián Hernando Puerta Zapata the next morning. All that trying and failing, those meals not prepared standing up or the dogs left to walk themselves, and it was all paying sweet dividends.

Into the quarter-finals at 4 p.m. that Saturday afternoon, Laura's team pursuit final an hour later. Focus on the race in front of you, not someone else's still to come. Aussie Patrick Constable beaten 2–0, straight sets, and I still couldn't give Laura's final much thought. I had to warm down, rehydrate, warm up again. I had a few worries for her – the US had come from nowhere at the Worlds and dominated, and the girls had failed to get their best ride out. If the US started strong again it could go the same way. When, instead, our girls ripped out the first 500 metres and then the first kilometre, I knew they would never relinquish it. All those hours in Laura's company, the counselling, the cooking, the washing-up and the rows about washing-up, and in the four minutes that made it all worthwhile I had to be less emotionally involved than a stranger who had never met her, as if I was watching it all on TV back home.

I don't think that potential distraction was the reason I hit my first speed bump in the semi-final. I knew Dmitriev would be a challenge but it never crossed my mind that I wouldn't beat him; I had been so much faster than him in qualifying. Maybe I was under-geared. Maybe I misread it, but he rode it perfectly. It just shows it doesn't matter how fast you are going, it is never a given. I knew he had a big gear on his bike and would be strong, but if you've got a big gear on, you want to be high up the track so you can use gravity to get it turning. When we were instead both on the black line at the bottom of the track I thought it would suit me, yet he just shot past me.

There had been a few fruity rides up to that point, but this was the first time I hadn't had an answer for what a rival had thrown at me and, to be honest, it left me shaken. The best-of-three format meant I would have to win the next two; one more slip, one more untethering of those horses from Dmitriev, and I would be left scrapping for bronze. You don't have long between those heats, and heated it became. Down there in the track centre, understanding how dangerous it had become, I bit Jan's head off. His point was simple: I needed to go harder at an earlier point in the race. So was mine: I was already going flat out. I couldn't go any harder.

You calm down and you think about it. I don't panic. I don't believe in nerves. What he was trying to get across was that I needed to start my effort earlier. I had qualified considerably faster, so the logical decision was to use that speed. I put on a fractionally bigger gear and made my decision: I am going to go really, really fast. From the front or from the back, I'm just going to make sure it's a whirlwind for him.

I started from the back, left a big gap with a lap and a half to go. I could tell he had a thought about going for a long one, going early with most of the race still to come, but he didn't commit to it, and that suited me fine – I could drive into that gap with everything I had, use his drag, use my speed. And I knew as I closed in that he had spent his biscuits. His strength versus my speed, my speed winning out.

The decider. I had to lead this one out, and that made it harder. I had to make it harder still for him, make sure I got loads of height, keeping the pace up, never giving him the chance to make that jump. If I kept the gap there I could swing high, and as he closed in I could swing back down. He needed that gap to overtake, for otherwise he had nowhere to go. It worked out. In the end he couldn't even get close. Into Sunday's final I would go, a night to sleep on it, a night to get it right.

**LAURA:** Watching but not watching. Jason's quarter-final had come less than an hour before my final, and I had been getting changed into my racing kit. When the semi-finals came around I was trying to get through the mandatory doping control all gold medallists have to undergo. In a team event it can be hard to know whether the individual is going well or if it's the team that's got you there. His qualification had made me hopeful. The first heat of the semi had made me anxious. With my omnium starting at 11 a.m. the day after next, Monday, I had to abandon him to it.

It was one of those nights when elite sport can feel like the loneliest profession in the world. My three pursuit teammates had gone straight out to celebrate, and I wouldn't see them until the next morning. You feel left out, almost jealous that their competition is over when you have to race on. You spend your life trying to get as many rides in as you can, fighting for the right to ride on the biggest stages. And then it can all be over after one day, if you are just doing the team event. The girls were kicking back and moving on. But I had to switch back on for the next race, when it started all over again.

**JASON:** That semi-final had thrown me. I wasn't anticipating being beaten in my first race against Dmitriev that way, even if we had then got it right. Even more unusually, when I woke up in the athletes' village that Sunday morning, my final opponent was snoring in the bed next to me.

Just as I had in Beijing at my own first Olympics, Callum Skinner had followed up team sprint gold by reaching the individual final too, and had come past Glaetzer in his own semi-final without recourse to a third heat. It was reminiscent of me going up against Chris Hoy, eight years before: the kid versus the champ, the outsider against the established force. When two teammates race each other the coaches say, 'We're just going to let you do your own thing, you pick your gear, pick your tactics.' You would even swap which coach pushed you to the start line to ensure the team's strategy was as fair-handed as possible. At least, with sharing a room, I knew that when I hadn't been sleeping that night he hadn't been sleeping either.

Seeing the man who was trying to beat you to Olympic gold walking around in his pants and brushing his teeth should have been disconcerting. So should have been sharing a bathroom. Ought one of us attempt to gain an early advantage by elbowing the other out of the way in the race to the toilet, or leave that smallest room in the least pleasant state possible before the other had to go in?

Instead, the familiarity of all those morning routines rendered everything rather normal. Breakfast together, as we had done before the team event, lunch together. We talked about Jess Ennis-Hill's silver in the heptathlon, we discussed Greg Rutherford's long jump bronze. We debated

Andy Murray's chances against Juan Martín Del Potro in the men's singles final later that day. The only weird aspect was that everyone kept telling us it was weird. Even Laura looked concerned when she bumped into the two of us coming out of our room to set off for the track, although that was more because she thought we both looked wrecked, having slept so poorly. She had messaged me the night before to tell me that I was going to win easily, but I wasn't so sure – that semi-final, the fact I knew the times Callum had been clocking in training, that he was going faster than I could go in certain efforts.

Training also gave me the advantage of knowing his tactical preferences inside out. It wasn't so much that I knew what he wouldn't want me to do, but that I suspected he would struggle to decide what to do. I thought I would struggle if I was him; even in retrospect I'm not totally sure what I would have done in his shoes. Callum's strength is the long sprint. So how was he planning to race someone who is faster than he is and could accelerate quicker? It made me think.

We didn't discuss the final on the way to the track and we didn't discuss it as we went through our warm-ups. All these habitual acts only added to the eerie sense of ordinariness: the usual coaches, the same mechanics, the established protocols for the last hours before a sprint final. I wasn't thinking about gold medal number five, or following on from what I had done in London or what Chris had done four years further back. By now, too, the Olympic Park felt familiar, the pale green livery around the velodrome seating, the shape of the roof when you glanced up and the brightness of the lights, the way crowd noise echoed around. The Rio 2016 logo blended into the background rather than nudging you in the ribs.

Pushed on to the track. Same dark blue skinsuits as when we had raced together rather than against each other. White track gloves for me, inadvertently giving me a rather butlerish air, rounded black helmet for Callum to squeeze in that giant Glaswegian head.

Callum has to lead the first one out. He doesn't want to. Quite quickly it opens up for me: I go for lots of height, he gives his own height up too easily and drops down too early, leaving himself a sitting duck.

He starts his acceleration and gets up to top speed fast, but he's still in a nightmare situation – I'm high, he's low, I've got more pace to come, he is flat out already. He needs to come back up the track to mess with what is even now looking like a certain outcome, but he doesn't.

At the bell I drop down and catapult into the gap between us. A hundred and eighty metres to go, and I know I've got it – all the momentum, coming up to him on the back straight as if I'm on a bungee, past his back wheel and level on to the final banking, ripping past him through the transition on to the home straight to sail past and away.

Race number two. No looking up to find my family, not getting ahead of myself and thinking how victory might feel. It's me to lead it, and I think about what I learned from that tussle with Dmitriev: trust my speed, get going fast.

I figure there's a strong chance that Callum is not going to want to take the front. I'm guessing he's going to want to stay at the back, make me lead out and die, because that's what I would do. And when, as we reach the final lap, the slow dance switches to quickstep, initially he has me in a bit of trouble – he's going fast and I have to react instantly, so I pick my point and go flat out.

He is closing in on me, and now I am turning myself inside out, trying to make myself as big as possible so he can't get round me. I want to be as aerodynamic as I can to make myself as swift through the air as possible, but I also want the airflow to be as messy and slow for him as I can.

He's coming at me, and I know without glancing back that he's there. I also know that this is not an easy track to overtake on because its shape means the transitions off the bends are short, and short transitions mean less speed off them, which is bad news for the rider trying desperately to come round the outside.

Callum tries to come round. He can't. He can't.

I am the champion.

Just 9.916 seconds for my final 200 metres, the fastest I've ever done.

After five gold medals you'd think you would have worked out how to celebrate, but this one felt different to the others. One hand out, that white glove now slightly regal as I let it flutter at the spectators as I swing past, but I didn't want to cut loose; I had just beaten my teammate. Instead, it was thoughts of my brother's girlfriend that filled my mind, albeit with the best possible intentions. Andreea was miffed not to have made it into the television images broadcast back home in the UK of the celebrations after the team sprint, so I was under firm instructions from Craig: if you win another, make sure she gets some prominent hug time. Next in my vision: what appeared to be the world's biggest Union flag, thrown from elsewhere in the crowd. I remembered seeing sprinter Ryan Bayley stood on the fence of the velodrome in Athens after winning keirin gold at the 2004 Olympics, silhouetted against the crowd and with a huge Australian flag behind him. He had looked so cool that I thought I should replicate the image. Call it a homage. Everyone there – Mum and Dad, brother, the coaches and mechanics and physiologists who had made the solo gold a team affair – everyone there except for one twenty-four-year-old woman.

**LAURA:** Back in the village, jumping around. Jumping around and then bed, on my own, into the mosquito net. I'd sleep to get in before the next morning's omnium. I sent a text before lights out: 'Jason, you're my hero xx.'

**JASON:** I missed Laura that night. I had a million texts on my phone, and I wanted to share it all with her in person. She was probably only seven or eight bike lengths away through those painted brick walls, but she may as well have been a thousand miles away. One of us now with two gold medals, the other with one and about to begin the hunt for another. We had done everything together for the past four years, never spent a night in separate beds when under the same roof and not competing, been both a support and an inspiration for each other. In the eye of the hurricane, we would have to be apart.

Lying there with the adrenaline and emotion of the final rattling through me, I couldn't sleep. There was a man in the bed a few feet away from me who I'd just beaten to Olympic gold. When Laura had been in bed by herself after the team pursuit final, she had tweeted a photo of her tucking her medal under the pillow. I put mine in my pants drawer. The time for reflection would come later. Two more days, and we could be together again. The first three events in Laura's omnium on Monday, the last three interwoven with all three rounds of my keirin on Tuesday.

**LAURA:** When you're racing the omnium, you need to start the day well. A breakfast of porridge, eggs, avocado and salmon. You don't get that in every apartment, but you do when Mark Cavendish is in town to ride the men's omnium. Cav does not believe in compromise. He makes sure the fridges are stocked to his satisfaction. If I benefited from that, using the massage bench as a table that morning, that was just fine.

I rode the few miles from village to velodrome with Paul Manning. Keeping it normal, not talking about cycling, dealing with my cycling worries by talking about anything else. And there were worries there. I had the team pursuit gold under my pillow, yet the knawing feeling came that the other three girls had carried me. They would have denied it. Paul would have denied it. Jason would have put me right.

The scratch race at 11 a.m. Jan van Eijden sits me down. When you need Jan, and I did, he always tells you the right thing. 'Laura, just remember you're a racer. The minute you get that number on your back, you will be fine.'

Paul and I had already decided the tactics. Put on a big gear, let me lead it out. The scratch race can look complicated, all eighteen girls on the track at the same time, but it's the most simple one of all – who crosses the line first wins – and that's how I try to keep it: simple. I was confident that once I got myself to the black line, they had to get round me. When I make that move with a lap to go, I hit it flat out and the gap just opens behind me.

Belgium's Jolien D'Hoore behind me, Sarah Hammer behind her, Annette Edmondson further back. My only worry was the one girl ahead of me, Belarus's Tatsiana Sharakova. I knew she was strong, but her results over the years had always been really inconsistent. When she lapped the field to give herself maximum points, she did it on her own. That's hard to do. But I had the legs on all the other girls, and I was mentally in a much better place to hold them off, and that was the order it stayed.

Down into the track centre to watch it back with Paul on his laptop. I saw the gap I opened on the other girls, and I thought: Laura, you're going all right.

The ride back along the same route that had seen me so stressed just a few hours before now saw me transformed. A smile on my face, the wind at my back. Lunch in my room all on my own. A lie-down, a sleep. A stressed woman does not sleep.

The individual pursuit at 4 p.m. I rode back in with Paul again. This time we did talk cycling. 'Laura, I think you're going to break the national record.' No wobble on the road and no wobble in the mind. Okay. Paul thinks that. I'm believing, at last, in my form.

No need for Jan this time. Lining up on opposite sides of the track to Sharakova, because she and I are one and two in the standings after the first race. We push away, and every time I come past Paul he's taken another step. I'm not just up on Sharakova, I'm eating into the gap between us.

Lightning is not going to strike in both the morning and

afternoon. If she was strong in the scratch, she is in pieces in the pursuit. After four laps I can see her ahead of me. Four laps further on and I go flying past her. The effort of it all hits me then, because suddenly I'm out of her slipstream, but I keep tucked and low and tight and fast to the finish, and then I look up and ... three minutes 25.054 seconds?

That can't be right. I've never gone that fast. I feel sick, but then you always do at the end of an effort like that. Sharakova, more than twelve seconds back, out of overall contention – and Hammer, after her race, more than a second back: Hammer who owns the pursuit, Hammer who I've never beaten in an IP. Where did that come from? Now Paul is all smiles, and so am I. 'Told you that you were going to break the national record ...'

The omnium offers little rest. Just over an hour later, out for the elimination race. The devil is back. And me and the devil – well, you know the story now.

It works out exactly as it should. Every two laps I am exactly where I want to be, and exactly where rivals wish I wasn't. There is one shaky lap, when for a moment it feels as if some of the other girls are trying to run me off the track. I look up and see the ambush happening just in time, and I squeeze under the riders coming over the top.

And then I just ride round. It's the Olympics, and I'm actually enjoying every pedal stroke. At the absolute pinnacle of my sport, I'm having a whale of a time. No longer is this pressure. It's fun, just as it was at Friday-night track league in Welwyn, just as it was when I was fourteen years old and on a bike my dad had saved up and bought for me.

Riders keep dropping. I keep coming through. When there

are three of us left – me, D'Hoore and Hammer – it feels simplified rather than troubling. If one of them goes out hard now, I'm on it. There is no way I'm going to get trapped on the inside. If you're trying to squeeze me in there, I'll slow down and then come round you.

Hammer drops. Me and D'Hoore and two laps to go. Jason, watching as a sprinter, must be shaking his head: she's an endurance rider, coached by endurance coaches, and yet at this point it's just a sprint. If someone tries to take me to the top of the track, that suits me all the way. I've got that power in my legs and they haven't.

I keep my speed. She keeps her speed. Mine is faster. Unless my legs blow, I'm away.

They don't. The race is mine, too.

Three events down, three events to go. I have had a second place, a first and a first. Thirty-eight points from the scratch, 40 from the IP, 40 from the devil. A halfway total of 118, D'Hoore on 110, Hammer 108.

Another ride with Paul, this time back to the apartment. Happy again, although you always want more, you always want a bigger gap. But it didn't matter, because I knew I had two of my best events to come.

One more day, two more golds for us to challenge for. One more day.

# Thirteen: **The Home Straight**

**LAURA:** I should have slept well on that advantage. Instead I lay there awake. Too much caffeine chewing gum that day to keep me sharp and focused for each of those three battles. I can't use the normal energy gels that most riders use. Anything with citric acid in it upsets my stomach, and I'll either be heaving or ready to heave.

When I did finally drop off, air-con on full blast, mozzie dome all zipped up, there were no omnium dreams. When I woke up on that Tuesday, a sketchy six hours later, the omnium was all I could think of. The 500 metre time trial in the morning, and the initial doubts about the bikes suddenly resurfaced. I don't want to use it, I don't want to use it. The sensible part of my brain was telling me it would all be fine. They had made the adjustments. The last run-outs had been fine. The handlebars were not going to break again.

But what if they did? What if a perfect omnium was ruined by an imperfect bike at the most inopportune time?

**JASON:** I felt weary on Monday morning. That day, as Laura had established her lead, I had gone out for an easy spin around the quiet roads on our side of Rio. There were no traffic jams on the western side of Lagoa de Jacarepaguá, mainly because few cars were allowed so close to the Olympic Park. We could follow the bike path set alongside Avenida Salvador Allende, south-west towards the coast and back again. Spin out the legs and then try to eat as much decent food as possible, for three keirin races in one day – having already raced hard on four of the previous five days – was going to take everything I had left.

My expectations were still in check. The two golds already in my underwear drawer didn't feel as if they carried all that much relevance for this last charge, because I would be coming up against some opponents who hadn't ridden the sprint or who had gone out early in that competition. They would be fresher, they would be totally focused. I had Germany's Joachim Eilers as the possible favourite, in part because he had looked so impressive in winning both the keirin and the kilo, the one kilometre time trial, at the Worlds in London back in March, and in part because I had seen him much more recently in training and he had looked good. He always did. I had no specific goal for myself beyond riding as hard as I could with what remained in the tank.

I wasn't like Laura. I didn't wake up thinking about it. I didn't even know who else was in my heat; although the draw had been made the previous evening, I felt no need to find out until I got to the track. I knew that seemed strange to Laura: she got so nervous about what lay ahead that she would almost overthink it, looking at old results to see who might jump into a gap in the points race, who she might want to steer clear of in the scratch. It was obsessive, but it worked for her, and what I did worked for me. My reasoning in the keirin was that it didn't matter who was in my heat. If you want to win, you've got to beat everyone anyway. So what was the point in thinking about it until half an hour before?

An ordinary breakfast on what would turn out to be an extraordinary day. Bircher muesli, eggs, an espresso from the machine in the carers' room. It had fuelled me before, so I trusted it to fuel me again.

**LAURA:** A wind had kicked up that night, which kicked on in the morning. Riding in with Paul, our familiar and practised route, we turned the corner into what felt like an invisible wall. I actually couldn't turn the pedals. Paul had to push me, an interesting look for a woman trying to become a four-time Olympic champion.

**JASON:** My first-round heat was at 10.15 a.m., Laura's 500 metres just under an hour later. During my warm-up I wasn't feeling great. It simplified my strategy further: take it on, lead it out, race against myself in the hope that it would be enough and I wouldn't have to ride in the repechage, the extra round that those finishing outside the top two in each heat would have to go through to reach the semi-finals.

It worked a treat. Me out top, Colombia's Fabián Puerta through in second, the rest – including Germany's Maximilian Levy, who had come so close to beating Chris Hoy in the keirin final in London – left trying to scramble through the back door.

I was straight back on my road bike and back to the village. Time to eat, time to rest. It meant I would miss Laura's 500 metres. At an Olympics, you sometimes have to be selfish. I knew she would understand.

**LAURA:** The 500 metres was horrible.

I committed to the new bike for this race. Even now I don't know what possessed me, given my fears before. Maybe I had got it in my head that it was faster because I had done one good start on it in training. But that was on a day when I ran a smaller gear, which will give you a better start anyway – it's easier to turn, and easier to get going. On this morning I had geared back up to give me more speed later in the effort.

My fear was that if I lost three tenths of a second by the halfway point, then there would be no way I could claw that back on the second lap. I should have gone with my gut.

I got out the start gate and straight away it just didn't feel right. I didn't connect at all with the bike. I had secretly hoped I was going to set another personal best, because everything across the first day had pointed that way. I knew Nettie Edmondson had clocked 34.938 seconds, and that was the time to beat, so looking up as I went through the line to see 35.253 secs next to my name was like a sharp jab in the ribs.

Gutted, but as my helmet came off in the track centre and the pigtails tumbled out, I could see silver linings rather than the silver-medal spot. It didn't matter that Edmondson had beaten me, because she had had such a bad start with her result in the scratch race. Much more importantly, D'Hoore was down in fourth and Hammer was fifth. Even in defeat I had extended my lead to 12 points over second and 16 over third.

I wanted more, of course I did. Had I bagged those extra two points by winning the 500 metres rather than coming second then it would have pushed the margin out to where my nerves wanted it to be. But it was the best I could have hoped for out of what had felt like a crap ride for me; not that it stopped me venting afterwards about that bike, as ever.

Paul got it in the ear. My parents got it in the ear. Paul in the track centre, agreeing that I should have gone with what I thought was best. My dad, all logic: 'It's done now, Laura, forget about it.' My mum, all maternal care: 'It's all right, love. It's going to be fine.' Mum, who texted me every morning to wish me luck; Dad, who had told me throughout my racing life that they didn't care if I won or lost, that they only wanted me to be happy.

I had to get it out of my head, and I did. I couldn't ride the race again, so just let it go. And I knew I had a flying lap to come, and I'd already taken two tenths off my PB at the holding camp in Newport, so something special was in there somewhere.

**JASON:** Laura came bursting into my room, where I was watching the keirin repechage with Phil Hindes and Liam Phillips, our BMX rider. It was a proper hissy fit: the bike this, the bike that. 'I'm nip and tuck with that Belgian, this could be bad, Jason, this isn't good.'

After all these years I knew to let it blow itself out. Her lead was huge. Nip and tuck? It was beyond comfortable. Only in

Laura's head was it so tight that she had to worry about it. Have some food, have a cuddle. It's going to be okay. It's going to be great.

Her flying lap was scheduled for 4 p.m. My keirin semi-final was half an hour later. Twenty minutes after that would be the points race, the last of her six omnium disciplines. Sixty minutes after that, the keirin final, should I make it. Just over two hours left of our four-year Olympic journey, two gold medals there to be won.

We thought it would be two hours. How could we have known otherwise? How could we have guessed the recalls and recriminations that were to come, that those two hours would stretch out, and out, and that almost 12 million people back in Britain would be strung out too, waiting and watching and wondering.

**LAURA:** I wasn't being fearful; I was being logical. I wanted a bigger lead over D'Hoore and Hammer, because if I sat in on every intermediate sprint in the points race rather than going elbow to elbow with them, that lead would not be enough to guarantee gold. The points race was my shaky one. It was the one I had least confidence of all in. I wanted to know that I could lose a whole lap to one of my rivals, given the extra points you get for a breakaway that size, and still be okay. Make it safe. Make it certain.

This time Jason and I rode back in together. A little extra comfort, a little more like an ordinary afternoon in the cool and damp Cheshire countryside than a hot and sticky one in a city that looks like no other.

Back in the velodrome, all noise and big support and Union

flags once more. I know Mum and Dad have managed to get tickets, even if it was a little last minute, and I'm excited again now, because I love the flying lap and so I'm feeling confident. I'm over the 500 metres. I had done the 200 metres in 13.8 seconds in training with power cranks on the bike, slowing me down, and I had ridden a 13.9 secs on a bigger gear, too. For this race, I drop it back down, and as Paul pushes me off, the lead-in – the gradual wind-up and acceleration that precedes the bell and the start of those 200 metres – feels so easy.

I know that France's Laurie Berthon has done a 13.9. I know that Nettie Edmondson has done a 13.87. I'm going round, and I'm thinking, this feels easy … and I'm getting quicker and quicker and I drop, throw it all in, and I look up and oh my God …

It's the fastest I've ever gone: 13.708 seconds. Sarah Hammer's had a shocker: back in fifth with 14.08 secs. D'Hoore has had an even bigger nightmare – 14.19 secs, only good enough for seventh.

The big screen does the maths. D'Hoore now on 172 points, Hammer on exactly the same. They're tied for second. Me? I'm on top: 196 points. I'm 24 clear with one event to go.

I'm not even thinking about alternative scenarios. Now a messy head has it clear. I've got this. I've done this now.

**JASON:** I see it all as I warm up. I don't think it has affected me, and then I go out for my semi-final. Waking up feeling average again, the legs not really there in the morning. And now, speeding up behind the derny, it all suddenly seems as easy as it had for Laura a few moments before.

I know from a long way out that I'm going to win. I'm not

remotely worried about it. There is some serious talent in the field – Malaysia's Azizulhasni Awang, silver medallist in the keirin at the 2010 World Championships; Holland's Matthijs Büchli, bronze at the 2013 Worlds; Aussie Matthew Glaetzer, former team sprint world champ; Michaël D'Almeida, my old French friend from the team sprint final at London 2012. They can't trouble me. My legs have come back, and I tell Laura the good news: Laura, I could still mess this up, but I think I've got the legs to win it.

**LAURA:** A hundred laps until the end of the omnium. There is still a danger. If D'Hoore or Hammer can get a lap up on me during one of the intermediate sprints that come round every ten laps, it'll be worth 20 points to them. That's a game-changer. Maybe the Netherlands will gang up with Belgium to try to put D'Hoore ahead of the pack.

Five points on offer for the first rider across the line in each sprint, three for second, two for third, one for fourth. I think back to all the lessons from Chris Newton, a few years before in Manchester. Get a point on the board in the first race. Mark your rivals. Dictate, don't wait. And then the first sprint comes round, and D'Hoore and Hammer are watching each other rather than watching me. They lay off me, I pick up a point.

Second sprint, I pick up two more. Fourth sprint, two more. Then three, and then five. It has dawned on me that they're no longer interested in me. D'Hoore and Hammer are no longer racing for gold. It's silver and bronze that concern them. Instead of the woman in second place attacking to try to get the lap to close the lead on me, she's worrying about someone attacking her. They're almost tripping each other up. A lot of the time, they just let me go and I can roll off the front.

There's no need for me to chase it, no need to battle at the front for any more points. After eight of the ten sprints my lead over Hammer in second is 29 points. With fourteen laps to go D'Hoore has one final desperate dive off the front. Hammer goes after her. For a moment I worry about them stealing a lap on me, and then when I get the chase on I close the gap to them so fast I know that it's over. They're not escaping from me now. Not with these legs, not with this beautiful form.

As I pass coach Paul at the end of every lap I smile. I have nothing else to do. I can just ride round. Coming in to the last sprint, the pair of them scrapping like crazy for the other two places on the podium, I wonder if I should contest it too. The competitor in me raises her head. And then I think: That's not my fight. They can do whatever they need to do. Do what the hell you want for the last ten laps. It's already over.

It was relief at the end, not immediate joy, not instant tears. Relief that nothing had gone wrong, that I hadn't punctured, or had a mechanical and had to use a spare bike that I'd never ridden before. I hadn't been taken out by another rider. In training I had been crashing left, right and centre, and had I gone down again I would have climbed back on to the bike and finished that race if I'd had a broken leg or splinters in every inch of my back.

The best omnium I had ever ridden. Hugging Paul and shouting, 'We did it!' Pulling off my shoes and running across the track to Mum and Dad and another of their fierce embraces. Dad crying again. Mum with the trusty 'Go Trotty Go' flag. I'd made a big point of not taking that flag after the team pursuit, because we were a team, and I wasn't going to celebrate it as an individual. After the omnium I could parade whatever flag I wanted. Go Trotty Go it was.

Down into the pit where Jason was waiting. Tears now, into his arms. I didn't think about being the most successful British female Olympian of all time – I wasn't even aware. I didn't add up all our medals from the past five days or even work out how many we had together from the past three Games. I just wanted Jason. I just wanted a hug.

**JASON:** Glenda loves that flag; it's travelled the world with her, and it has never been lost. When Laura brought it down the track with her I kept a careful eye on where it went. Her carer Luc made sure it got stashed somewhere safe. Then came the cuddle, but it could only be a brief one, because Laura had to prepare for her medal ceremony and I had to prepare for one final race.

I didn't find it hard to switch my head from boyfriend to racer. I have done it so many times now that I don't have to think about it any more. Instead, I talked to coach Jan: about who was in the race, what each might want to happen. You can usually split a keirin final in two – the riders who will be frontrunners and the ones who want to be late chargers. One set will want to lead it out. The others want to find a wheel and get the late finish. It affects where you want to be. You don't want to be sitting on the wheel of someone who's going to be a late charger. You don't want to get in the way of a frontrunner and lose the chance of them leading you out.

Such tactics are Jan's real strength on race day. Once we worked our way through those scenarios, I didn't think about it again until I climbed on my bike. From Justin Grace came a nice little phrase that he used before every keirin I rode: 'React and then reassess.'

It helped get me in the right mindset. I had a few other little buzzwords to repeat to myself as Justin helped me on to the track. Be decisive. Be confident.

You are so physically close to your coach as you get clipped in to your pedals, and you need to be mentally in sync, too. If the rider is secretly thinking, I'm not sure I've got the legs for this, I'd better find a good wheel, and the coach is whispering in your ear, 'Come on, you've got this – hit out, take it from the front', then you'll do neither and go nowhere.

**LAURA:** I wasn't thinking about a sixth Olympic gold medal for Jason. I had started thinking like my parents. I cared so much about his success, but I cared more about his happiness. If coming away without a gold medal in this race would still leave Jason happy, I wasn't going to worry about a defeat.

Yet I was also thinking about perfection. This had been a flawless Olympics for us. Every final, a gold medal. Every race the champion. What if we could close it out in the same way? What if we could make it five races, five golds?

I had confidence in him, too. Especially after that semi-final ride; I could see it had all suddenly clicked. The legs were there.

**JASON:** Six and a half laps behind the derny motorbike, two and a half in a free-for-all when he leaves the track. The derny our pacemaker, a white and green electric bike ridden by a straight-faced man in a yellow polo shirt and white helmet, coming past us at 30 kph, gradually picking the pace up lap by lap, getting up to 50 kph and then stepping aside to let the real fun start.

In Japan, the home of the keirin, it's all about gambling. At the Olympics it's all about tactics: where to position yourself, who to follow or hold off, when to go go go.

There are six of us in the field. Büchli and Awang from my second-round heat that morning. Eilers, the reigning world champion. Fabián Puerta of Colombia, silver medallist at the 2015 Worlds; Poland's Damian Zieliński, the veteran, going for a golden handshake twelve years after his Olympic debut.

I don't know that BBC One is holding back its ten o'clock news. I don't know that millions of people who have absolutely no idea what the keirin is or how it works have been watching Laura's long night of triumphs and are now hanging on to see if her boyfriend can do the same.

All I'm thinking about is that, in his semi, Eilers had gone for it as soon as the derny had left the track. I'm thinking that it means he has the confidence to lead it out in this final as soon as the derny pulls out of the way and we go for it. If he's going to go, I have to make sure that I'm not boxed in on the black line. If that means sticking my nose out straight away, then so be it.

Held in my place on the track by Justin, his left hand on my bar and right hand on my seat-post. The gentle hum of the derny building up speed. Here it comes, whizzing up inside us. As it passes, the gun sounds, and into a brisk line we form.

Awang and Puerta at the front. That's fine. Me in third. Büchli next, Zieliński second from the back, Eilers at the rear. Awang and Puerta both want to lead this out, so I leave a little gap ahead of me so I have somewhere to accelerate into and follow them away as they come over the top. As soon as I see them step out, I have to make sure I am the first to react.

Getting up to pace now, the derny accelerating, everyone doing the same as me and leaving a little space. Here it comes. Here we go.

**LAURA:** I can see that Eilers is coming out. I'm thinking Jason needs to get to the front. Now I'm thinking, 'Hang on, they're going way too fast coming out of the home straight, there are riders up almost level, they're going too quickly compared to the derny ...'

Crap. The starting gun has gone off. That means a restart. A cold flush in my guts, because from where I'm standing, it looks horribly close. Horribly close to Jason crossing the derny's back wheel.

**JASON:** This had always been the rule: the derny leaves the track at the start of the back straight. Then that was deemed too vague, so they changed it to the pursuit line – the point where a team pursuit quartet begins their race. The point the derny left had been drifting back, and back, and throughout this competition the races have been kicking off earlier and earlier.

My immediate reaction when the gun goes is that no one has moved early. If they had run it on, no one would have batted an eyelid. I'm not worried in the slightest. If someone has gone early, it's not me.

A stare up at the slow-motion video replay on the big screen, and it all changes. It's really close.

**LAURA:** I'm watching the same replay from inside the track. I don't want to watch it any longer. I just want to know what's happening.

'Jan. Did he get disqualified?' I ask.

Jan is very unsure. Unsure whether it was the derny going too slow or the riders overtaking.

Head coach Iain Dyer into the pits. Iain getting our video footage.

**JASON:** Nerves. I don't let myself feel them. Panic. Not for me – not at the wheel of a spinning car at Brands Hatch, not in my first Olympic final in Beijing at the age of twenty, not now, eight years on, when a gold medal might be disappearing in front of me.

The logic, always the logic. These Olympics have already gone so well. Being a five-time Olympic champion has given me a deep and rich satisfaction. If it goes wrong now, it might seem like the end of the world to some. My world will go on.

The racer's logic too: if this gets restarted and I'm still in it, I need to be ready. Panicking won't help that. Pedal round, free the legs, prepare the mind.

Years ago I won a big keirin race, only to be relegated after crossing the line. The rider in front had swung out over the red line, I had launched down the inside, he had come back down the track, clattered me and then wiped half the field out. When I crossed the finish line I hadn't celebrated, and I had waggled my palm at my coach to indicate that I thought I might be in trouble. Afterwards he had given me a severe telling off. You've given the commissaires a steer. They might have let you go.

I remember that now, and I stick on a poker face instead. If I am pulled from this race, I'm not going to argue; they won't reverse it. But I won't hand it over on a plate, and I won't stop riding, even though my shoes are getting tighter, and the skinsuit's getting hotter, and everyone in the track centre is jabbering away like armchair experts.

I try not to look at the screen too much, try to keep my head down. Laura's face keeps popping up, and she looks terrified. Iain is arguing really well, and keeping a sneaky eye on the replay. I'm thankful he is; I can see that I've committed to Eilers' move, as I wanted to, but it is really tight.

It's a vague rule, and I don't think it's ever really been applied consistently enough. No matter. Those millions of people watching back home are getting a deep immersion in the minutiae of keirin racing.

I can't regret it. I knew I couldn't afford to hang about, and I knew I had to be aggressive. I did what I thought I had to. As I wait, as Laura slumps in her chair, as Iain jabs his finger at the officials' slow-motion replays, I think of what I'll say in my interviews if I'm pulled.

**LAURA:** They keep looking at the replays. They haven't got the right one. The officials have got footage from a head-on camera, but that doesn't show anything.

Up in the stands we've got two data analysts from British

Cycling, Will Forbes and Debs Sides. They have got footage, and it's side-on from across the track. Iain's telling the chief commissaire, an official from Germany called Alex Donike, that it's much too tight to be able to justify disqualifying anyone.

I'm staring at the pair of them. Donike nods. Iain nods too. Thank God. He's safe. He's in.

**JASON:** My poor mum. She must be in bits. She can't watch at the best of times, and that was almost the worst of times.

I'm actually a bit annoyed. I'm irritated rather than ecstatic, because they've fired the gun for no reason, and that race was going well for me at that point. It had been unspooling exactly as I'd wanted. With a restart everyone's got a chance to rejig and change strategies based on the way others have just ridden.

Justin doesn't say much as he pushes me back to the line. A little clean of the tyres. My concern is that the truncated race has in effect shown everyone each other's hand. Now that this is a fresh race, someone might sense an opportunity that wasn't there before.

In the event, however, it's like riding the same race all over again. Round goes the derny. Same order of riders, although Awang is being slightly more aggressive.

Same move by Eilers. Gun goes again.

Now I'm convinced that Eilers has gone. Why else would they fire the gun? A glance up at the screen. Hang on, why have they fired the gun? It's not even close.

**LAURA:** I'm not even slightly worried this time. If someone's getting pulled, it's not Jason. It's the most relaxed I've felt all day.

**JASON:** This has worked out for me quite nicely. I have been so patient in this race that I got jumped by Zieliński. I'd missed a move and might have ended up stuck on the inside with nowhere to go. Eilers had timed it beautifully: he was getting over everyone else exactly as he wanted.

Time to sit down, time to take the shoes off. Stay inside that skinsuit too long and you feel as if everything is expanding. Deep breaths, a brief meeting for the managers in which they're told that once again all the riders are in the clear. The poor derny rider is now probably concerned about the amount of charge left in his electric battery. The BBC must certainly be concerned, because they've put the ten o'clock news on hold for what they thought was going to be a few minutes, and at this rate it might have to be retitled the eleven o'clock news instead.

Back up. Back out. For a third time we are lined up for keirin gold. Puerta in white on the inside, Awang in bright yellow and black. Me in my dark blue kit, white lid and reflective visor, then Büchli on my right all in orange, Zieliński outside him in the red and white of Poland and Eilers highest up the track in his white top with the colours of the German flag across his chest. Dropping down on to the bars, a cheer going up from all around the stands as the derny begins its slow progress on the far side of the track and picks up pace towards us.

Exactly the same positions all over again. Awang to the

front, Puerta jumps on his wheel. Büchli sits behind me. Zieliński and Eilers, the big kickers, bide their time at the back.

Round we go, pedalling but frozen in position. The gearing I've chosen feels good. A hundred metres before the derny swings off, and Awang accelerates, and I move alongside Puerta so the late chargers behind me have to go the long way round.

Now Eilers moves, at the perfect time, and although I'm looking behind me for exactly that move, I'm still surprised by how hard he is going. He's almost caught me out, and now Zieliński is following his wheel too. I drop in behind the German and hug the black line. No extra distance for me, no wasting of what's left in these legs.

I think Eilers has just decided he can make it all the way. There is no point in him getting tangled up in a race he doesn't need to be in if he can lead it out.

Two laps to go, and now Zieliński throws it all in the pan. Straight over the top of me, straight past Eilers. I didn't know he was there, and I hadn't thought he would make this move, because round the outside is a long way to go. I have to make sure there is no gap between me and Eilers so he can't drop in there and mess everything up for me, and I've got to be aware if he's dragged anyone with him. No, this is solo. Now he doesn't have a choice because he's committed and has to find the black line, so all the way to the front he goes.

I'm going to sit on Eilers' wheel. He is the horse I've backed. I don't expect anyone else to have a go yet. Awang is backing me, so he's staying on my wheel.

The bell clang-clangs, and Eilers goes again. Out wide, out

past Zieliński, and the pair of them have gone so hard and gone so early that my confidence is surging. They're just racing each other. They're surely going to run out of gas.

Just 220 metres to go. I'm coming round the penultimate corner on the black line so I've got all the speed. I'm going to pop out on this back straight, and Eilers has made it easier for me because he's trying to get past Zieliński and now it's a smaller obstacle for me to get round.

A hundred and fifty metres to go, halfway down the back straight, and now I'm laughing. There is no stress, because they are all stacked up exactly where I want them to be. Eilers is the perfect target, and I am past Zieliński and round Eilers and here's the final bend, those two now at the back, and Awang is on my wheel but not close enough, and down the last stretch, orange inside me as Büchli makes a late charge, bumping into me, finishing really strong, but I'm home – driving it hard, bike shoved out in front of me, pushing my front wheel to the line.

There is no wheel ahead of me.

**LAURA:** I've got my hands pressed together in front of my face as if I'm praying. There are tears popping out from the corner of my eyes. Down the back straight I don't know if he's got it. Round the bend I think he might have. Through the final metres, I know. He's got this.

Jumping around and clutching my face. Coach Justin with his hands over his mouth, laughing in disbelief. Now the tears really come. Our psychologist Ruth Anderson grabs me and gives me a huge hug. The coaches are in tears. Photographers swarming, me dabbing at my face with the sleeve of my white tracksuit, whooping at Jason as he swings round the track with his arm out wide.

**JASON:** I'm so impressed with how Laura and the girls celebrate their gold medals. In that moment I always feel a bit awkward. All the attention on me when I've been locked into my race.

But I can't keep the big grin from spreading across my face. My target had always been the team sprint, because that was winning gold with my friends. The solo sprint was a beautiful bonus. And this keirin gold is the most delightful surprise on top of that already beautiful feeling.

I gradually slow down the revolutions. Justin looks shocked. Jan is so giddy he only just manages to catch me as I come to a halt. I climb off the bike, and here comes Laura.

We are laughing, we're looking into each other's eyes with happiness and disbelief. She throws her arms around my neck, and then we pull back for a moment, laugh again and steal a cheeky kiss. She's sweating more than I am.

**LAURA:** The first thing he says to me: 'Why are you crying?'
So British. So male.
It is over. But so much else is just about to begin.

# Fourteen: **Aftermath**

**JASON:** And so my night went from flat-out speed to slowed-down sleepiness. Everything felt as if it was taking forever: the pee for anti-doping, the getting changed into official Team GB podium wear, the medal ceremony itself.

It didn't matter that this was now the sixth time I had stood atop an Olympic podium and watched the Union flag go up: I still felt slightly uncomfortable. I never felt like crying, although I'm not too proud to cry; I just preferred having my teammates alongside me.

And then the real glamour kicked in. Cycling back to the village with Laura, desperate for some bad food after all that being good. Laura wanted McDonald's, but we were too late. It was shut, and the McDonald's in the athletes' village does not open especially for Olympic gold medallists, for otherwise it would never shut at all. Pizza it was instead, sitting there with our medals in our tracksuit pockets, and crap pizza it was too – we barely managed half. Champagne? The athletes' village is dry. There's no pub, no cocktail bar. You can bring in your own, but who would have dared to bring five bottles of champagne in with them?

To Laura's room, to try to sleep in her single bed under that mosquito net. It clearly wasn't big enough; it took all my core strength not to roll off on to the floor. Halfway through the night I cracked and went back to my own room. Back to all those stinking piles of kit, back to put one last gold medal into the pants drawer.

The day after, we had lots of media commitments. Again the boy from Bolton found the attention a little too much. Halfway through I started sloping back into the crowd of people being interviewed, hoping no one had noticed. Play it casual, play it cool, and before anyone knows it you're hidden in the middle of a lot of other people looking in several other directions at their interviewers and you're on your way out of the back door. A drink with our parents, and then I fly back to Britain – not aboard the specially chartered British Airways Boeing with the gold-painted nose cone, but as incognito as you can be when you're in full Team GB kit.

The day before, I had been a five-time Olympic champion. It was a good thought to have in my head. Now that I was six times Olympic champion it was like someone had flicked a switch. After a lifetime of carefully constructed anonymity, suddenly hundreds of people wanted pictures and autographs and selfies.

The satisfaction was a slow grower for me. Those achievements would take a long while to sink in, and they didn't change at all how I felt about myself. I didn't think I was suddenly a better man because I had now won as many Olympic golds as Chris Hoy and slightly more than anyone else. For me, making the list in the first place had felt fantastic. I found it more satisfying that I hadn't been a one-hit wonder, as I had always reserved special admiration for the champions who kept coming back to triumph afresh: Chris, Bradley Wiggins, Roger Federer, Steve Redgrave. When you spend so much of your adult life in elite sport, you develop an intense appreciation of how hard that is to do.

**LAURA:** When I was told I had now won more Olympic golds than any other British woman I was genuinely surprised. It also felt weird that I was on the all-time list of gold-winning British athletes. To me, the names I am ranked alongside are the greatest athletes we had ever had. To be among the people I used to idolize was maybe the most satisfying thing of all. The great shock was being on the list at all, and once on it you don't compare across events and eras. You just respect them all.

Everything that comes with success can still be a surprise. When we each got back to our little cottage in Cheshire from the heat and thrills of Rio, there were photographers camped at the end of our road waiting for us. They stayed for four days. Others hung around longer, or kept appearing in their cars at the end of nearby roads, pretending to be asleep in their seats when we stopped to ask them what they were doing. We had to live our lives with the curtains shut. We didn't dare leave our underwear hanging on the washing line after finally washing it.

As a sportsperson, you don't ask for such attention. We're not true celebrities. Celebrities want fame; we want gold medals. We understood the attention that came with the success and we didn't want to appear ungrateful, but it often felt like an invasion of our privacy. Frequently we felt trapped, sitting in the house on a summer's afternoon with the curtains shut. When I was on my own it could become scary, as if I had stalkers. When stories came out in the newspapers that just weren't true, I worried that millions of people might actually believe them. The story from 2012 that Jason had a child with someone else resurfaced. So too did the one that claimed that he had been married before. Jason's mum actually phoned to check, having read the reports. 'Is there something you haven't told me?'

**JASON:** You've come home, you want to relax, hang your laundry up, walk the dogs. Be normal. Instead, Laura had to go to our other house in Cheadle to be able to get a shower. When I had picked her up from Manchester Airport, it became a big deal in the papers. 'Man picks up fiancée in the car they own.' We thought of ourselves as cyclists. It was still rather startling to be seen as anything else.

Our wedding date was set, the invites had been sent out months ago. What we didn't want was the big day being mobbed by photographers and reporters. We had turned down an offer from a magazine that would have paid for five weddings, twenty if we'd stuck to my budget, because we wanted to keep the occasion for us, our family and our friends. The money would have been forgotten in a few years' time; the day never would be.

**LAURA:** I am the girl who used to pull my sister's hair. I am the girl who used to race her up and down my nan's road on our scooters. That's who I feel like now. Not a huge star, not someone for whom everyone in a pub should start applauding.

A girl who loves riding her bike, a girl who loves a boy who loves to ride one too.

**JASON:** Saturday 24 September, a day we had been looking forward to for more than a year and a half, a moment we had both been thinking about for much longer.

Laura woke up at Hilltop Country House in Prestbury, about eight miles east of our home, Emma there with her, Adrian and Glenda in another room. I was at my parents' house, preparing with the groom's traditional pre-wedding full English. The service was at 2 p.m. in Macclesfield, in the same church that I had been quietly sneaking into every Sunday for months. The thing about a big fry-up is that it leaves you unwilling and unable to move for a significant period afterwards. At 10.30 a.m. not a single one of us was ready: Mum, Dad, or my brother and his girlfriend. Cue a classic Kenny family fluster. Just get me to the church on time, would you, Craig?

**LAURA:** I was operating a tightly planned schedule, Trott-style. I only had a few more hours of being a Trott. Might as well do it properly.

All the girls up at 7.30 a.m. to get ready in Mum and Dad's room. Me starting my metamorphosis at 11, finishing at 1.30 p.m. Sprint versus endurance once again. Jason goes for the sudden dash; I let it go long.

I didn't want to be late for my wedding day. I'm all for tradition, but this had been years in the making, and everyone had told me how it goes so fast. I didn't want to waste a single minute. Even the opening of presents was scheduled in, and there weren't going to be many of those. We had asked instead for donations to be made to the charity Dementia UK. My nan had suffered from the disease, and Jason's nan was still battling it.

My parents, always fantastic, had outdone themselves in the weeks before. Flying my sister over from New Zealand, and always there to help with small details and big omissions. Part of my maternal nan's own wedding dress was sewn into the sleeve of my dress. Dad gave me his mum's wedding ring to wear as my something borrowed. My big day, but nothing without everyone else, a piece of all of them with me.

My hair was done by my friend Jennifer. Nails, in blush pink to match the dress, by my friend Lucy. Make-up by Hannah from the cosmetics company Bobbi Brown. Together they made me feel beautiful.

By 1.30 p.m. I was ready to go. My dad came into the room to see me and started to cry, the sight of his little girl all ready to get married too much when he was already wobbling on the edge. Mum looking absolutely beautiful in a lilac dress, Dad in a grey tweed suit to match Jason's dad and brother.

I didn't feel nervous at all. With my sister back by my side it was time. Into a car with Dad; Mum and the three bridesmaids in the one behind. Time to see my groom.

**JASON:** With half an hour to go, standing outside St Alban's in Macclesfield, I began to realize the gaps that my laid-back approach to life had left. I hadn't organized ushers. Laura's uncle, an obvious Trott, thankfully knew the score and got on the case. I had thought about enlisting my uncle, but being from my side of the family he arrived just five minutes before the start, so no luck there. One side of the church for family of the bride, one for family of the groom. No, hadn't planned that out either, or worked out how many copies of the order of service we actually required. Another task to hand across to the stand-in and surprised ushers.

I was also keeping one eye out for paparazzi. We wanted to be able to leave the church through the front door so we could take the traditional photos. If we were mobbed – and we had paid for security to keep them at bay – the back-up plan was a sharp exit to the rear. I was also slightly unsure how the security would work. You wanted it firm but you wanted it subtle. No one wanted to see an aged aunty rugby-tackled and pinned to the ground in a half nelson because she had moved in late from stage right with a handful of confetti.

**LAURA:** We needn't have worried. Our strategy of fibbing in media interviews about the exact date for our wedding ('Oh, not decided yet; probably next year, when it all settles down') had paid off. There wasn't a rogue photographer in sight.

We had kept it intimate. Sixty guests, Justin Grace's daughter Cadence (the other one's called Madison – that's what you get when your dad's an Olympic cycling coach) played 'Over the Rainbow' on her violin, accompanied by her friend on the cello, as I walked down the aisle.

The church was decorated simply with lanterns down the aisle, and we had compiled the order of service ourselves. Giggles when the one we were handed had two of the same page. I blame the Kenny side of the partnership.

**JASON:** I had wanted to drive ourselves to the reception. Laura had agreed, and I was going to hire a Morgan but – surprise, surprise – had never got around to it. At the last minute, a local company had stepped in and offered to lend us a car instead; Laura and I agreed on an Aston Martin. Very classy, until I received an email a few days before, saying they had been unable to get one. Instead, I revved up in the car park round the back of the church and appeared in a bright green Lamborghini Hurricane. Classier still.

Of course you test out the performance of a bright green Lamborghini when you've only got it for an hour. But, naturally, all speed limits were strictly observed. Relatively strictly, anyway.

**LAURA:** It was the most uncomfortable car I've ever sat in. You try getting in and out of a bucket seat wearing a one-off wedding dress. I had already put my foot through the front of it trying to squeeze into the car. I took it in good humour, I've been assured.

**JASON:** A secondary benefit to driving a Lamborghini to your reception is that you tend to get there first. It gave us time to have some photos of just the two of us taken, and to spend a few moments together on a day when we were otherwise trying to ensure everyone else had a good time.

Our choice of wedding banquet was entirely appropriate. Prawn cocktail to start, and then bangers and mash – three proper big sausages too, on a par with anything I'd ever rustled up on the bangers and mash nights we'd had to ban in the build-up to Rio. Pudding was the wedding cake;

the topper was a model of the two dogs, one dressed as a bride, the other as the groom. Pringle got the short straw as the bride. Well, he is already white.

The speeches brought a little of everything. From Adrian we had exactly the approach you would expect from an accountant: planned out carefully, written down in advance, straight from the textbook of bride's father's speeches. Whereas mine was exactly the approach you'd expect from a man who had forgotten to organize ushers: nothing at all written down, nothing prepared in advance, powered by five glasses of champagne in advance and then another chinned between being called to stand and actually starting to speak. I'm not quite sure what I said, but people seemed to be laughing.

As brother, like brother. Craig, my best man, also hadn't prepared a word. Realizing the potential for problems, we subbed in Emma, who had an idea for a speech, and she did a wonderful job: thanking the bridesmaids Dani King and Kristi, talking about how lovely my family were (triggering more tears from my mum), delivering all the emotion that the afternoon required. Between us, we nailed it.

**LAURA:** The first dance was a simple choice. 'Total Eclipse of the Heart', Bonnie Tyler.

We used to sing it to each other in the cottage, dancing around the kitchen using spoons for microphones. It works a treat. You can take a line each, even when neither of you can sing very well.

The dance itself was poor. We're really not very good, so we held each other and swayed a little, as couples on their wedding day generally do. No one came out on to the dancefloor to help us. I think they left us out there for laughs.

**JASON:** Afternoon tea was served from the back of a pink VW campervan, in time for the evening arrival of all those from British Cycling who weren't there already. A fair number of Olympic gold medals represented: Chris Hoy, Jo Rowsell, Dani King, Philip Hindes, Callum Skinner, Katie Archibald; coaches Jan and Justin and Paul, only Iain Dyer away on holiday; physio Phil Burt, Hannah Crowley, doctor Richard Freeman. We wanted a proper party and we wanted everyone to be able to let their hair down, which made it all the more surprising when Laura stopped it all to show a video on the projector screen of an artist telling the story of our relationship through the medium of sand. Not a staple of weddings for lads from Bolton. The dancing had only just got going and she wanted to chuck everyone off.

**LAURA:** It was supposed to be cute, our love story told in a different way. I think it went down well with the older guests, anyway.

That was the theme of the day: half-planned, half-winged. My dad spent most of the afternoon crying. Lorraine only paused occasionally. Pringle and Sprolo were dropped off with us before midnight, and we took them up to our room. A perfect day, and a perfect ending.

**JASON:** I felt more grown up on my first morning as a married man. I hadn't imagined I would feel different, but

I did, and not only because the feeling of a ring around my finger was so unfamiliar.

We already had a campervan packed. Across Sunday and Monday we drove down through England, crossed the Channel and then carried on through France. From the expressions on the faces of the other drivers, we must have been the fastest campervan on the continent. It's possible I may have taken the Lamborghini mentality into the camper world.

I drove. Laura looked after the dogs, mainly by sleeping while I sat behind the wheel for kilometre after kilometre. Down to the Mediterranean, down to a villa on the coast that was big enough for ten people. Laura had found it and booked it in July 2015. It's always easier to wing it in life if your wife is obsessed about long-term planning.

And that was us: feet up, together, alone, campervan on the drive, a month ahead of us to talk, ride, bicker, cook, not wash up, sleep, drive a lap of the Monaco Grand Prix circuit, stop Pringle and Sprolo spoiling the look of the internal furnishings. Together, everything would be fun.

**LAURA:** Jason scraped the bottom of the van on a mini roundabout. He was mortified. I wasn't going to complain, not after our year, not now I was Mrs Kenny.

I felt more grown up, too. I loved sharing that surname. Finally alone, finally truly together.

# Acknowledgements

We would like to thank all of the following: our wonderful families and all our special friends for being alongside us every pedal stroke of the journey; our teammates from the early days at Eastlands Velo and Welwyn, all the way through to Team GB, for sharing every moment of racing and training with us, and sharing the same cycling dreams; to every single coach that has played a part in developing us from skinny kids to Olympic champions, in particular Paul Manning and Iain Dyer; our mechanics Mark Ingham, Ernie Feargrieve and Adam Bonser, plus all the others who keep our precious bikes working and put up with all the annoying changes we like to make at the very last minute; to the brilliant support crew that the public never hears about but are so critical to our success, including Martin Evans, Joe Hewitt, Len Parker Simpson, Conor Taylor, Hannah Crowley, Hanlie Fouche and Luc de Wilde, and to all the other unseen heroes at British Cycling; to our sponsors, for their generous support; to Clare Tillyer, Clara Nelson, George Maudsley and the talented team at Michael O'Mara, plus David Luxton, for their hard work and dedication in making this book happen; to our ghostwriter Tom Fordyce for drinking our coffee and bringing flapjacks as well as words (sorry your typing fingers are now wonky); to our agent Luke Lloyd Davies and all at Rocket Sports for their expertise and dedication. To all of those who have cheered us on in velodromes across the world and in front of their televisions: thank you so much, we appreciate every single shout, whoop and waved Union flag. And finally to Sprolo and Pringle, for just being dogs, but for bringing so much happiness to our lives.

# Picture Credits

All images courtesy of Laura Trott and Jason Kenny, apart from those listed below.

Page 7: Stewart News / REX / Shutterstock (top right)

Page 9: Andy Hooper / Daily Mail / REX / Shutterstock (top); Mark Pain / REX / Shutterstock (bottom)

Page 10: Tim Ireland / PA Images (top left); Stephen Pond / PA Images (top right); Phil Walter / Getty Images (bottom)

Page 11: Offside / REX / Shutterstock (top); Cameron Spencer / Getty Images (bottom)

Page 12: Paul Grover / REX / Shutterstock (top); Pascal Le Segretain / Getty Images (bottom)

Page 14: Bryn Lennon / Getty Images (top left and bottom left); Alex Whitehead / SWpix.com / REX / Shutterstock (top right); Odd Andersen / AFP / Getty Images (bottom right)

Page 15: Miles Willis / Getty Images (top); Bryn Lennon / Getty Images (bottom)